Getting Up AGAIN

Getting Up AGAIN

Surviving Unemployment and Pursuing Destiny

Philip H. Page, Jr.

ISBN 978-0-9823069-0-1

Published in Hampton, VA by Kingdom Living Day By Day, LLC. For ordering information or to contact the publisher, please visit www.kingdomlivingdbd.com or address correspondence to:

Kingdom Living Day by Day, LLC
P.O. Box 9003
Hampton, VA 23670-0003

Cover design and book layout by David "3D" Ferreira of MASTERGRAFIX.com.

All the stories in this book are true, but most of the names have been changed to protect the privacy of the companies and people mentioned.

First Edition
10 9 8 7 6 5 4 3 2 1

Dedication

Understanding that God is the center of my life, the source of my strength and the power in my purpose, I give honor to Him in all that I do. I also thank Him for my wife who is the personification of God's deep and rich love for me. Throughout our 18 years together, she has celebrated with me at my absolute best and she has cried with me at my utter worst. Regardless of the situation, her love, support and respect for me has never wavered. For that alone, I wholeheartedly dedicate this book to Robin Fletcher Page. I would not be half the man that I am today without you.

Acknowledgments

There are so many people that I wish to thank for their support and encouragement through the time covered in this book and the resulting publication.

To my Savior and Lord. You are indeed Jehovah Jireh, the God who sees and provides.

To my beautiful wife Robin. I can't begin to explain how important it was to have your support during my time of unemployment. I also want to thank you for encouraging me to finish and publish this book. You continue to amaze me with your love and I will gladly spend the rest of my life becoming the husband you deserve.

To my family. Thanks for always believing in me. To my mom and dad, thanks for raising me to know no limits. To Dinah, thanks for being an excellent role model to follow and emulate. To Cleo, thanks for being a big sister and a best friend. To Daniel, thanks for looking up to me and pushing me higher. To Jennifer, thanks for challenging my mind and my intellect.

To my pastors, Bishop Steven W. Banks and Dr. Keira Banks. I have deep respect, love and admiration for both of you. You have blessed every area of my life and I consider it an honor to be a part of Living Waters Christian Fellowship.

To Bishop Carlton Pearson. Thanks for the excellent instruction and life changing messages during my time at Higher Dimensions Family Center. You always challenged my thinking and caused me to know the Bible for myself.

To Fred Hammond. We have never met but I thank you for a ministry that's more than music. I can remember too many nights where I cried out to God and it was your words that helped me voice my feelings. Thank you for being there.

To the publishing team at Kingdom Living Day by Day, LLC. Thanks for your hard work editing, proofreading and praying that God would refine this work. I'm so glad you are on my team and I look forward to working with you again.

Table of Contents

Foreword

Of course I think *Getting Up Again* is wonderfully inspiring because I lived it out with my husband. But you may ask, why should I read it? Have you ever experienced times when nothing seemed to go your way and wondered "why, oh why God are You allowing this to happen to me"? While some of us wonder "why", we do nothing. While others decide, although I may not know "why", I know I can't stop trying so I must get up again. It's in the getting up again that we eventually obtain destiny. So, if you ask the question, why should I read *Getting Up Again* – I give you my answers below:

- If you need to be inspired: Read it.
- If you need wisdom: Read it.
- If you enjoy a good love story: Read it.
- If you have ever wanted to ask God "what in the world is going on?": Read it.
- If you ever asked the above question and did not like the response: Read it.
- If you have ever looked at someone else's life and asked, "why can't I be like he or she?": Read it.
- If as a man, you have had or currently are experiencing feelings that you would never put to words: Read it.

I know if you must "Read it" you will truly enjoy *Getting Up Again.* You will be inspired, you will gain wisdom, you will have a better understanding of God's love for you and you will also be able to love better. Maybe most importantly, you will feel free to voice and / or share what you are experiencing on your way to destiny.

This book helps you to see God's love and what He is willing to allow in your life for your ultimate good. He really does have a plan for you. God's plan is for your good and it will give you a future and a hope (Jeremiah 29:11 – NIV).

You will also see the importance of having people in your life that love you unconditionally. I hope if you are married, you will be inspired to support your spouse in whatever he or she encounters. Realizing that no matter what either of you deals with, it is much more bearable if you two really become one. It is so worth it!

Please sit back and enjoy. You may cry, I trust you will laugh, I think you may see yourself and I hope you will cheer knowing that Philip got up again and you can too.

Enjoy & God Bless,
Robin F. Page

Introduction

If you have ever been knocked down by life then you know that there are really just two responses. The first response is to just lie there. Just remain in a fetal position and keep hoping that someone will pick you up. Keep hoping that God will miraculously propel you to success. This is, by far, the easiest response and, unfortunately, the one most often chosen.

The second potential response is for those who believe that lying down is simply not acceptable. Although they feel the pain and the hopeless despair of failure, there is a little reserve of power, a small shred of faith that won't leave them alone. For those people, the only response is to fight as hard as possible to get up again.

The book that you are about to read is for anyone who has been knocked down by life and needs the power to get up again. My specific situation deals with the tragedy of a layoff but you may be facing an illness, a failed business, a lost loved one or a divorce. Whatever the situation, I believe that the lessons learned through this book will help you overcome your current adversity and begin to thrive in this time of your life.

During my time of despair I believe God taught me four skills for success. They are *Waiting on God, Hearing from God, Receiving God's Provision,* and *Pursuing your Purpose*. Although they may appear simple, each one is Biblically sound, universally proven and applicable to any situation where your current reality falls short of your desired goal.

This season of your life may be the most trying you have ever experienced. Yet I firmly believe that if you learn and apply these skills, you will be empowered with keys to success that will open doors in every area of your life. I am living proof that, no matter how hard you have been knocked down, you can, indeed, get up again.

Chapter One

Before The Fall

The Good Life

April means many things to many people. For some, it marks the real beginning of spring. To others, it's the beginning of Major League Baseball. For me, it was the official end of tax season. Of course, there were still some late filers who spent every April 14th rushing to the Post Office in search of a postmark. But for most normal people, the reign of Uncle Sam and his feeding frenzy was over. The IRS has stopped bugging taxpayers. Taxpayers have stopped bugging their CPA's. And, most importantly, those CPA's have stopped bugging me. Life is Good!

You may be wondering why CPA's would be bothering me during the most important season of their year. Well, I was a Tax Development Specialist for TaxOn Software Corporation. In plain terms, I created tax software for New York and New Mexico. Or at least, that's what I told my friends at parties and social gatherings. In all honesty, I was the personal whipping boy for several hundred CPA's, Enrolled Agents and Tax Practitioners. Since I was the lead programmer for the software they used to file tax returns, I got to field their calls, answer their questions and try to convince them that the bugs I overlooked were really just features that they didn't know existed. So goes the life of a Developer. But alas, that life was over and I could begin a long summer of relaxation.

Out of my six years at TaxOn, I needed this break the most. This past year was the first that I was responsible for testing and programming. Before that, I just tested the software that someone else created. Prior to that, I sold the software that someone else created. Either way, it was much easier for me because I always had someone to blame. But this year, it was all on me.

In addition to that, I had become a Supervisor. I was in charge of three other programmers with duties similar to mine. I often complained about the added responsibility and the increased workload but, in truth, I loved it. I had been trying to become a Supervisor in three different departments over six long years and I had finally made it. The Masters of Business Administration (MBA) classes I had been taking were finally paying off. I had become a member of management.

Notwithstanding my recent promotion, my career was about five years late. According to my internal career calendar, I should have become a supervisor about five years ago. Not that I deserved that level of advancement, but it was necessary to fit my long-term career plans. The way I saw it, the plan was to get management experience by the age of 25 so that I could break off and start my own business. Then grow that business to over $1 million in sales in order to get into a national business magazine. At that point I should be able to slow down my career and start having children. By 30, I should be a millionaire and able to invest some capital into other businesses. And by 45, I should be able to retire. I know it sounds a bit incredible but that was the plan. And I was five years behind.

Faith, Family and Finances

The good news was that my career was the only thing keeping me from the total Quan – the Quan is the pinnacle of life described by Rod Tidwell in the movie Jerry Maguire. For me, the total Quan was a mixture of Faith, Family and Finances. Although my finances were a bit behind, my faith and family were right on track.

Actually, my family was ahead of schedule. While I was in high school, I met the girl who would become the love of my life. We didn't actually start dating until our freshman year at college. By then, we had become good friends who were completely comfortable with each other. We were comfortable enough to talk to each other, comfortable enough to flirt and comfortable enough to go to a formal banquet when I couldn't find a date. I didn't realize this at the time but we were also comfortable enough to end the date with the most passionate kiss I had ever known.

Since our first kiss, Robin has owned my heart and mind. The strange thing about that night is that it was so spontaneous and pure. Up to that point, I had never done anything significant without planning it three days in advance. But Robin seemed to give me the courage to be spontaneous and the strength not to second-guess myself. She immediately became the best thing in my life and marrying her was the easiest decision I ever made.

At that point, Robin was the only family I wanted or needed. We both wanted to have children but not immediately. When asked about children, our standard response was "we're going to start in about five years". Of course, we had been saying that for a while. It's not that we were scared, although Robin admits to being a little nervous about being a mother. I was mainly concerned with being as financially prepared as possible. I could look at my wife and begin to imagine how adorable my daughter was going to be. I realized that she would immediately capture my heart and deserve lots of lavish gifts. I figured it would take a few years of hard work to be able to spoil my daughter properly but she would deserve nothing less.

The faith portion of my life was also where it should be. At least, that was my opinion. I was still growing closer to God on a daily basis. And I still wrestled with deep theological questions but my foundation was sure. To put it plainly, I believe that Jesus Christ is the Son of God who loved us so much that He died on the cross to set all men and women free from the eternal agony of Hell. I know that there's more to religion than this, but I don't think God cares about the other stuff. As I said, my foundation is sure and the rest will come with time.

My wife and I attended a non-denominational Christian church in the suburbs of Tulsa, Oklahoma. The praise and worship was lively, the congregation was racially diverse and our pastor was a true leader. During our time there, we had volunteered in the Children's ministry, the Youth ministry, the Greeter ministry and more. Basically, our church was the best thing about living in Tulsa and we couldn't have been happier.

Our excitement about our church completed the faith portion of my life rather nicely. And with two out of three parts on track, I was sitting pretty. Of course, things would have been even better if I had all the things I had asked God for already. But in this brief moment of realism, I had to admit that life was good.

Chapter Two

The Fall

A Joyous (Working) Vacation

Now that tax season has wound down, we were getting ready to start the nine-month preparation process for next tax season. In reality, we were going to gripe and complain for a month, talk for two months and then start the six-month preparation process. This was the well-deserved break that I had been anticipating. We started with a recap of last tax season.

While we were working on our review of the past season, rumors persisted about the future of TaxOn. For the most part the rumors were just an irritation coming from the Sales and Support department. Like most issues that originated from the Sales department, we dismissed them with an arrogant chuckle. Before I go any further, let me explain the relationship between the programmers in Tax Development and the people in Sales.

Generally speaking, relations between the Sales department and the Development department were similar to most companies. There were times when we needed to work together so we reluctantly tolerated each other (and the undercurrent of tension that seemed to always be present). I thought it generated from each department thinking that they were the lifeblood of the company. I understood this tension as well as anyone because I had worked on both sides of it. When I was in the Sales department I was convinced that the company couldn't exist without the orders that we generated. It didn't matter that we were selling a quality program. In our minds, no one would buy the software if it weren't for us. Besides, I had once sold software that wasn't programmed yet. Who needs programmers when you sell programs that don't even exist? Anyway, as a Sales person, I was motivated by the belief that my work was paying the salaries for the entire company.

Of course, my belief changed when I moved into the Tax Development department as a software tester. Being a tester gave me input before the product was shipped and being a programmer gave me creative powers that I had not imagined before. I felt as if I had evolved and was now at the apex of my (TaxOn) career. So, when I heard rumors coming from other departments about the company being offered for sale, I disregarded them, as usual, and continued my nine-month well-deserved break. Besides, how could a rumor be credible if it didn't come from my department?

Loud Whispers

As I tried to enjoy my break, the rumors about the company's future continued. Perhaps the worst rumor was that there was a big Sales meeting where the Vice President told everyone that there would be no raises this year. Evidently, a portion of the people walked out in protest after hearing this. Now I could imagine the owner making the alleged statement but not the VP. When TaxOn was in a smaller building, the owner once said that he might alleviate our cramped quarters by taking space from lazy employees. I think he intended to motivate us, but the VP, who was also the dedicated schmoozer, had to spend the next few days settling a revolt by people who were offended that their hard work was not being appreciated. Although, I never really trusted the VP or his schmoozing abilities, I didn't think he would be foolish enough to tell a meeting-room full of people that their work would not be rewarded with raises.

There was going to be a meeting on April 17th, the official end of tax season. I was really looking forward to it because it would finally put the rumors to rest. The owner was going to address everyone in his usual blunt manner and we would know where we stood for the next year. Unfortunately, ominous signs began to appear before the meeting. For example, I received a call from the HR secretary. She said that she needed me to turn in my receipts for school early. In the past, the tuition reimbursement process had been run with military-style rigidity. Payments covered only tuition and required books (no workbooks or supplements) and checks were dispersed only after a transcript had been properly submitted. Now, I was being told to turn in my receipts in order to get paid in the middle of the semester.

The signs continued and the rumors persisted but I continued to deny that TaxOn would end on April 17th. The conversation at work was always about who would buy TaxOn and how much the employees would receive in proceeds and severance. The employees with children were mostly concerned about their jobs. All of them were looking for other jobs and some jumped ship before the meeting. I continued to hold my belief that TaxOn would continue for another season (at least) and everyone would feel silly after the meeting. I expected it to be like January 1st, 2000 when people realized that Y2K was an overblown fear within the IT industry whose worst outcome was scaring companies into updating their computer equipment sooner than necessary.

I can't really say why I thought TaxOn wouldn't end. At the time I just thought that the company ending was too good to be true. I could sense that my career at TaxOn had reached a plateau and a layoff would be the thing to get me going in a fresh new direction. And since our blunt, but generous, owner had always said he would share the proceeds, selling TaxOn would be an ideal situation for me.

Nonetheless, I expected the worst. In my mind, the worst thing that could happen would be if TaxOn was sold to the management. The VP would run the new company and nothing would change. No payout. No growth. No change. Since this seemed like a real possibility to me, I didn't let myself get excited about the more real possibility of life after TaxOn. I simply waited and let life happen to me.

Spiritual Preparation

In the midst of the crisis over our future, my immediate boss started to have regular meetings to try and calm some fears and remove some doubts. He admitted that he didn't have much inside knowledge but he would be open and honest with everyone and let us know what he knew. As you might imagine, the meetings were well attended. Everyone took it as an opportunity to state the latest rumor. Fortunately, he shed the light of reason on each rumor and we all felt better in the end.

In addition to the meetings, my boss also planned a special session to discuss the importance of having an individual purpose for our lives. He was going to show a video from Dr. Myles Munroe regarding "Purpose" and give us the opportunity to discuss it afterwards. I must say that this was the classiest thing I had ever seen done at TaxOn and my respect for my boss increased tremendously when he mentioned this. I had already seen the video but I decided to see it again because it was so awesome and appropriate for this time.

In my opinion, the most important concept in the video was that purpose is the key to fulfillment. Just as King Solomon instructed, "To every thing there is a season, and a time to every purpose under the heaven". (Ecclesiastes 3:1) I realized that, without knowing your purpose, you couldn't ever really be fulfilled. We have all been taught to make goals and set dates for reaching those goals, but goals must be based on our purpose. If not, we won't ever feel the passion or desire to fulfill those goals. Well, there's much more to say on this topic but I'm probably not the one to say it. I would strongly encourage anyone interested in this issue to seek out the books by Dr. Myles Munroe.

THE END

Well, April 17th finally came. We all gathered downstairs in the meeting room full of excitement and fearful anticipation. I saw many people from other departments that I used to work with so we made light conversation. Once we piled into the meeting room, the head of HR picked up the microphone a little before the meeting started. Evidently, we were supposed to pick up a personal packet before entering. So we had to leave the meeting and get in a line based on our last names. As I waited in line, I couldn't shake the reality that something was definitely different about this meeting. I had fooled myself for as long as possible but I couldn't do it any longer. Things were going to change and it was only a matter of how much.

After we reentered the meeting room, the owner approached the microphone and began the meeting. The first words out of his mouth were, "Well, I don't want to prolong anything. TaxOn has been sold." He kept talking after that but I'm pretty sure the world stopped for at least five minutes. Our company had just been sold. And, even worse, it had been sold to our sworn enemy in the tax software industry. This was the company that had been our rival. The one that our sales staff always fought the hardest to out sell. And now, they owned us, lock, stock and barrel.

After the world started moving again, I found out that, in addition to being bought by another company, we were all being laid off. This was supposedly for our good so that we could have a fresh start. That was a bunch of crap but I couldn't really do anything about it. The packet that I received before the meeting was a formal letter stating what had just been said in the meeting. But it didn't say anything about the severance or payout. After answering a few questions, the owner finally said that we would receive information about severance and payout in a month or so.

Although everyone was being laid off, a "lucky" bunch of 30 or so individuals were being rehired. Our packets would tell us whether we were among the chosen few. Despite my tenure, hard work and marketable skills, I was not being rehired. I would receive the federally mandated severance amount of two months pay shortly. Until then, I was directed to clear out my cubicle and go home.

We were given the rest of the day to say our good-byes and clear out. The new owners had also brought their human resources people to the meeting. The "unlucky" masses were given the chance to wait in line for an opportunity to apply for a job. It was probably a nice gesture but, at the time, it felt like a double-handed slap in the face. I had been abruptly dismissed from the place I had worked for six years. Now the new owners, the company I had been trained to hate, were giving me the chance to wait in line to beg for a job. It was more than my pride and self-respect could handle.

I went upstairs to get my stuff. On the way, I noticed the security on hand to ensure that we didn't steal a computer or try to strangle anyone as we left. This was becoming more than I could bear. The irritation of the day had come to a head. My flesh had had all it could stand so my spirit started to take over. I began to think of two scriptures. First, Luke 17:1 "Then said he unto the disciples, It is impossible but that offences will come: but woe unto him, through whom they come!" Then Romans 8:28 "And we know that all things work together for good to them that love God, to them who are the called according to his purpose."

The scripture didn't really give me peace because I wasn't accurately applying these scriptures to my situation. First, no one had done anything wrong by selling *their* business. Especially when they had given every inclination that they would sell. Second, I don't believe that everything is God's intended purpose. He just works things out for His eventual glory. Still, the scriptures gave me a sense of knowing that the situation I was in was fine. I definitely wasn't excited about how things worked out, but I knew I was in God's hands and everything was going to be all right.

After the Fall

After I packed up my things and left, I called Robin. By this time, I was pretty happy. I started to think about the implications of this moment and realized that things weren't too bad. I was now free to pursue my purpose in life and start a business of my own. I could do things my way and, hopefully, I would have a nice wad of cash from my severance package to get started.

I wasn't sure how Robin would respond when I told her the news but I was hoping for the best. Robin isn't a worrier and her faith is usually stronger than my faith. But, she is still a woman and most women I know don't typically react well to uncertainty. So, with reserved optimism, I called Robin and told her that I had recently joined the ranks of the unemployed. Of course she reacted only with concern for me and what I was going through. After I assured her that I was all right, we said good-bye. After Robin got home from work we spoke more about TaxOn. Evidently, she was more confident that TaxOn was being sold than I was. As an HR expert, she took the early payment of the tuition reimbursement as a sure sign that the end was near. The more we talked, the more we began to get excited about the great possibilities that lay ahead.

The faith and optimism that Robin and I share really express the blessing of being married to a Christian. I can't imagine what it would be like to tell someone without faith that you got laid off and you don't know what to do. Unfortunately, I was about to realize what that would be like when I went to class in the evening. This particular class, Analysis of the Internet Enterprise, was one of my favorites. It was taught by one of the best professors on campus and I knew and/or worked with several people there. I was looking forward to pouring my energy into the last year of my MBA program and this class was the beginning of that effort.

Entering the class was like attending a funeral mid dejected faces and stares of pity. I arrived to class a little late and found out that the closing of TaxOn had been the early topic of conversation. My former coworkers had a grimmer picture of being laid off and they were sadly discussing the details of the day. I was initially shocked at the despair in the room. I was glad they cared enough to ask me how I was doing but I was surprised that they didn't believe that I was all right. They must have thought I was still in shock or something. Nevertheless, I continued to convince everyone that things were going to be fine and the class continued.

After class, I drove home with a friend of mine that left TaxOn a few weeks before the end. I always thought he jumped ship too early but as the single breadwinner for a family of three, with one on the way, he could not afford to wait and see. I knew he was concerned about me not having a job, but he also seemed very interested in what was said about the payout to employees. It seemed that he asked the owner to remember him when he left but no promises were made. At that point, the payout was the only thing I could think about too but I didn't have any new information for him.

Chapter Three

Philip The Cat, Always Landing On His Feet

The Leadership Conference

So far, unemployment wasn't that bad. I think the newspapers got it wrong; being out of work can be a real blessing. Or maybe it's only a blessing when you have a loving (and working) wife and you're expecting a nice cash payout in order to start a business. Actually, I never considered it to be unemployment. My business training taught me that the only people who were considered to be unemployed were those who were actively looking for a job. That didn't include me. My job title was "Entrepreneur". I just hadn't started a business yet. I realize that this is an oxymoronic concept but I was enjoying life to this point and feeling good about the future.

The first week of my new life was spent at the end of a leadership conference. This was an annual event sponsored by my church in April of each year. Since I was at the beginning of my new life, I would definitely need spiritual encouragement. Specifically, I wanted supernatural insight regarding what to do. I didn't receive it through a burning bush or anything but I felt encouraged spiritually and my faith got a much needed boost.

JUBILEE FUNDRAISING

After the conference, I spent my days either volunteering at church, studying for school or working on business plans. The business plans were the hardest project because I hadn't picked a business yet. For as long as I could remember, I had come up with business ideas on a weekly or sometimes daily basis. The sheer volume of these ideas had almost become a distraction in my marriage. Many of them were variations on previous ideas but together they were a large collection of potential moneymakers. In order to stop boring Robin with the details of these businesses we decided that I would have to store them up and only describe the "Business Idea of the Week".

Now that I would finally be in position to act on one of my business ideas, I couldn't pick just one. To me they were all golden. Eventually, I made a list in my head and whittled it down based on which one was 1) most in line with my desires for life 2) took the least amount of risk and 3) had the biggest upside potential. The winner was the *Jubilee Fundraising* program.

The idea behind *Jubilee Fundraising* was to create a Christian-based fundraising company that would use coffee and coffee products to raise money for nonprofit organizations. I realized that fundraising was not a novel idea, but in my years as the Fundraising Chair for my church's youth outreach I never found a good Christian fundraising company. As a result, we were always in the position of selling a product that people only bought because they wanted to help us out. *Jubilee Fundraising* would sell coffee that would spread the Gospel through its packaging. The bags would have scriptures and miniature devotions on it that would encourage customers on a daily basis.

Now you may be thinking that this isn't exactly a golden idea but keep in mind that *Jubilee Fundraising* wasn't designed to make me rich. It was designed to support a lifestyle of helping nonprofit organizations. This was something that I felt passionate about and very capable of doing. Plus, I could have leveraged my new business with my then current hobby – I had been hosting The Jireh Café.com as an Internet destination for urban Christians. The Jireh Café already had a great website (built by me) with devotions and other Christian content and I could use this to get a jump-start on *Jubilee Fundraising*.

Work on *Jubilee Fundraising* took much longer than I expected. The main reason was that I scrutinized over every detail. This was my first baby since "The Fall" and I was determined to treat it right. Aside from that, I had several years of undergraduate and graduate business classes to utilize. I had business models in my head on everything from tracking direct mail response to production management of consumable goods. I wanted to use all of it whether I needed to or not.

Unfortunately, too much of a good thing isn't good. My vast database of business information caused action to suffer significantly. Things that should have taken minutes took days. Like when I went looking for a mailbox to use as a corporate address. I went to the US Post Office and then to almost every shipping franchise in Tulsa, OK. Then I cross-checked the prices of the franchises with a second location to make sure I didn't miss out of any local deals. I calculated the length of time it would take to get to each location to pick up my mail and adjusted the relative price of mailbox rental accordingly. Then I considered the intangible benefits of how different address variations would look on the mailers I was sending out. The final decision was in line with the decisions of a large, bureaucratic corporation. However, it was overkill for a $50 expense in a single employee company with zero revenues.

Suffering for Christ in Orlando, FL

When I wasn't working on my business plan or homework, I was spending time with family. My oldest sister was graduating soon with a Doctoral degree in Adult and Occupational Education. My younger brother was graduating from the same university with a Bachelor's degree in Finance. The focus on education came from having a mother who was a teacher, principal, head mistress and guidance counselor. I always appreciated how she encouraged (i.e. forced) us to celebrate all great academic achievements. As usual, my entire family got together to celebrate the graduations and had a wonderful time.

After the graduation festivities, Robin and I had planned a trip to Orlando, FL. Actually it was a business trip for her and a business trip/vacation for me. The whole thing looked like it was going to be a great blessing. Robin's company was paying for her airfare and a single room for a week. I had frequent flyer miles to cash in so I accompanied her and shared a beautiful room overlooking International Parkway. During the day, Robin went to meetings and I worked on my business plan.

Nights in Orlando were pretty awesome. Since our room and travel were covered, we spent our money on food and entertainment. After Robin's meetings, we went shopping at the malls, visited the amusement parks and went to the themed areas that were downtown. We also partied at the clubs that were run by the large theme parks. The food at each place was just awesome. After the conference was over, we rented a three-bedroom house for the weekend. Since the property management company gave us a lower rate than a typical hotel room, we took the money we had saved and rented a sports car to drive to the beach. We truly lived it up and had, probably, the best vacation (I mean business trip) of all time.

Powerful Little Prayers

Aside from the fun and celebration, I did manage to have times of prayer. At about this time, a very popular book on prayer was sweeping the nation. It was based on a scripture in the first book of Chronicles.

> *And Jabez called on the God of Israel saying, "Oh, that You would bless me indeed, and enlarge my territory, that Your hand would be with me, and that You would keep me from evil, that I may not cause pain!" So God granted him what he requested.*
>
> 1 Chronicles 4:10 (NKJV)

It's amazing how life changing a single scripture can be to millions of people. I think it was based on the fact that there is nothing else known about Jabez except that he was born, he prayed and he eventually died. When my brother-in-law introduced me to the scripture I was pretty skeptical. But his uncharacteristic enthusiasm won me over. He told me he had been reading it daily for a week and almost every day since then someone had been coming up to him with an opportunity for him to help. To be honest, I wasn't all that interested in finding more people to help, but I was very interested in having God "bless me indeed" as Jabez put it.

Well, I bought the book and Robin and I read it. Nothing magical happened immediately but it did give a sense of encouragement that was different from what I had experienced before. This increased the importance of prayer in my life (since it was the only thing Jabez was known for) and gave me a way to consistently focus my faith. As I prayed and read the scripture in Chronicles, I extended my faith towards God blessing my business. I prayed that it would grow beyond

Tulsa into larger territories. And I prayed that it wouldn't hurt anyone in any way. At the end of the prayer, I expected God to do His part and grant my request.

Chapter Four

Money, Money, Money

The Big Payday

For the most part, Robin and I are practical people. Actually, I'm a bit excessive but Robin's influence brings balance to our marriage. With this in mind, we tried to apply this modesty to our expectations regarding the final severance/bonus payout from TaxOn. We failed.

We had already received the federally mandated monthly salary and promptly used it to take care of our regular expenses.

In the final TaxOn meeting, we never found out what, if anything, we would get in the form of a payout. No one ever officially mentioned a dollar amount, a percentage or whether the amount would be based on seniority or the last salary. Without any parameters to guide our thinking, employees' imaginations ran wild. Since we were a company full of accountants and tax specialists, you can imagine how serious our calculations became.

At one point, there was a rumor that a competitor offered $150 million. We quickly figured that $150 million split between 400 employees would be $375,000 each. Great! But we conveniently forgot that the person who founded the business would probably want more than 1/400th percent. OK, if we gave him half, our portion would still be $187,500 each. That was still a pretty good piece of change. The sessions continued for a while as the sales price and percentages were adjusted to estimate a final amount.

During these calculation sessions at work, I am proud to say that I was often the voice of reason. As a prospective entrepreneur, I realized that the one who incurred all of the initial risk should get all of the reward. I wasn't present when the business was being run out of a condominium and, when I did arrive, I always received a decent salary for the work I performed. So, I determined that anything I received would be a blessing. (But the $187,500 would be nice.)

THE PACKAGE

On one particularly average day, I went to the mailbox and found a nice large envelope. It was from the entity that was handling TaxOn's final arrangements. I had been maintaining my composure pretty well and today was no different. I casually walked into the house and looked through the rest of the mail. It was like I was trying to prove to God that I wasn't going to be overwhelmed by the amount no matter how large or small. I finally opened up the big package and read.

The package contained all types of federal papers regarding COBRA and statistics on who was laid off. I kept reading through. Yadda yadda yadda, blah blah blah, then I finally saw the amount of $23,000. At first I was kind of numb. I wasn't giddy and I wasn't depressed, just numb. Then I kept reading through the papers and there it was again. Final amount, $23,000. I tried not to be affected but I began to think about how much money this actually was. Slowly a smile crept upon my face and stayed there until Robin got home from work.

When I told Robin, she was as happy as I was. We didn't have the actual check yet but we knew we were going to get more money than we had ever had at one time. We could actually do something substantial like finally start our dream business or pay off some bills or *start our dream business*. Now that the amount was set, we allowed ourselves to make plans.

Receiving the information packet took a big weight off of me. Before I knew how much money to expect, I was cautiously optimistic and too afraid to plan ahead. Knowing the amount of money gave the freedom to plan. And plan I did.

First we tried to be sensible. We have always tithed faithfully, the practice of giving 10% of your income, and we were actually excited to be giving a tithe of such a large amount. Some people seem to do well with small amounts then forget about God's Word when larger amounts come. We were dedicated to returning at least 10% to God through our church so that was the first amount we set aside.

Next, we wrote down other things that we wanted to do and ranked them by their importance. We estimated that the final check would be about $20,000 after taxes. We were allowed to change our exemptions in order to minimize our tax deduction but I preferred to be conservative. In addition to paying tithes, we maintained our sensibility long enough to devote money to paying off at least one big debt. Since Robin's car was close to being paid off, and it represented a dependable asset, we chose to pay it off.

After reducing our debt, we planned to fulfill a pledge we had made to another ministry and give an offering to our home church. Some money would be spent for fun things and another big chunk would go to starting a business. All in all, we had spent the entire $20,000 on paper and awaited the check. In the meantime, I continued to plan for the *Jubilee Fundraising* program.

THE CHECK ARRIVES

For as long as I can remember, I enjoyed going to the mailbox. It seemed as if there was always the possibility of good news there. Maybe this had something to do with the fact that my father delivered mail for the post office. Either way, I hadn't missed an opportunity to go to the mailbox since the age of five. This day, however, was even more special because I was anticipating the arrival of a big fat check with my name on it. On May 31st, I went to the mailbox and found another envelope like the one that contained the information packet. A big smile came over my face and I quickly walked back to the house to open it up. I tried to hold back my enthusiasm but it was no use. I was just so excited to be opening my check for $17,000. Hey, wait a minute. I had calculated that the check would be no less than $20,000. But this was far less than $20,000; it was $3,000 less to be exact.

I can't really explain the disappointment I felt when I looked at the check. I was upset and confused at the same time. I didn't believe the check was accurate so I called the accompanying phone number to inquire further. After much prodding, I found out that the amount was indeed accurate. Evidently, the IRS has special rules for lump sum payments that require more to be withheld. This only made me mad at the IRS and mad at myself, a self-proclaimed tax expert, for forgetting the special tax treatment of lump-sum payouts.

Even though I was a victim of my own expectations, I turned my anger towards God. Although I understood the logic behind what happened, I felt betrayed by God in some way. It was as if He refused to do anything supernatural on my behalf. I had often quoted the scripture in Ephesians 3:20 that says, *"Now unto him that is able to do exceeding abundantly above all that we ask or think, according to the power that worketh in us."* This scripture had always been a reminder of the blessings and benefits that Christians enjoy, but now it was mocking me. There was no "exceeding abundance" in this. I was getting the same puny payout as everyone else and the IRS stole a big chunk of it.

As I pondered my frustration, I realized that it didn't begin with this check. I had always expected some measure of abundance simply for being a Christian. I felt, and still feel, entitled to an elevated status. It's not that I think I will get by without effort, the Bible routinely speaks against laziness, but shouldn't we see some benefit from having the Almighty God working on our behalf? Well, my circumstance was telling me that the answer to that question was NO.

Jubilee Fundraising II

Well, it took a while, but I finally got over the disappointment of receiving a payout that was much lower than expected. Actually, I didn't get over it; I just got through it. I still didn't understand why God allowed it to happen – couldn't He have reminded me of tax law – but I decided to be happy that I got something. My classmates and friends who were laid off from another company only received two weeks pay. And they were working for a much larger company in a much bigger industry. Besides, I was not dead so there was still time for God to bless me.

Speaking of blessings, I was ready to launch the *Jubilee Fundraising* program and this was a perfect time for God to come through with His supernatural power. The products had been chosen, the order forms were created, the advertisements had been designed and the initial direct mailing list had been selected. I had planned the launch with meticulous detail and it was finally time to go.

Initially, I had decided to send out a postcard since people would have to look at it before they threw it away. If I sent a letter, I could include more information about the background of the business and its purpose, but I couldn't be sure that anyone would open it. At the last minute, I chose to go with the envelope and include a letter and order form. Even though I was sending more information, it was going to be cheaper due to the expense of meeting the Post Office's regulations for sending a postcard. So, I printed and stuffed 150 envelopes and sent them to churches and nonprofit organizations in the Oklahoma and Texas area.

In a few days I started getting responses. I can't tell you how excited I was to see mail in the box I had rented. My excitement turned to disappointment when I realized that I had only received returned mail due to improper addresses. But I remained encouraged. My research in direct mail showed that this was to be expected so I continued to check my mailbox on a daily basis.

After a few weeks, it became hard to maintain my enthusiasm. I continued to check my mailbox and continued to get either returned mail or junk mail. The daily trek to my box became more and more pitiful. I was convinced that the clerk who worked there avoided eye contact with me out of pity. I thought she actually put someone else's mail into my box just so I would have something to open. It was as if I had written a letter to Santa Claus and was waiting for a response that would never arrive.

I waited several weeks more and then I finally gave up. There was not a single response to my mailer and no reason to expect that there would be. *Jubilee Fundraising* had failed. More to the point, I had failed. Despite my faith, despite my business training and despite my effort, I had failed. The only thing left to do was to box up the remaining materials and move on.

I didn't fully mourn the loss of the business but I was really sad and confused. Why didn't it work? I was trying to start a business that would help non-profit organizations to raise money and I didn't get a single bite. I just couldn't figure out what God was doing. A few years ago I started a business selling information about government auctions. This information was freely available from the government but, due to my fancy website and promotions, I managed to sell it for around $50 a piece. How is it possible that I could sell a borderline scam but couldn't sell a valid business idea designed to help nonprofit organizations? (By the way, I have repented for my past lapse in judgment and I believe God has forgiven me.)

WHY BUILD WHAT YOU CAN BUY?

Although the sting of failure was painful, there were many lessons that I learned. The biggest lesson I learned was that the name of God is not like magic pixie dust. Association with God's name won't make a bad business good any more than the Ark of the Covenant was a sure-fire method to success. In I Samuel 4, the Philistines defeated the Israelites even though the Israelites had the Ark of the Covenant. The Israelites looked to the Ark instead of looking to God. In hindsight,

I realize that I expected the fact that this was a Christian business to overcome the fact that fundraising was a mature and crowded field.

Among the other lessons I learned was that it's often expensive to build a business from the ground up. All of the details that must be tended to make it more convenient to buy an existing business if one is available. By the grace of God, I found an available business a few miles from my home. It was a coffee shop that was being sold because the franchisee couldn't keep up his end of the agreement.

I was really excited to find a coffee shop, of all businesses, that was actually available. I had written more business plans for coffee shops than any other business. And I did a long-term study on the specialty coffee industry for an MBA project. I knew all the major competitors, the major vendors, the profit margins and the key cost components. This was a custom made situation for me and I was determined to jump on it.

In the next few days I scouted out the location to get an idea of how I could improve it. I came up with all kinds of ideas and met the franchisor. Then I found out the price was only $60,000. I didn't have that much money but I figured seller financing would be an option. It was, so I submitted an application. I was a bit hesitant to fill out an application for credit because my credit history was pretty poor. Actually it has been perfect for years now but I sunk deep into debt while in college and ended up filing for bankruptcy. Since then, I've contacted my creditors to offer repayment. I think God is pleased with this voluntary offer of restitution but, somehow, I didn't think the owners of the coffee shop would be impressed.

After a few days of not hearing a response from the coffee shop owners, I started to get worried. It only takes 15 minutes to check credit and they seemed to be in a hurry to sell. Besides, I had great credentials and could surely run a single location coffee shop. I called to find out what was holding things up. I couldn't get through immediately (another ominous sign) so I left a message. After my contact didn't call me back, I figured the worst. I finally reached him the next day and he confirmed that they had chosen another applicant. Even though we both needed to borrow to buy the business, the other applicant offered "a better overall package". Yeah Right!

This disappointment was a bit easier to take than the *Jubilee Fundraising* mishap. I was accustomed to being denied things on the basis of credit and I figured it was my cross to bear. I mishandled my credit and I would have to pay the consequences no matter how long they lingered. I also began to realize the problems with the coffee shop that I was too gung ho to admit before. There were problems with infestation and the location wasn't near a high traffic business to draw customers. Worst of all, there was a rumor that a huge competitor was opening a block or so away. All things considered, this was a situation where God saved me from my self-confidence.

A month later, I found another coffee shop under the same franchise that was selling its location. During our negotiations, the owner told me that the reason she was selling was because the franchisor drove her out of business by forcing her to carry products that no one in her area wanted. She strongly recommended that I never do business with this franchisor under any circumstances. I took this as further confirmation that God's mercy had saved me from severe frustration.

Chapter Five

Spiritual Nourishment

A Gathering of Men

A few years ago, two of my coworkers and I went to a large ministry event for men in Dallas, TX. This was a really great event for many reasons. First, the host organization was a pioneering ministry for men. They were the first organization to fill a football stadium full of men when there wasn't a game to watch. Second, this trip was one of the few times that I hung out with guys and enjoyed it. I usually don't care much for male bonding, but the preaching during the conference and the conversation afterwards really gave me a fresh perspective on what it takes to be a man, husband and father. All in all, it was a once in a lifetime occurrence that I really enjoyed.

The momentum behind the host organization dwindled, but thankfully, another men's conference arose in its place and began to have annual meetings in various locations throughout the United States. This particular year, the conference would also be in Dallas, TX. As I saw advertisements, I began to think back to my time at the previous event. Although I fell out of touch with my previous road trip buddies, the good memories from Dallas made me interested in giving male bonding another shot. Besides, I was at a crossroads in my life and I needed direction. I wanted to start another business but common sense told me to just start looking for another job. I needed help.

My church was sponsoring a tour bus but, like a typical man, I didn't feel comfortable traveling unless I had control of the transportation. Thankfully, one of my two best (and only) male friends, was also interested in going. So on July 12th, we left Tulsa for Dallas, TX.

The conversation was pretty good as we drove to Dallas. I had forgotten how interesting men could be. I also forgot that I'm still pretty interesting even when I'm not around Robin. We arrived in time for the night session, which was as good as I could have imagined. The presiding pastor opened up the conference with an awesome message to get us fired up and eager to come back. His text was Genesis chapters 12 and 22 (Abraham's preempted sacrifice of Isaac) and the message was about the marks of a great man. I have heard many messages on Abraham but this one really gave me some key attributes that I needed to understand. I guess the most appropriate was how Abraham followed the voice of God without knowing the specifics of where he was going. And many people know about how Abraham was going to sacrifice his son but, even more impressive, was how Abraham stayed aware enough to immediately hear the voice of God and stop. No matter what you believe or whose voice you heed, Abraham's example is an awesome one.

THE ALTAR CALL

On the second night of the conference, we heard from another one of the speakers. This one pastored a large church in a major city but I hadn't heard of him before. When I found out that his ministry had recently bought an NBA stadium, I immediately started paying closer attention. I figured anyone who was preaching in the place where Magic Johnson, Kareem Abdul Jabar and James Worthy played must be all right.

The message was from Joshua 4:18-22 where the Israelites were on the brink of entering the Promised Land. Before the battle of Jericho, they crossed the Jordan and stopped at a place called Gilgal. According to the teaching, they did this for three reasons.

> *And the priests came up out of the river carrying the Ark of the Covenant of the LORD. No sooner had they set their feet on the dry ground than the waters of the Jordan returned to their place and ran at flood stage as before. On the tenth day of the first month the people went up from the Jordan and camped at Gilgal on the eastern border of Jericho. And Joshua set up at Gilgal the twelve stones they had taken out of the Jordan. He said to the Israelites, "In the future when your descendants ask their fathers, 'What do these stones mean?' tell them, 'Israel crossed the Jordan on dry ground.'* Joshua 4:18-22 (NIV)

As the speaker went on, I continued to see parallels between my life and the message. Gilgal was presented as a place of rest, a place of remembrance and a place where the Israelites washed off the shame of slavery. My life does not compare with the plight of the Israelites but I still felt that there were obvious similarities that God was using to speak to me. Mainly, I felt that the six years I spent at TaxOn were a form of slavery. Please understand that I am not claiming that TaxOn was an oppressive environment with substandard work conditions. I worked at TaxOn voluntarily but, during that time, I was being transformed from an entrepreneur to an employee. The longer I remained there, the harder it became to maintain my vision of starting a business. My dreams were slowly dying inside and, before I lost my vision completely, God freed me in the form of a layoff.

The speaker closed with an altar call and I immediately responded. I usually avoid altar calls but this one spoke to me directly at the point of my need. I had been freed from a form of career subjugation and I wanted this night in Dallas, TX to be my Gilgal. This would be a place of rest, renewal and remembrance that I would never forget. For years I had been draining my body and mind for the good of the corporation instead of moving in faith to accomplish the vision God gave me. By settling for jobs that didn't fulfill my life's purpose, I had chosen finances over faith. From this point on, I would never again prostitute the gifts God had given me. This was my Gilgal.

Chapter Six

Finding Purpose

The Afterglow

I left the men's conference feeling fired up and excited. In my twenty-plus years as a Christian, I don't think I've had as good a time at Church as I did there. In the presence of thousands of men, I praised God more elaborately than ever. Maybe it was because I didn't know anyone there, but I was extremely expressive and unashamed. I also received direction from the Lord that was timely and catered to my situation. The messages I heard over the weekend were fulfilling on a very deep level. All in all, I was remarkably blessed.

When I got home, I was determined to capitalize on the enthusiasm that was sparked by God's word. I hadn't forgotten about the disappointment of *Jubilee Fundraising* but I had released it to God. I had too much faith to let a minor setback paralyze me. God was preparing me for great things in the future and I didn't want to be caught looking back. In some ways, my current situation was similar to that of the Israelites shortly after they were freed from slavery in Egypt.

> *That night all the people of the community raised their voices and wept aloud. All the Israelites grumbled against Moses and Aaron, and the whole assembly said to them, "If only we had died in Egypt! Or in this desert! Why is the LORD bringing us to this land only to let us fall by the sword? Our wives and children will be taken as plunder. Wouldn't it be better for us to go back to Egypt?" And they said to each other, "We should choose a leader and go back to Egypt." Then Moses and Aaron fell facedown in front of the whole Israelite assembly gathered there. Joshua son of Nun and Caleb son of Jephunneh, who were among those who had explored the land, tore their clothes and said to the entire Israelite assembly, "The land we passed through and explored is exceedingly good. If the LORD is pleased with us, he will lead us into that land, a land flowing with milk and honey, and will give it to us. Only do not rebel against the LORD. And do not be afraid of the people of the land, because we will swallow them up. Their protection is gone, but the LORD is with us. Do not be afraid of them."*
>
> Numbers 14:1-9 (NIV)

After meditating on this scripture, I gave up on the idea of finding a full-time job. I kept my eyes open for something that was entrepreneurial but I wasn't going to jump back into a 40 hour-a-week position doing something I didn't enjoy. Robin and I still had enough money to pay our bills and her support for me was consistently strong. (Thank God for a virtuous woman.) Even though things didn't look great for me in the natural, I was determined not to give up.

Finding Purity, Finding Purpose

Several years ago, Robin took a 12-week course at our church that was designed to strengthen and heal women spiritually. I have heard it described as a Christian response to the feminist movement but it had been updated and improved for both men and women. Robin became a facilitator of the program and, over the years, had helped countless women find healing from their past and become positioned to pursue their purpose in Christ.

Since Robin was such a strong facilitator, people naturally assumed that I should take the class. Although Robin realized that the course was best suited for those who were desperately seeking purpose, I had to constantly tell others that I wasn't yet ready to take the class. This continued for a few years but in August of 2001, my desperation was at a peak and I was finally ready to take the class.

Over the 12 weeks, I learned more things about myself than I care to list. I also became free from habits and practices that have hindered my progress during the course of my life. The class was something that must be experienced to be understood so I can't really explain its benefit. But I can say that by the time I graduated, I had a renewed since of purpose and a much clearer direction for my life. At the graduation ceremony, each of us gave the meaning of our names and the purpose of our life. Here is the meaning of my full name and my life purpose:

> Philip – Lover of horses or lover of strength, power and beauty.
> Howard – Sword guardian, nobleman.
> Page – An assistant to a knight.
> Jr. – This appellation signifies that my purpose is connected to my father's purpose, although I don't yet know how.
> My Purpose – To help God's people obtain wealth using the talents and abilities that He has given them.

After our statements, we received some words of encouragement and then our pastor prayed for us. I won't dictate the pastor's comments in detail, but I will say that it reaffirmed my purpose statement and highlighted the definition of my name. Specifically, he commented on my role as a protector, which is the meaning of my middle name. He also said that there were great business deals in my future, but that they weren't the main focus of my purpose. Whether they were the main purpose or not didn't matter to me, I was just happy that they were included somewhere in there.

Ordinarily I didn't get excited about prophecies or prophetic comments. I couldn't really figure out the purpose of God telling someone else something for me. Why doesn't He just tell me? I could only assume that prophecy was for wimps, or at least those who weren't spiritually mature enough to hear God for themselves. Of course, when you hear a prophecy that says what you want to hear then your attitude changes. Thinking back on the day of my graduation, I was glad that the prophet mentioned the business deals. I was reasonably concerned that I had missed God's instructions regarding business since I hadn't yet found success in that area. But this prophecy reinforced my desire to start and run a business. It also reminded me of a similar prophecy that I had received about a year prior during a trip with my sister. Both strengthened my resolve and propelled me back into business.

A New Business

Fresh from my graduation, I came up with another business idea. This one actually came to me during the class. As an exercise for writing my purpose statement, I had to take a personal inventory of myself. I was instructed to look at the knowledge the Lord had allowed me to gain and consider how it could be used for His glory. Naturally, I put my six years of tax experience at the top of the list.

While working at TaxOn, I was well aware of the thousands of tax preparation companies that tried to benefit from the most complicated tax code of any developed nation. Aside from the independent tax offices that were customers of TaxOn, there were a handful of big players with household names and locations in every strip mall. Still, I felt that there was room for a very small, nimble, independent tax preparation company with low overhead. Me.

I figured that the established players had a lock on the good locations and I couldn't afford a fixed location anyway. My plan was to get even closer to the customer by starting a door-to-door tax service that caught customers before they even left home. I would start by doing taxes in the common areas of townhouse and condominium complexes. Instead of renting office space and shelling out money for advertising, I would only need a laptop, a printer and a friendly leasing agent willing to let me camp out in the clubhouse. In my opinion, God had given me a great idea that was not only profitable, but also extremely creative and capitalized on the unique talents and abilities He had given me. I felt rejuvenated and started planning immediately.

ANOTHER NEW BUSINESS

There was a lot of work in planning a new business. I had learned a valuable lesson about over planning during the *Jubilee Fundraising* fiasco. But there was still a lot of work to be done. I had to find inexpensive (i.e. cheap) tax software, buy supplies and find a willing condominium complex. In the middle of my planning, however, I felt the need to put on the brakes a little. I realized that faith is necessary for success in Christ, but part of me was running on sheer excitement. This was the same excitement that blinded me before and I wasn't going to let it happen again. I slowed down and made a point of taking a more casual approach to this business.

As I was slowing down, I had another idea for a similar business. Instead of actually doing people's taxes, I could write some sort of software program to assist people in preparing their own taxes. I had already created a raw version of a program to help my sister and brother-in-law. I could just revamp it to help teach the basics of taxation. And instead of charging for it, I could just upload it to one of the websites that holds amateur programs and let people download it for free. If they liked it, they could send me a nominal amount. If not, then they haven't lost anything.

The more I thought about this second idea, the more intrigued I became. This was less a business and more a labor of love. For once, my goal wasn't to be rich but to help people. I legitimately wanted people to understand the entire tax process and feel empowered by this information. Of course, getting rich would be nice so I took the remaining months in the end of 2001 and worked on my first solo program – *Stater's Quick Tax*.

Chapter Seven

A Little Help Can't Hurt (Can It?)

Working Man's Welfare

Towards the end of 2001, things were going great spiritually but we were being stretched financially. We had spent the majority of the payout from TaxOn and were living mainly on Robin's salary. It was at these times that I was more grateful that Robin was finally getting paid close to what she was actually worth in the marketplace. Still, money was tight and I wanted to find a way to ease the burden.

When I was first laid off by TaxOn, I rejected the notion of filing for unemployment. There was just a stigma attached to it for me. Actually, in my mind, there was a stigma attached to any government program whether it was unemployment, welfare, WIC or anything else. Back in middle school, I could remember one of my classmates describing the way a welfare check looked. What he described scared me because my family received a check like that every month. I began to think about the impression people would have of me if I was actually on welfare. Would they pity me? Would I become a charity case? These thoughts bombarded me through the rest of the school day and all the way home until my Mom assured me that she was only receiving disability checks from her time in the Navy.

Notwithstanding my foolish pride, I didn't think I qualified for unemployment because, in my mind, I was "self-employed." Some people may be comfortable lying to the government but I wasn't going to jeopardize my integrity when I needed God's blessings on my business. Besides, the maximum amount of unemployment I could get didn't compare to the lowest sales estimate for my business. Well, that was then and this is now.

The more I thought about unemployment, the more I realized that I probably qualified. I can't tell you how much I didn't want to qualify. To qualify for unemployment meant that I was financially at the bottom of the barrel. I always thought that only those people who were broke and without options qualified. Well, suddenly I was "those people". I hadn't made any money since I was laid off from TaxOn and I wasn't working now. I figured I owed it to Robin to check with the local unemployment office to see where I stood.

Asking for Help

Everything was pointing towards me applying for unemployment but I still wasn't sold until I talked to my other best friend (the one who couldn't attend the men's conference). He was moving to Texas and I went to help move boxes even though I wasn't looking forward to seeing our mutual TaxOn friends that were sure to be present. During one of our moving breaks, the conversation inevitably turned to unemployment and I was asked if I was receiving money. I said no, but didn't seem to have a good reason. Being too proud to take money from the government seemed inadequate in the presence of my peers who freely accepted it. The clincher was when my friend said, "Philip, if the government was offering me free money I would be quick to take it." As usual, his logic represented someone who spoke the plain truth with no pretense. So, at that point, I realized that I needed to give up my pride and accept help.

When I called about unemployment, I was greeted with a barrage of questions by an automated telephone application system. The system started asking me very personal questions so I hung up. Why did they need to know my name and address? I wasn't ready for my information to be a matter of record so I called back and, this time, I opted to wait until I could speak with a customer service representative. After waiting on hold for what seemed like an hour, I reached a representative that was pretty pleasant considering she talks to desperate, unemployed people all day.

I questioned her about my situation in order to make sure that I wasn't abusing the system (and to give me a reason not to apply). I told her that I tried to be self-employed but it didn't work out. She then asked, "Did you make any money?" I paused for a minute and reflected on the disappointment of not making a single dime on my business idea. I wished again that I could change the past but I couldn't. I swallowed a little bit more of my pride and then answered, "No". She quickly responded, "Then it doesn't matter" and began to take the rest of my information. Her politeness really started to get on my nerves.

At the end of the application process, I was told that I needed to have a meeting with a live representative. I guess they needed to show me the resources of the employment commission to make sure that I wouldn't live lazy on the few hundred dollars per week they were giving me. I thought how crazy it was that I was doing all of this for a fraction of my previous salary. I wanted to back out now but I couldn't find a reason. I wasn't working, I qualified for unemployment, and to not take it would be to refuse money for the sheer sake of pride and pride was no longer a luxury that I could afford.

Humility is like Humiliation, only more Painful

I drove down to the unemployment office in the middle of the day to miss the rush. I hated arriving at government offices early in the morning or at noon when most people tried to run errands. When I arrived and saw a line back to the door, I realized that my reasoning only held true for employed people. Everyone filing for unemployment was unemployed so there was no early morning or noontime rush. We were all "in between" opportunities with very little to do while in between.

When I got into the building, I noticed a familiar face. This was a bit unnerving because I had intentionally gone to the office furthest from my house. I was in a part of town that I almost never go but I still ran into someone who had attended the purpose class. This guy was almost 7 feet tall so it was impossible to avoid him. When we made eye contact I just greeted him politely and kept filling out my paperwork. I really wasn't in the mood for a long conversation and, evidently, he wasn't either.

While I filled out my paperwork, I thought about how pathetic this whole situation was. A year ago I was a DINK (Double Income No Kids) family and my biggest worry was timing the purchase of a car with my next promotion. A few weeks ago, I was attending a class to help me clarify God's ultimate purpose for my life. A few days ago, I had received prophecy about how I was going to protect others and receive financial blessings from God. And on this day, I was sitting in the unemployment office petitioning the government for financial assistance. Oh how the mighty have fallen (or so I thought).

Sitting in the unemployment office with "unemployed" people was a strange experience for me. I was surprised that everyone else seemed so common and I began to feel out of place by comparison. Then each passing face brought a deeper realization that they weren't common and I wasn't special – we were all just regular people who were in a bad situation and needed help to get out. This new insight made me see how pompous and arrogant I was. Despite growing up with friends and family at all levels of the economic ladder, I had become a snob. A big fat snob.

After filling out the paperwork, I met with another representative. She was as polite as the woman I spoke with on the phone. She was pretty encouraging as she introduced me to the resources that could be accessed. Back when I was employed, I always thought that the unemployment office was just a place to get unemployment checks. Who knew that they were actually serious about helping people find employment? In my current predicament, I was happy to know that, at least, the government wasn't as bad as I thought. I left there thinking about all the other resources that the government had to offer. *Maybe I could start a business that acted as a fee-based directory of governmental resources.* I was too drained to create a new business plan so I made a mental note of the idea and saved it for another day.

Chapter Eight

You Can't Buy Happiness (But You *Can* Rent It)

Deductive Reasoning

I had gone through a lot at this point. I had been on a high from the anticipation of God's blessings and had hit a low as my expectations went unfulfilled. This had happened over and over again but I hadn't given up and I hadn't given in. As the days went on, my lows got lower and I often found myself crying out to God in desperation. I was determined to see God's blessings and abundance but I didn't know how. All I could do was hold on to my faith in Him. His Word declared so many good things and I figured that they had to eventually come true. To get myself through the lean times, I started to write down scriptures that reminded me of God's promises.

But remember the LORD your God, for it is he who gives you the ability to produce wealth, and so confirms his covenant, which he swore to your forefathers, as it is today.

Deuteronomy 8:18 (NIV)

But my God shall supply all your need according to his riches in glory by Christ Jesus.

Philippians 4:19

Blessed shalt thou be in the city, and blessed shalt thou be in the field. Blessed shall be the fruit of thy body, and the fruit of thy ground, and the fruit of thy cattle, the increase of thy kine, and the flocks of thy sheep.

Deuteronomy 28:3-4

There were many more scriptures than this, but they all followed the same pattern. Basically, I was trying to get as much proof of prosperity as possible from the Bible. I thought back to my "Introduction to Philosophy" class in college. I remember being concerned that the class would be anti-Christian so I took it under the Pass/Fail option. As it turned out, this was one of my favorite classes because it taught me how to make a clear-cut, deductive argument that could withstand any challenge. My goal now was to make an argument for God's blessings using His Word.

The unfortunate reality of philosophy is that it doesn't mesh well with the Christian faith. While Christianity has no problem standing up to philosophical criticism, the life of the Christian is not as direct and straightforward as a good philosophical argument. So no matter how much I used logic and reasoning to prove God's desire to bless me, I could never create an argument that would force the manifestation that I craved. It was as if God nodded and agreed with me when I talked to Him about His blessings but then chuckled every time I tried to pin Him down to a specific time or method.

The Holidays

The holidays posed a unique situation for me. They were a welcome break from the monotony of my life but they were also a reminder of the fact that I wasn't where I wanted to be. Robin and I were still living on her salary, plus unemployment, and we didn't have any extra money. That meant the usual excesses of the holidays would have to be reigned in this year.

On Thanksgiving, Robin and I usually spend the day at my sister Dinah's house. Traditionally, she and her husband take care of the meat and we bring many of the side items. Our two most popular items are my macaroni and cheese and Robin's collard greens with salt-cured ham but we also bring a variety of other sides and desserts. On this Thanksgiving, however, it would be a stretch to try to bring as much as we normally would. Dinah understood our financial situation but it still bothered me. I hated not being able to participate in something as good as Thanksgiving. I can see why God would make us go through the process of giving up the excesses of life. But Thanksgiving is probably the purist holiday ever and it was going to be hard for us to participate.

Aside from not being able to buy as much food, this Thanksgiving was humbling because I felt like I lost some of my role in my family. Growing up, my sister Dinah was the oldest and naturally she was the ruler of the kids. I have another older sister, but she didn't try to rule so, by default, I became the second in command. This role commanded a certain amount of respect from my siblings and I enjoyed it. I know this sounds weird but I had cherished this role since birth and now it was being threatened by my inability to bring food to our family function. I was on the verge of being demoted beneath my younger brother who almost never brought anything to family dinners except a hearty appetite and a doggie bag.

Christmas was a little worse for me than Thanksgiving. It was fairly easy to tell my family that I wasn't going to be buying expensive presents like normal, but it was very difficult when it came to Robin's present. More than anyone, she knew the details of our financial situation. Even though she said she didn't care about presents, I couldn't bring myself to rob her of a gift during the holiday. I know that everyone thinks Christmas has been commercialized, but I didn't care. So, despite our income, I cashed my unemployment check and took Robin shopping for clothes.

It wasn't very smart to spend as much money on Christmas as we did. It was like a business owner that is contemplating layoffs but still gives everyone an end-of-year bonus. If we hadn't bought anyone a Christmas gift, they wouldn't have thought any less of us. In the end, I think I just didn't want to admit how dire our financial situation was or how bleak the prospects looked for the future. By buying gifts, using money we didn't have, I managed to fool myself into believing that we were still as successful and prosperous as before I had been laid off.

Chapter Nine

Back In The Game

Focusing My Personal Life

The new year brought about a refreshing change of pace. As with each new year, Robin and I looked back on the challenges and accomplishments of the previous year in order to position us for the future. Overall, I must admit that 2001 wasn't all bad and it wasn't nearly as bad as it could have been. Sure, I was laid off, failed in my attempt to start a business, and failed in my attempt to buy an existing one. But I also received a fat check, made huge offerings to various ministries and significantly reduced our debt. Best of all, Robin and I are still together and that was the most important thing to me. Being broke had not hurt Robin's respect for me or tainted our love for one another in any way. God is good.

During the holidays, Robin and I talked a lot about our future. We lived in Tulsa for five years before we started calling it home but we had always intended to move back to Virginia. Tulsa may be the buckle of the Bible Belt but it's not exactly the picture of diversity. We wanted to raise our children in a place where they can be spiritually and culturally nurtured and Virginia offered a lot more than Tulsa in the way of diversity. It seemed possible that this was the proper time. Robin still enjoyed her job and her coworkers but the work had become less fulfilling. I, of course, just wanted to be doing something somewhere and moving to Virginia was a very small price to pay.

Robin and I weren't clear in our decision to move. We knew that we wanted to move but we didn't know how. If we sold the house and moved without jobs, there may be two of us looking for work instead of one. If we just looked for jobs, we may have to live apart while one of us worked in Virginia and the other sold the home in Tulsa. For someone as mentally dependent on his wife as I am, that wasn't an option. So, we decided that I would look for jobs in Virginia and we would see what happened. Our hope was that, after graduating with my MBA, I would get a six-figure job in Virginia with relocation expenses covered. Until then, we would just continue our life in Tulsa.

The Certainty of Death and Taxes

We've all heard the statement that there is nothing as sure as death and taxes. Well, that may be true but I was determined that, at least, taxes wouldn't be as tragic as death. I had almost finished programming my personal tax software program and was putting on the finishing touches. In all modesty, the program was pretty neat. It was simple but still very helpful. Instead of trying to create an all-encompassing program to do all types of taxes, I created a guide that would help an individual taxpayer to estimate their taxes for the year. In the process of estimating your taxes, you would learn the basics of taxation.

After finishing the program, I intended to upload it to the most popular website for software downloads on the net. There was no charge for storing your program listing on their site and millions of people visited the site to try new software. When someone looked for a program that matched yours, they could download it. My program didn't have a cost so people could download it and use it free. If they liked it, I asked them to send me a small registration fee of $7.90. Don't ask me where that amount came from. Since I was depending on the benevolence of the general public, I just picked a number that wasn't too high and hoped for the best.

Door to Door Taxes

Having finished my tax software, the digital portion of the tax business was on autopilot. Now I needed to put my 'door-to-door' tax business in place. As I mentioned before, the beauty of this business was that it didn't require a large investment of money. I could use my personal printer and tax expertise and borrow my sister's laptop but I would need to obtain professional tax software similar to what TaxOn used to sell. Unfortunately, that type of software cost upwards of $1,000 and I no longer had connections in the tax industry that would allow me to obtain software free. There was a package sold by the company that bought TaxOn that allowed you to pay for each return as you prepared it. The pay-as-you-go approach was great but shipping was still expensive and the program required you to connect to the Internet to get an access code before you could print. I couldn't be sure I could do that consistently from a remote location.

The cost of purchasing tax software caused me to have second thoughts about starting the business. I began to question whether taxes were the way I should go. I had a background in taxation but I never really liked taxes. I don't think anyone likes taxes. Maybe I should focus more on moving to Virginia or finding another coffee shop since that's where my heart was. Before I put the idea away for good, I brought it before the Lord as God tells us to do in Philippians 4:6. I asked the Lord to provide money for software if it was His desire that I pursue this business. I didn't hear a voice from God or feel compelled to stop so, after praying, I called a few tax companies to collect prices. I knew I didn't have any money to buy anything but I knew that faith required an action on my part and it couldn't hurt to call.

The prices were just as I expected, which was more than I had. After a few weeks, I figured that God was telling me to let this idea go. He hadn't made provision for the business and there was no way I was going to go into it without a clear sign from the Lord. Then, I received an offer in the mail from the company that bought TaxOn. I had requested a sample of their software but never followed up with a purchase or any additional questions. Well, now they were offering me their complete line of software FREE! The letter stated that they were offering me this free trial in hopes that I would purchase next year. I reread the offer a couple of times to make sure I understood the deal. I couldn't find any fine print that caused me to change my long distance or buy anything else at a later date. In response to my prayer, they had sent me an offer I couldn't refuse and I called them to make arrangements for them to ship me the software. I was back in business!

The failure of *Jubilee Fundraising* was still fresh in my mind so I wanted to make sure that I didn't make any of the same mistakes. Instead of over planning and trying to get everything in order simultaneously, I followed a process called Milestone Planning that I learned in a small business class. It's really pretty simple; you just list the steps that are absolutely necessary to start your business in the order that they must be completed. This way, you never overspend or over plan. With my tax preparation business, the first thing I needed to do was to find a luxury apartment or condominium complex willing to let me sell my services to their residents. It was strange calling places before I had all the details in place, but, based on Milestone Planning, nothing mattered until I found potential customers.

Success Doesn't Look Like I Thought It Would

The one thing I realized about living in Tulsa was that it was full of transients. It seemed very few residents were actually born in Tulsa, they either got transferred there by their job or they were just living there while they went to college or Bible school. The good part about this, for me, was that Tulsa had a large number of affluent apartment, condominium and townhouse communities. I went to the convenience store to pick up one of the free apartment listings and started calling the properties that appeared to have the richest tenants.

At TaxOn, I spent my first two years as a salesman making and receiving telephone calls all day. I really hated the idea of making sales calls again, but it was necessary to make this business work. I was prepared to beat my record of 150 outgoing calls in a day but the Lord gave me grace on just the third call. The second property manager I spoke to recommended one of their sister properties and, when I called them, the leasing agent was more than willing to let me come by for a visit.

The leasing agent met with me and was excited about what I was doing. She hosted a monthly breakfast on Saturdays as a way to meet and greet the tenants. She had been looking for something to offer the tenants to help distinguish her property from others and she thought an in-house tax professional would be a good draw. So, on Saturday I would meet for breakfast, mingle with the tenants and hopefully drum up some business.

Things were moving pretty fast at this point. I didn't have the software or the laptop and there were a hundred things I needed to do. I didn't expect to have a gig so soon but I definitely wasn't going to turn it down. I just needed to get started and let things work themselves out. God had already shown His favor and I didn't need to get anxious now. Besides, this was a bootstrapped business that was started with no financial investment whatsoever. The only thing that was at risk was my faith.

The software finally arrived and I loaded it on my computer. It didn't seem as good as the software I produced at TaxOn but, as my Dad always said, "free is better than cheap". I started a practice return and found out the software was much better than I thought. Next I started to create order forms and information sheets to process my potential customers. I had no way of knowing how many people would want me to do their taxes but I didn't want to turn anybody down. Just in case I had more customers than I could handle, I called in reinforcements in the form of my youngest sister. She had experience doing taxes for one of the big tax preparers and, more importantly, she was always willing to help her big brother. God just continues to provide.

The Day of Reckoning

When I arrived at the apartment complex I was pretty excited and very nervous. I had planned to call my little sister only if I needed her so I started the day alone. Robin offered to help me, as she always does, but I wanted to do this myself. In all honesty, I wasn't sure that this would work out and Robin's presence would make me more nervous. I could eventually handle failure, but failure in front of the woman that I love more than anything on this earth would be unbearable. I couldn't imagine what it would be like to lose her adoration and respect.

Once I was set up, the day started off pretty slow. People came in and headed for the food so I had to wait until most people were finished eating before I could start a conversation. I'm an introvert by God's design, but I can do a pretty good job of imitating an extrovert in most social situations. The problem was that it wasn't a social setting. I was trying to sell myself, in the figurative and literal sense, and that carries an extra measure of personal exposure. Thank God the people were pretty open.

After an hour or so, I got my first real nibble. I met a couple who had recently relocated to the area in order to go to Bible school. The husband had a few questions about multi-state returns and deductions for his daughter's private school tuition. I was so excited that I could answer his questions I practically fawned over the guy. He probably thought I was flirting with him or something. At the end of the conversation, I gave him my homemade business card, my price sheet and a thousand thanks.

I didn't actually prepare any taxes on that day but I still considered it a success. I had one great lead and I talked to some other people. Once I got over my nervousness and anxiety, I figured I could do this at a lot of other places. And the leasing agent agreed to let me come back for another try. Other than wishing I hadn't dragged in my big all-in-one laser printer, things went pretty well.

Chapter Ten

Keeping My Head Above Water

Produce!

One of my managers at TaxOn used to walk through the office during tax season and yell, Produce! He was a nice, mild mannered guy so it was kind of funny to hear him try to crack the whip. Instead of sending fear, he offered much needed comedy relief. As I tried to balance my two tax businesses, I thought about his attempt to motivate. I yelled, Produce! to try to get something going. Just like at TaxOn, nothing happened.

By now I was getting a pretty good response to my software. Almost a hundred people had downloaded it and I was feeling proud of my creation. Unfortunately, no one appreciated it enough to send any money. It was only $7.90, what's the big deal? I calmed myself down by remembering that the software was a labor of love. I wanted to get rich but I knew it was a long shot. My main motivation for finishing the program was to fulfill my purpose and "train God's people how to obtain wealth" by helping them understand taxes.

The tax preparation business was a different story. I had started off so well that my expectations were pretty high. But I couldn't seem to duplicate my early success. The first apartment complex was unique in that the leasing agent had the flexibility to invite people to community functions. The more people I called, the more I realized that this flexibility was rare. To make matters worse, I was shut out of the majority of properties because they shared the same corporate parent company that had a policy against any business in the clubhouses. I had called about half of the properties in the local apartment directories and no one was willing to work with me.

The early promise of tax preparation turned flat. Although I had one successful outing, I didn't make any money from it. My one good lead wasn't good enough. The truth was, since I was still accepting unemployment, I wouldn't really make any money until I earned more than the weekly allotment of $290. Anything I earned during the week would be deducted from that amount so my effort would be meaningless. I coordinated for my lead to get his taxes done free but that didn't make me feel better. I was beginning to think like a man on public assistance. I used to look down on people that *seemed* to be leeches on society but now I was the societal parasite.

THE DAILY GRIND

After not being able to secure another venue for tax preparation, I gave up. Maybe I didn't try hard enough. Maybe I shouldn't have tried to make a business out of taxes. Either way, my efforts failed to yield fruit so I purged the vine. I stopped trying to sell tax preparation services and started volunteering my time for free. I felt bad about the failure but I was more confused than anything. Once again, I felt like God's promises didn't come through. This wasn't a 'Christian' business but I started it in faith and only moved when I felt His urging. It was like He started me up fast then dropped me hard.

The lack of financial success for my software program was equally hard to take. On the one hand, I was pretty happy about the consistent growth in downloads. I was up to several hundred downloads so evidently somebody appreciated my work. On the other hand, no one had bothered to send me a dime for my effort. I didn't even get an email saying Thanks. Without any positive feedback, my mind created its own negative replacement. I started to wonder if anybody even used my program. What if they just downloaded it because I wrote a good description then deleted it right after they looked at it? Or what if some computer is downloading it over and over again as a test? The more I let my mind wander unchecked, the worse I felt.

My list of faith scriptures, and other sources of spiritual nourishment, were pretty helpful. But I still ran into times where the pitiful reality I faced on a daily basis seemed more than I could bear. The only thing I had going for me was the MBA program. Thank God I was still making A's but I even started to question them. How good of a student could I possibly be if I had failed at every business I had attempted? Nonetheless, my schoolwork was a therapeutic alternative to the rest of my life so I proceeded as best I could.

Aside from studying, I spent most of the day in a pity party or looking for work. I wanted a job that would allow me to fulfill my purpose but it didn't seem to exist. With the stalled economy, and other major layoffs in Tulsa, I wasn't finding anything. I got pretty desperate and started to apply anywhere that fit my skills. I did this on a daily basis but to no avail. My daily routine became so monotonous that it was stressful.

To spiritually prepare myself for the day, I began to have more intense devotions in the morning. I would read my Bible as usual but I would also spend time in praise and worship. I can't sing very well so I mostly relied on my collection of urban contemporary gospel music to lead me into God's presence. I'm not very emotional at church but, in my daily praise and worship, I was an emotional basket case. The trigger for my breakdown was when a song would begin to repeat a lyric about the greatness of God. Sometimes the song would go into an endless loop on God's goodness. I realize that this is the purpose of praise but it was painful for me.

The more I thought about God's awesome power, the more frustrated I became with my present situation. Eventually I got to the point where I was just furious with God for betraying me. He has all power and all authority and, somehow, He is content with one of His children in total despair. I had done all I knew to do and I was still left with nothing. No money. No job. No success in anything I tried. Every time I thought about His great power and strength my blood boiled. When I came to my senses, I tried to reconcile His great power with my failures but it was just too much to comprehend.

Help in the Time of Trouble

My angry praise and worship continued for a long time. After seeing Robin off to work, I would try to praise God, get mad, start crying, try to praise Him again, then give up and read the Bible. That was my morning ritual for longer than I care to remember. Afterwards, I would start searching for jobs. I didn't really care at this point so I just applied to anything that had the words computer or Internet in the description.

To break up the monotony of my day, I would work out at the gym. I figured if I was going to be jobless, I could at least lose some weight. On the way to the gym, I would often try to praise God again. In the middle of some songs I would burst into tears. Sometimes the tears just streamed and I had to drive around until I could get myself together. The gym was such a masculine place that I didn't want to be caught whimpering in the parking lot.

After a while, I noticed something different about my praise and worship. Although, I continued to cry, I realized that my tears were no longer angry. I had begun to cry tears of pain and sorrow over the recent events of my life. While I cried, I was able to praise God in the midst of my circumstance. I gave Him praise for being alive and for simply giving me the opportunity to live on His Earth. I stopped blaming Him for the things that went wrong in my life and just praised. In these times, I started to feel God's peace. I felt drained afterwards but, somehow, I felt better. It was as if the act of exposing my feelings allowed Him to reveal Himself to me.

My situation didn't change, but I finally understood the benefit of having God beside me. One day, when I was listening to the gospel artist, Fred Hammond, in the car, I heard the following words, "*I will live and not die. For every need there is supply. For the Savior says just ask, just ask and believe that you will receive. He can do what seems impossible, somebody say, Yes He Will! Yes He Will! Oh, Yes He Will!*" My pastor used to say, "Sometimes God brings you out of a situation and other times He stands beside you and walks through it with you." This never made sense to me. I used to always wonder why God didn't just put me in a new circumstance, but at this point I was just thankful that I wasn't alone. God was with me. And no matter what happens, I will live and not die!

A Word of Encouragement

By now, I had given up on a lot of things but I hadn't given up on God. I had decided to stop dreaming up business ideas in order to concentrate on finding a job in Virginia. Robin and I wanted to move and it was just too unlikely that I was going to start a successful business in Oklahoma and somehow move it to Virginia. The decision to stop creating businesses was not easy to make. After Robin and I discussed it, I went into our home office and cried. Actually, I mourned more than I did when my favorite Aunt died. I felt like my heart had been cut out with a spoon. The very thing I loved was being sacrificed and I couldn't see how it was ever going to be resurrected. I just tried to have faith in God and focus my energy on starting a new life in Virginia.

Shortly after I sacrificed my business dreams on the altar, one of the assistant pastors of my church asked me if I would do her taxes. She was getting married soon and didn't have the time to take them to a tax preparation office. I was honored that she asked me because I knew there were other, more qualified people in the church that would have done it. She told me to charge her whatever my rate was but I refused. Robin and I simply adored her and there was no way I was going to charge her for anything.

I got her tax documents and started on her taxes immediately. It was a little different doing a pastor's return so I had to get some guidance from a CPA friend of mine. I also didn't want anything to go wrong. I couldn't take it if she got audited based on my work. After much effort, I finished her taxes and found out she was getting a pretty sizable refund. I called her to tell her the results. I wasn't sure how much she was expecting so I just calmly told her the amount. She thought she was going to owe so she got really excited about the refund.

I was more excited about the refund than I have been about anything in a long time. When you're unemployed, you often feel as if you don't have the chance to contribute anything of value on a regular basis. I realized that I didn't create a refund that wasn't already earned, but I was ecstatic that God gave me the opportunity to be the one to give her the good news. And when I gave her the return, she shoved a check into my hand. I told her that I wasn't charging her but she said she just wanted to bless me. And she definitely did because when I looked at the check I realized that she had given me $100. I REALLY appreciated the money, but, more than that, I felt like God was using it to talk to me. It was as if God was saying, "I haven't forgotten about you." I had given up on business but He hadn't given up on me.

The Return of Good Things

After blessing us through our pastor, God blessed us even more directly. Robin and I filled out our taxes and realized that we were also going to get a refund. A big refund. We were going to receive about $5,000 between our state and federal taxes. This was a big deal for us because, normally, our goal was to break even. We always believed that getting a tax refund means that the government has been using our money, interest free, for a whole year. So we have always adjusted our exemptions to break even. But this year, my overestimation of the TaxOn payout resulted in an unexpected increase in our tax return. The refund was based on the IRS requirement to withhold a fixed percentage of the lump sum we received.

I remember thinking about how dejected I was when the

payout amount was so much less than I anticipated. I acted as if someone had just robbed me at gunpoint or stolen my life's savings. In actuality, the only difference was that the government would hold on to a portion of my money for a while. Thinking about this made me feel so stupid for the way I sulked around and accused God of not doing all He could to make me happy. I was moved to embarrassment then to repentance.

In my thinking, this refund was really the rest of the payoff from TaxOn. We had spent the first part of the money and we really needed this last part. But during the wait, God had changed our thinking regarding money through a 12-week small group Bible study designed to help Christians take control of their finances. Through this course we were learning, among other things, that God wanted us to be debt free. This made perfect sense to me until I realized how much it would affect me. Everyone wants to be debt free but no one wants to stop spending.

> *The rich rules over the poor, And the borrower becomes the lender's slave.*
>
> *Proverbs 22:7 (NASB)*

> *You were bought with a price; do not become slaves of men.*
>
> *1 Corinthians 7: 23(NASB)*

There are many scriptures that attest to God's desire for us to be free from financial bondage, but the ones above say the most to me. Basically, if we were bought and set free by the blood of Christ, why would we sell our selves as slaves to lenders? Slavery is a strong word, especially to an African-American, but what else would you call it when another party so strongly influences your actions. Debt takes God out of control and I felt convicted that it was time for that to stop. So, when Robin and I finally received our tax refund, we used it to wipe out the last of our credit card bills. This took us one big step towards freedom and left only my school loan and our house as the final remnants of bondage.

Chapter Eleven

Be Careful What You Wish For

One is the Loneliest Number

The life of an unemployed person is really busy. It was not that I exerted so much physical effort searching for work, it was that I was preoccupied with unemployment all day. By the time Robin came home in the evenings my mind was pretty drained from trying to find work. I hadn't worked that hard since I was putting in 50 hours a week a few years prior. And I refused to take a break until something happened. In my mind, breaks were for employed people. I needed a job and I needed it immediately.

In addition to my desire to have a job, I also had a desire to overcome the stigma of unemployment and the stereotype of the lazy male. Being unemployed is like having a disease. Everybody tells everybody else about it and people feel sorry for you. You can't hang around your old friends because your job search immediately becomes the topic of conversation. Then people try to diagnose you by telling you about every job listing they've ever seen. It doesn't matter that you're not qualified to do any of those jobs (or you may be overqualified) they still want to help. I know their heart is in the right place, but the last thing I wanted to hear was "Have you found a job yet?" for the thousandth time.

My initial response was to avoid being around do-gooders who wanted to "help" me find a job. By nature, I'm not a people person so this wasn't too difficult for me. Of course, when I have to be in social situations, like at church or Robin's office parties, I was forced to be creative. I started telling people that I was consulting but that only generated more questions that I didn't want to answer. My new skill for these situations was called "Attention Deflection." I basically stored up a series of generic, open-ended questions. When I ran into someone I couldn't shake, I would inundate him or her with a barrage of questions to keep them talking. Inevitably, they get tired of talking and leave. This worked better with some people than with others but I would eventually wear down even the most self-centered person.

The danger in avoiding people was that my perception of reality got skewed. Since I conducted my job search mostly on the Internet, I spent several hours a day without speaking to anyone. My interaction with people was often limited to the one hour of TV that I allowed myself during lunch. I did, however, work on my communication skills through my cover letters. I had it down to a science. I could create a custom cover letter for practically any position using templates that I created. Whenever I managed to find a job my written communication skills would be incredible.

Sure, I Can Do That

Strange things happen when you write cover letters all day. The more cover letters I wrote, the more poetic license I took. My resume was even worse. I never lied to anyone and I always used the titles that I actually held, but the descriptions for those jobs changed dramatically based on the position for which I was applying. Since I spent such a long time in a small company, I had experience doing mostly everything. In my six years at TaxOn I was a salesman, tradeshow presenter, trainer, recruiter, technical support representative, software tester, programmer and manual writer. If the job description called for it, I could do it.

This zealousness caught up with me when I was actually called to interview for a job for which I forgot I had applied. As it turned out, I had applied to a state-sponsored health organization for a job that had been filled (thanks a lot). But they wanted to interview me for a related job as a Technical Researcher for an anti-smoking campaign. I wasn't overly sympathetic to anti-smoking campaigns but I needed a job. And if I could do something to clear the air of smoke in restaurants then that was icing on the cake.

The first interview was absolutely horrible. I did my usual preparation on the organization and I researched the job title but I was still unprepared for government agency questions.

The interviewer, my potential boss, was a nice person but her questions stunk. There was no emotion in them and no room for me to use my personality to hide the weaknesses in my experience. They just wanted to know how long you've done this and when did you start that. At one point, they asked me to define mean, mode and median. I thought to myself, "what kind of question is that?" Even if I could define mode (which I couldn't at the time) it wouldn't make me a better employee.

After the interview, I picked up the remainder of my ego and went home to look for more jobs. Up to that point, my job search had gone nowhere and I was about to be ineligible for unemployment checks. I wouldn't miss the money as much as I would feel like a loser for reaching the maximum unemployment benefit. Strangely enough, I got a call for a second interview. I couldn't think of any reason why they would call me back unless they just needed a good laugh. This was a situation that only God could have put together.

The second interview went much better than the first, but it was not my best work. I'm not sure exactly what the problem was. I'm normally pretty good with interviews. I just couldn't seem to find the right words to say. I think I actually said that I wasn't the best candidate for the job. Despite my performance, I left the interview feeling good. I was grateful that they gave me a second chance and I enjoyed the challenge. This was good practice for the rest of my job search.

A few days after my second interview, I got a call with a job offer. This took me completely by surprise. Someone was offering me a job. A real job. I was kind of dazed on the phone, but I did manage to hear that a long time friend of the family had made a call on my behalf. Although I flubbed up the hiring process, I was awed by the fact that God had still made a way for me to come out successful...until she told me the starting salary.

The starting salary for this position was going to be much lower than I had made before. My potential boss knew that it wasn't a lot of money so she told me that there would be opportunities for raises in the future and that there were great benefits. This sounded good but I just couldn't get over the amount. The amount was more than a 20% pay cut. I knew I should have accepted immediately but I asked for some time to think about it.

I talked the job offer over with Robin. She thought it was a decent offer, considering the circumstances, but she wasn't as eager for me to accept as I thought she would be. The more we talked, the more amazed I became that Robin wasn't telling me to take the job. This gave me the freedom to think about the job and whether it was right for me. On the plus side, it was a job with long term potential (the average employee had been there over 10 years). On the negative side, it wasn't exciting work and the pay was low. Additionally, I found it hard to commit to such an important job in Tulsa when I really wanted to move soon. Finally, I came to the conclusion that this wasn't right for me so I declined the offer. I decided that God was just giving me something to chew on while I looked for the real job. I would take this as a learning experience and look for something I could get excited about.

HE'S THE GOD OF A SECOND CHANCE

It took me about a month before I got another interview. During that time I applied for jobs at a faster rate than before. Finally, I got a call from another company that I didn't recognize. I talked to someone's secretary, said "yes" a bunch of times and set up an interview for a programming job. I remember her asking me about my minimum salary requirements. I thought this was strange, since I hadn't been in an interview yet, but I was happy to have a chance to scare off any low bidders. I told them what my minimum was and started preparing for the interview.

The company, Digital Money, Inc. (DMI), was a third-party payment collector for several regional utility companies. They accepted payments through kiosks, over the phone and on the Internet. I would be working for the VP of Information Technology, and helping the company to build and maintain e-commerce websites. It actually sounded like a job that was above my head but I wasn't going to admit that. I figured the purpose of an interview was to see if they could figure that out themselves. And it would take a great job for me to put off moving to Virginia.

From the start, I realized the interview wasn't going to be easy. The conversation was laid back and relaxed. This seemed good at first, but I had never gotten a job offer from this type of interview. Without structured questions, the applicant has few ways to distinguish himself and the job goes to the guy with the nicest shoes. Knowing this, my marketing experience took charge and I started throwing out bullet point advertisements about myself. I wanted her to have something easy to remember and I wanted her to like me. She helped me out a lot by telling me about the slothful ways of her previous employees. I figured if I could just prove that I was the opposite of those guys, then I would have a great shot.

As it turned out, I had a fantastic shot. They called me a few days later and offered me the job. This job offer didn't place me in a state of awe, but I was really happy. The happiness remained for a few seconds until she told me that the starting salary was the same amount I had just turned down (here we go again). I told her I had to think about it.

Once again, I had gotten through a difficult interview and somehow been offered a job only to find out that the salary was comparable to what I made several years ago. These companies were obviously taking advantage of the fact that the economy had dumped tons of qualified workers on their butts. Why did they even ask me what my minimum was? I wasn't going to take this much of a pay cut, especially not for a job in Oklahoma. It wouldn't be right to take this job knowing that my heart was somewhere on the east coast. And to accept that salary was like agreeing that I was only worth that amount. It was an insult and I couldn't do it.

When Robin and I talked about the offer I found it harder to hold on to my, so-called, principles. It wasn't anything she said, it was just that the argument inside my head sounded better than the one that left my mouth and reached my ears. As I heard myself speak, I remember thinking about the unemployment checks. I had tried to justify not accepting unemployment but I finally admitted that my pride was not worth losing out on the money. Now, I had to admit that my pride was definitely not worth losing a job. The reality was that instead of taking a pay cut, I was actually getting a raise from my current salary of $0. But I wasn't going to give up without a fight.

I called the VP back and tried to give God a way to let me out of this situation. I know God is omniscient, but I wanted Him to have options. I told her that I was not happy with the salary. I said that I couldn't accept it in good faith because I knew that I would still be looking. She agreed that it wasn't in her best interest to hire me in this situation. (Great, I knew God would appreciate this.) She had taken the bait and backed away from the job offer. Then she did an about face and raised the salary a little more than 5%. She said that this salary, and any commitment I could make, would be better than the expensive consultants she had been hiring. In that one statement, she killed both of the objections that I wanted God to use to get me another opportunity. I frowned for a moment as I held on to the phone. I realized that God was giving me a chance at a job and it simply wasn't going to pay as much as I wanted. I told her I could start working on Monday.

No, I Can't Do That

I spent the weekend brushing up on my programming. I had been doing odd website jobs for family and friends but nothing that really helped me to maintain my skill. The more I thought about my interview, the more I remembered the things I said I could do. I really stretched myself during that interview. I mentioned every programming language that I had ever looked at or read about. She never asked me how long I had worked in a certain language; she just asked me if I knew it and I said yes.

I showed up for work giddy and nervous. I was happy that I had somewhere to go in the morning but I was scared of the job itself. When I arrived, my fears were justified with the first task I was asked to do. The VP wanted me to reroute the program files for one of the main applications we used. Before I started that, she also asked me to write a batch file (a series of instructions) for a utility that wasn't working properly. What happened to the orientation? What happened to the two weeks of training where you sip coffee and get to know the other new hires? They actually wanted me to work on the first day doing most of the things I said I could do in the interview. How crazy was that?

Apparently, small start-up companies don't have time or money for luxuries like extended training. Nor do they have patience for lazy employees. Realizing this, I started on the first of my projects. I stared at the files that I was supposed to move. I didn't even understand half of the terminology she used when she was telling me what to do. Then I thought about the fact that these were real files and not backups. If I made a mistake, everyone would know it instantly. I was paralyzed by fear and embarrassed before I even made my first mistake. Actually, I think the mistake was when I accepted the job. Obviously, I had missed God or misread His signs. I got my briefcase and went to her office to quit.

He's The God of a Third Chance

On the way to the VP's office I was filled with emotion. I was nervous, worried, embarrassed and relieved. Mainly, I just wanted to get out and go back home. I went in the office and told her I didn't feel comfortable and I didn't think things were going to work out. I started to tell her that it was better for the company if I leave now when she interrupted me. She must have seen the desperation in my eye because she stood up and said, "No, this is going to work."

I couldn't figure out why, but she really wanted me to stay. She just met me and at some point I must have made an impression on her. Or she just didn't want to go through the process of hiring someone else again. (I found out later that I was the third person to be in that position and the other applicants requested 50% - 75% more salary than I did.) Either way, she wasn't going to let me go without a fight so we went back to my cubicle and she walked me through my duties. Apparently, the reason she asked me to work on network related issues was because my new computer hadn't arrived yet. When it came, she intended for me to do what I was comfortable doing, programming.

After I got over the embarrassment of my first day, things started to go much better. I never got my two-week orientation but I managed to learn how things were supposed to run. The only problem that remained was with some of the programming that had been done before I arrived. The previous programmers used code that I wasn't familiar with and did things I didn't know could be done. Once again, I started to feel as if my resume writing and interviewing skills had put me in a position that I couldn't compete in. This caused me to struggle a lot so I asked the senior programmer a lot of questions. I soon realized I was asking too many questions about things I should already know. I was in way over my head and the water was rising.

My lack of programming success caused me to go to God in prayer. Before I realized it, He answered my prayer in a strange way. I was selected for jury duty. At first, I complained and tried to get out of it. The last time I was selected for duty, I spent a week sitting in a white room in the basement of the courthouse while waiting for my name to be called. It never happened. I agree that defendants should have the right to a speedy trial, but I don't think the government should do it by kidnapping 200 innocent people. I started to think about all of that wasted time and then it hit me, I needed as much time as I could get to become the programmer I already said that I was. So, I borrowed the company laptop and a couple of programming books and went to jury duty. By the grace of God, I was never picked to sit on anyone's jury. God used the wasteful wheels of justice to give me a weeklong study break.

When I returned from jury duty, I settled into my job. I also came to realize how much this job was an expression of God's mercy and grace. I really didn't want a "regular" job in Tulsa – especially not one that paid less than I was accustomed to making. I tried to sabotage it before I got it and then I tried to leave on the first day. And even after all that, I was still there and doing a pretty good job. My boss often told me that I was working out as well as she had hoped. This job is God's provision for the time; it's my manna from Heaven. Manna is not as spicy as jambalaya or as seasoned as catfish but it is daily sustenance that will keep me going until we can make it to Virginia.

Chapter Twelve

The Biggest Move Of Our Lives

Pomp and Circumstance

As I continued to be blessed at my new job, I moved closer to graduation. I had been in the part-time MBA program for three years and I was going to graduate in May of 2002. Best of all, I was going to graduate with a cumulative 4.0 GPA. This was especially significant for me because my undergraduate GPA was embarrassingly low. I didn't start studying in undergrad until my third year. By then, the A's and B's that I earned couldn't overcome the D's and F's that were permanently affixed to my transcript. The overall undergraduate GPA left me looking as if I was drunk half the time I was in school. But leaving graduate school with a perfect GPA would reinstate me to the ranks of the mentally gifted (or at least let people know that I didn't drink).

Even though I was looking forward to graduating, I wasn't

excited about graduation. I don't really like to be celebrated. I'm not sure if this is due to a low self-esteem or just the curse of being an introvert, but I tend to get uncomfortable when people make a fuss over me. I decided that I would only send out a few invitations to family and close friends. Pretty soon, I started to get some monetary gifts in the mail. My uncle in California, who I had not seen since I was a kid, sent me the most. And both of my dads, Robin's and mine, said they were coming from Virginia to be a part of the festivities.

I expected my Dad to come to graduation. (I can still remember the look of pride he had at my undergraduate commencement.) But I didn't expect Robin's Dad to fly to Oklahoma for me. After eight years of marriage, I didn't think he ever really forgave me for stealing his daughter and moving 2,000 miles away. I'm sure he just missed Robin but I was really touched that he was coming. He's a former D.C. cop who doesn't get mushy often so his visit was the equivalent of getting a big bear hug from someone you love and respect.

Robin's Dad stayed with us through the weekend and we really enjoyed having him there. I'm sure it helped that he no longer carried a loaded weapon but I actually lost most of my awkwardness and talked to him like a normal person. When we went out with the family, my two dads hung out together bowling and going to the movies. We all had a lot of fun. Since my siblings and Robin and I aren't usually in the same city as our dads on Father's Day, we decided to have a joint Father's Day Party at our house. All in all, it was a great weekend that I will never forget.

Virginia on my Mind

By the first few months of 2002 we had resettled in our Oklahoma life. We were both working. We were highly active in a great church. My family was mostly settled around us and everything was going well. The only problem was that we wanted a Virginia life. After eight years in the Midwest, we still remembered the nature, the culture and the family that was in Virginia. We wanted to go home.

Speaking of family, I was really looking forward to being with the Virginia portion of my family. My Dad was still in Virginia and all of Robin's immediate family was there. Although I grew up in the same house as my Dad, I never really spent time with him. This is mostly my fault because I was always into other things. Seeing him during my graduation made me miss him more and moving to Virginia would give us a chance to catch up. As a bonus, we would also get to spend time with Robin's niece. She was about 12 and she looks just like Robin. I've always had the best fun playing with her because it's like playing with my future daughter without any of the responsibility.

When we told Robin's family about our tentative plans, they were really happy. Robin's sister, who lived in Virginia, started to help us plan immediately. My Oklahoma family, as expected, had mixed emotions. In their minds, we were leaving them, but in our minds, we were returning to where we came from. We were returning to Virginia; the place where we were born, the place where we met and the place where we wanted to raise our kids.

My brother-in-law seemed to be the one who would miss us the most. This was hard to understand because he is a big, tall former college linebacker that doesn't usually express sensitivity externally. But he really wanted us to stay close. He wasn't crying or anything, but he was really giving us a hard time about moving. It was strange at first, but we began to realize that he was simply saying I love you and we appreciated it.

Overall, the rest of the family was OK. I guess they remembered the beauty of the state we were all born in and understood our desire to move. Of course, we would all miss the Sunday family dinners, the Birthday parties, the holiday celebrations and all night board games. There would be a ton of things we'd be leaving back in Oklahoma but Virginia was calling us. And the call was getting louder.

BURSTING AT THE SEAMS

Aside from our desire to live in Virginia, we were ready to move from our current home. Even if we stayed in the same city, we were outgrowing our 3 bedroom, 2 bath house. We wanted more space for entertaining inside and outside. We managed to cram up to 30 people in our home but it was tight and the temperature wasn't always adequate.

The outside of our home was equally insufficient. I needed more land to get away from our neighbors and their kids. The children in my neighborhood didn't seem to understand the purpose of property lines because I couldn't look out a window without seeing some kid playing in or through my yard. These kids had yards of their own with better grass and fewer trees but, somehow, our yard was like a magnet for bikes and skateboards. It was probably the large sloping driveway that attracted them but it drove me crazy. I thought one of the benefits of owning property was being left alone.

The final reason for selling our home was the current shape it was in. This was our first home, so we didn't fully appreciate the amount of upkeep that was required. We kept the grass cut and swept the walkway every now and then. But we never got around to painting the exterior or starting any landscaping projects. Our privacy fence in the backyard had fallen almost completely down and I couldn't patch it because the beams were rotted. Even worse, we hadn't been saving for any of these major expenses in the four years we had been there. Our only choice was to get a home equity loan or just sell the house. In order to not assume any new debt and position ourselves to move, we chose to sell the house.

Timing is Everything

The timing of our move was the biggest issue we faced. We wanted to find jobs, sell our house and find a place to live in a duration of a week. Our prayer was that God would direct us in the way we should go and coordinate our steps. It didn't seem as if we had direct control over any of the things that had to happen so we thought the best thing to do was to plan what we could and let God work it out.

The first thing we did was to call a realtor for advice on selling the house. Since agents are paid at the closing, and we could always turn down an offer, we figured that working with a realtor held little risk. We were comfortable with the realtor that sold us our current house. He went to our church and had become a friend of the family. But we wanted to be good stewards of our resources (another lesson learned from the financial Bible study) so we called two other agents to be sure we were getting the best deal.

The first agent we talked to arrived to our meeting late and didn't have much experience in our neighborhood. She was ruled out quickly. The second agent was very professional and had sold most of the homes in our neighborhood and gave us a ton of information about what our home was worth. They both gave us the exact same sales pitch, "Most agents in this area charge 7% commission but I only charge 6%" but this guy was pretty sharp and gave us a lot of information. He offered a lot of extra services and we were impressed. We just wanted to talk to our original agent before we made a final decision.

We made an appointment to meet with our previous agent at our home. I must have given the impression that we were ready for him to sell the house immediately because he showed up ready to go. My wife, always the pragmatist, let him know that we were just interviewing agents at the time. Although we loved him as a friend, business is business. As it turned out, he proved that he could do as much as the previous agents we interviewed. Plus we thought the process would go more smoothly with him since we had a history. As a bonus, he tithed to our church so we had the benefit of knowing that 10% of his 6% commission would go back to our church. He was the one.

In my opinion, the only thing worse than giving up 6% commission was having hundreds of strangers walk through my house. I knew it was necessary but it would destroy the peace that I valued so much. We talked to our agent about this and he told us that he would be sensitive to this in the showing. In addition to striving for low traffic, we also wanted to net $20,000 from the sale of our home after closing costs and commission. Our mortgage was about $75,000 and our market analysis told us that we could sell it for around $100,000. Even though there were things that needed repairing, he told us there was a decent chance that we could accomplish this. We were set to sell our home.

A Seller's Market

Our agent got to work very quickly. Before he put the For Sale sign in our yard, he called us to ask if he could show our home. The clients were a couple that was new to the area. They were about to be married and were looking for a home to start their life together. They came by the very next day and liked the place. They had questions about the repair spots, the painting, the plantations shutters, etc., but they made us an offer. Getting an offer on the first try was far beyond my expectations. The offer wasn't what we wanted, but it showed us that we had something worth selling.

I was ready to dismiss the offer immediately because we didn't end up with our goal of $20,000. They wanted us to pay for the repairs on the house, build a fence and pay for their closing costs. They even wanted us to throw in our washer, dryer and refrigerator. Our agent told us that these were typical requests but I didn't care. I had lived in the house the way it was and I wasn't going to fix it up for someone else to enjoy. And I definitely wasn't going to pay for anyone's closing costs. It just didn't make sense to pay almost $10,000 to sell a $100,000 house to the first offer.

Robin and I rejected the first offer and then they sent a counter offer. The counter offer was kind of irritating because it wasn't much better than the first offer. I was also irritated that the agent seemed to think it was a good offer. He kept working with numbers but I wanted to be done. The numerical output wasn't going to change unless the inputs changed. He was representing both parties and I figured he was just trying to close quickly with little effort. I started to doubt his loyalty.

I held on to my bottom line throughout the discussions. Robin didn't seem as dogmatic as I was but I was stubborn enough for both of us. We were currently making enough money to pay our bills and not much more. In order to move to Virginia, we needed money for the move and for our next place. Then we had to pay deposits and have money to live on until we found jobs. The only way I figured this was going to happen was through selling the house for as much as possible.

You Can't Serve God and Mammon

I had a big problem with the deal that I never really discussed. I wouldn't admit it out loud but I was actually jealous of the guy that was trying to buy our house. He wasn't even married yet and he was already in a position to buy a house for his bride. And the house was the one that we had been in for four years. Our first home was a one-bedroom apartment and he was making requests, which suggested that our standard of living was beneath him. I even fell short when I compared myself to him in current times. This guy had just moved to Tulsa due to a job promotion while my career was regressing and I was making less money than I had made a few years ago. This was killing me.

Towards the end of the negotiations, I started to realize that something else was bothering me. Aside from the numbers in the deal, I was holding on to the goal of getting $20,000 as if it was my only salvation. We needed big things to happen and it didn't seem like God was going to move in any supernatural way. Even with the payoff from TaxOn and the tax return, we still had about $15,000 of debt, our savings were depleted and we were just barely getting by. It was like God was sending us a sign saying, "Save Yourselves!" In actuality, I had lost my faith in God and was putting my faith in money.

The discussions with our agent continued and I began to soften my position. Robin wasn't seeing things the way I saw them and this made me reevaluate. I started to appreciate the benefits of the second deal such as the limited repair work (we only had to fix the fence) and the fact that only one client would have to visit our house. The big benefit was that they were going to let us stay in the house after the close and rent from them until they were married. This gave us the flexibility we needed to coordinate our cross-country move. I still wasn't happy about the deal but I was convinced that it was the best situation given our strange requirements. I put my pride aside again and we decided to accept the deal.

The deal made sense in plain terms, but, yet again, there was no miracle to be found. I wanted God to make this move easy for us but He seemed conspicuously silent. I kept thinking that God was going to use my faith and do something to knock our socks off. Instead, we had to just keep hoping that the other things that needed to happen for our move would fall into place.

MAKE YOUR REQUESTS KNOWN TO HIM

Being disappointed by God is a strange thing. We all know that it's not God's fault so I needed to find out what I did wrong. Did I have enough faith? Did I meditate on the right scriptures? I knew all of the prosperity scriptures and I was determined for them to work in my favor. I needed God to find us jobs and coordinate our move and I didn't want to be disappointed again. I began to put my prayer requests before God and trust that He would bless us. My desire was for Him to help me get a job that would pay for our relocation expenses. Hopefully, this would allow us to move directly into a home and give us some stability when we got there.

Robin and I both started looking for jobs as much as we could. We wanted to move to the Hampton Roads area so that's where we concentrated our search. Hampton Roads is the eastern section of Virginia that includes Hampton, Newport

News, Norfolk and Virginia Beach. Each city offers a great amount of social and cultural events, a bustling business sector (or so we thought) and family friendly environments. Either Hampton or Newport News would be good areas for us because they are close to my Dad and near the place where Robin and I went to college. Hampton is also where Robin's sister and brother-in-law live so we would be close to some of our family.

I had been looking for a job in Virginia since before I graduated two months previously and nothing was opening up. I was hoping that having the MBA behind my name would be the advantage I needed to get noticed. So far, it didn't mean anything to any of the companies that I sent applications. Not seeing any interest in the area of my choice, I widened the search to include Northern Virginia. We didn't really want to live there but there were lots of companies there that I would love to work for. Everybody seemed to have a headquarters in Northern Virginia. And if my dream job was there then I would just find a home and try to move again at a later date.

After several weeks of job hunting, neither Robin nor I had a job. Before we reached the point of frustration, Robin found two good leads. She had a phone interview with one company and it looked like things might work out. This company wasn't a nonprofit, Robin's organizational preference, but its core business was to keep information reports on other nonprofit companies. The other job was at a customer service subsidiary of a large insurance company. It wasn't her dream job, but it gave us hope for our move.

Chapter Thirteen

The Leap of Faith

Mountain, Be Moved and Cast Into the Sea

As our job search continued, we tried to make arrangements to finish our home repairs. Before we could close on our home we had to fix the fence in the backyard and we could not find anyone to do the work. Estimates to repair the fence were more than we could afford and it seemed we were about to run out of options until Robin ran into our next-door neighbor. As they chatted, she told him about our situation and he offered to build the fence for about 2/3 of the lowest estimate. We thought this was a great option until he stopped working in the middle of its completion. The deadline for finishing kept moving and I started to stress. Meanwhile, my neighbor's dog was running through my exposed backyard and pooping on a daily basis. My faith for moving to Virginia was in a fragile state and I really didn't have the patience to deal with this stupid fence.

To add to the stress, I had just rear-ended a car on my way to renew our car tags. It was a déjà vu experience that was eerily similar to when I first moved to Oklahoma and ran into the back of a truck after a sudden stop in traffic. In my mind I had put up with random, immediate stops for the past eight years and completely disregarded the fact that I constantly trailed too close to the cars ahead of me. After slamming into the truck, I started to think about rising car premiums, being sued and paying my deductible. Not to mention the ticket I was probably going to get. I looked to God and wondered why He couldn't have done something to help me avoid this big mess. It was completely my fault but I was just begging for an extra helping of God's grace at this point. We were already short of money and now I had cost us more by not paying attention to the road.

The auto repairs took a complete month to finish and I didn't have car rental coverage. I couldn't believe the ineptness of the body shop but there was nothing I could do. Whenever they were supposed to have the car ready, they called to tell me they had found something else wrong with it. Everything, except the deductible, was covered by insurance but the inconvenience of getting rides from my family and friends was killing me.

Things were getting too stressful for me by this point. I prayed daily for God to intervene in the circumstances but nothing seemed to change. Ultimately, I realized that instead of changing the circumstance, He changed me. In the midst of one of the most confusing times in my life, God gave me the strength and resolve to keep plugging away at work while the situation unfolded.

I finally got my car back only to find out that it had been scratched in the shop. Since it was their fault, I got to drive their brightly colored courtesy car for a few days. At home, our neighbor eventually finished the fence and hauled away the mess. As an added bonus, our neighbor on the other side agreed to pay half of the cost of the shared fence. He didn't have to do it, since we had to have the fence up in order to close, but I'm really glad he did. He saved us a couple hundred dollars and we needed every penny. Slowly things had started to come together.

Money Money Money (Again)

Once the fence was up, I forgot about the frustration that I endured while it was being built. I actually started to enjoy it because it made the backyard look better. It was a shame that we didn't put up a decent fence until we were about to sell the house. Our neighbor would have probably shared the expense if we had asked him years ago when we had two incomes and didn't care about debt. Oh well, we had finally finished our requirements for sale and we were ready to close.

The closing process is so much easier for selling a home than when buying a home. When we bought our home we signed a stack of papers about two inches thick. My hand started to hurt and I think we took a lunch break in the middle of it. As sellers, all we had to do was sign a few papers and pick up our check. It was kind of odd and sad since we were about to sell our very first home. Fortunately for us, the check made us feel much better.

The net gain for us at closing was $19,581. After getting a partial refund for the amount in escrow, we had netted over $20,000. When Robin brought the final amount to my attention I was dumbfounded. She started praising God for His goodness and His faithfulness but I felt a little ashamed. I remembered the big stink I made during the negotiations and how I thought our realtor and the buyers were taking advantage of us. Now, I had to admit I was wrong (Again!) and join Robin in recognizing God's faithfulness.

The first thing we did with our check was to pay tithe on our gain. It always makes us feel good to return our tithe on a lump sum of money. Paying tithes is such an awesome reminder of what God has done in your life. It's even better when you're doing it in church while the music is blaring and everybody is praising God. We took even more joy in the fact that this was probably the last time we would be doing anything this significant in our church in Tulsa.

After we paid our tithes, we let our new found financial training kick in and started planning based on our understanding of God's word. We wanted desperately to be free of all debt but we didn't want to be broke again. Our debt load was still pretty high and we still needed money to make the move to Virginia. We also didn't have jobs in Virginia and weren't sure when we would find them. In our worst-case scenario, we would have to move without jobs and pay rent from our pocket indefinitely. Even the Bible seemed to warn us to maintain an emergency reserve and not use our final dollars to pay off our debt.

Even though we wanted to save some of that big wad of money, our desire to be free of debt was too great. We had a lot of debt and we felt impressed by God to get rid of it. It was as if He had built our faith over the past year to get to this point. If we trusted that He was leading us to do this, and that He would supply our needs, then we could pay off our debts and still have a small reserve to make it to Virginia. It would be two big leaps of faith to knock off our final two creditors, but we could do it. So, in the beginning of June we took the first leap of faith and wrote a check for almost $9,000 to our credit card company. A few weeks later, after a little nudge from God, we wrote a $10,000 check to the U.S. Dept. of Education. We were a little nervous and a little shaky but we celebrated the 4th of July weekend by becoming completely debt free. How wonderfully appropriate.

Robin the Scout

By late June, we were still renting our old home from the new owners. They weren't ready for us to leave but we knew things couldn't remain this way. I hadn't found any job prospects in the technology or programming field but Robin seemed to have much better success with human resources positions. We decided to send Robin on a scouting trip to Virginia to look for places to live and, hopefully, find a job.

Robin had an interview scheduled and planned to spend some

time looking for businesses that weren't actually advertising jobs. Her scheduled interview went well but the company CEO was a bit unorthodox. When they spoke later by phone, he displayed some controlling tendencies that made Robin concerned about the peace of the work environment. That type of boss could make the life of a Human Resources Director miserable but it may be necessary to get where we wanted to be.

The housing search went a lot better. We had hoped to move directly into a house but our quest to be debt free left us without a sufficient down payment. Plus, we didn't want to jump back into a big mortgage in a place that was unfamiliar. So, Robin looked for condominiums or townhouses for us to rent for six months to a year. She found a handful of places and one, in particular, stood out.

I hadn't seen the townhouse Robin picked, but it seemed like a nice place in a nice neighborhood. It was close to Sheila, Robin's sister, and Robin knew someone else in the area. There was only one problem but it was a big one. There was no garage and we had grown accustomed to having a cozy home for our cars. We didn't look forward to getting out of our cars in the rain or scraping off snow and sleet in the winter. But Robin was hooked and it seemed like a good place for us.

When Robin returned from her trip, we had a lot of leads to pursue. She had found a job and a townhouse for us but neither was a done deal. We were waiting to hear back from both parties in order to proceed with our move. I was really hoping to hear from the job first. The job seemed like a necessary step for the rest of our plans. I knew we would need a place to stay, but finding a place to rent seemed much easier than finding a job. And I still wasn't crazy about the place without the garage.

As we waited to hear from Robin's potential job, we found out that the townhouse Robin found had been rented. We were disappointed (actually just Robin was disappointed) so we put our efforts into finding a new place by conducting a search using the phone and the Internet. We found a few places but no one seemed to want to rent to us. Leasing agents wouldn't call us back and no one wanted to rent to us unless we were already in the area. I thought we were facing some type of housing discrimination but no one had seen our faces. There was no basis to discriminate except on our location. Maybe that was enough.

The Big Leap

Robin continued to look for places to live and I kept focusing on work. We had sold our home and were looking for a place in Virginia but I hadn't told my employer about my plans. I was a little uneasy about my lie of omission. I trusted my boss, but, as someone who had been laid off before, I didn't trust any company enough to tell them I was planning on leaving unless I was prepared to be fired immediately. I intended to hold out until we were about to pack the moving boxes.

While I kept my secret from my boss, I found out that one of my coworkers was looking for a new house in my area. I kept thinking that he would see an old listing for my house and ask me about it. I wasn't sure what I would say so I tried to devise a strategy that would keep my plan a secret without telling any lies.

I tried to work in peace and avoid my home searching coworker. The more I dodged him, the more I felt like a liar. I also felt like I was beginning to doubt that our plans would be successful. The final deadline for us to get out of our house was just weeks away and I was holding onto a natural source rather than holding onto God. Robin had already told her employer that she was leaving and we had to move. Our options would soon be to either live on my income in a new place in Tulsa or take another big leap of faith and move to Virginia.

This situation reminded me of a sermon I heard about finishing well. The message highlighted the importance of ending a season well and was based on the third book of Matthew.

> *But when he saw many of the Pharisees and Sadducees coming to where he was baptizing, he said to them: "You brood of vipers! Who warned you to flee from the coming wrath? Produce fruit in keeping with repentance. And do not think you can say to yourselves, 'We have Abraham as our father.' I tell you that out of these stones God can raise up children for Abraham. The ax is already at the root of the trees, and every tree that does not produce good fruit will be cut down and thrown into the fire.*

> *"I baptize you with water for repentance. But after me will come one who is more powerful than I, whose sandals I am not fit to carry. He will baptize you with the Holy Spirit and with fire. His winnowing fork is in his hand, and he will clear his threshing floor, gathering his wheat into the barn and burning up the chaff with unquenchable fire."*
>
> Matthew 3:7-12 (NIV)

From this message I remembered the "principle of finishing". According to Matthew, it doesn't matter what you or your descendents did in previous times, God looks at the choices you make today. My failure to tell my employer about my moving plans was simply a lack of faith and I had grown in my faith too much to end my season in deceit. If I ended this season of employment without faith then much of what I had overcome would be for naught.

In addition to the issue of faith, I was really ready to stop programming and do something that was more in line with my life's purpose. So, on July 15th, I went into my boss's office and gave my two weeks notice. I told her the whole truth; I was moving to Virginia but I didn't have a job or a place to live. I was a little concerned because I figured she would think I was crazy. She also could fire me on the spot to protect the company since I worked with sensitive data files on a daily basis. As it turned out, she didn't fire me or laugh at me, she just asked me about my plans.

As we talked about my lack of plans for the future, she asked me if I would be interested in consulting for the company from Virginia. I was a bit overwhelmed by this because it seemed like an answer to a prayer that I never actually prayed. Continuing to work for DMI would give me guaranteed income while Robin and I got settled in Virginia. We could also find a place easier with a source of income to list on our applications. This was just a great thing and it took all of the control I could muster not to jump over the desk and give her a hug.

Encouraged by God's recent move on our behalf, Robin and I decided that we were definitely moving to Virginia at the end of July. Our plans had been confirmed by God's actions and we were ready to jump. We still didn't know where we were moving or how we would get there. We just knew that God had sold our home to the first client, gotten us out of debt and provided a way for us to keep an income stream. We compared our situation to the call of Abraham.

> *The LORD had said to Abram, "Leave your country, your people and your father's household and go to the land I will show you.*
>
> Genesis 12:1 (NIV)

When God spoke to Abraham, He didn't give him a specific location. He simply said, "Go to a land I will show you." Likewise, we didn't have a specific address to go to. We were just prepared to go. There were many reasons not to make this blind leap. When we told a few friends what we were doing, the blank stare on their faces seemed to say that they thought we were crazy. Maybe we were. But we had done too much to stay in Tulsa and God had done too much for us to back down now. Whatever we did must be done in faith so we blocked out the negative indicators and made plans to move to Virginia.

I Believe, Please Help My Unbelief

It's astounding how someone can have so much faith on one day, and start doubting God on the next. I thought I was done with this but I found myself vacillating on our decision to move. I knew we needed to take a step of faith before God would reveal His power on our behalf. This is what happened on each step of the moving process so far. But, although I acknowledged the power of God in our lives, I didn't necessarily like the way He had worked so far. I started to get scared that the actual move wasn't going to go the way we wanted. There were just so many issues and unknowns.

Our biggest problem was finding a place to stay. Even with a job, no one was interested in working with us. We would look up listings on the Internet and call the leasing office. But either no one would return our call or they would just tell us that we had to see the place before we could sign a lease. Without being able to sign a lease, we couldn't secure a place. And without a place, I didn't want to move to Virginia.

Both my Dad and Robin's sister offered their homes to us while we looked for a place to stay. This was a great gesture but moving into someone else's home was on the top of my "Things I Don't Want to Do" list. It was just so embarrassing.

And it seemed too easy for God to pull another miracle out of heaven and find us the perfect place in the perfect city on the perfect street. I just couldn't fathom the idea of living with someone else at this stage of my life.

I kept thinking about a comedian that I had heard making fun of people that didn't know they were homeless. He was referring to people who lived with their parents or men who lived with their girlfriends. He made me laugh out loud when he listed some of the ways you could figure out if you're homeless. He said something like, "If none of the utility bills are in your name, you're homeless. Or, if you have to ask for permission to use the telephone, you're homeless." I laughed like a hyena that night but I wasn't laughing now. If we didn't find a place soon, I was going to be homeless.

We'll Help You, But It Won't Be Cheap

The other problem Robin and I faced was paying for the cost of the move. I had called for estimates on moving trucks but they were extremely high. The prices were almost $5,000 for a full-service, cross-country move. Even if we packed the truck ourselves, it would costs thousands of dollars to have someone transport our belongings from Oklahoma to Virginia. It would cost almost a thousand dollars more to transport one of our cars. We had originally planned to hire professional movers to take our belongings and one of the cars while we drove ourselves in our other car. We then had to realize that this wasn't an option.

We went with the "rent a truck to drive" plan, which was the most affordable. This option meant that we were going to be responsible for packing the truck, driving the truck, unpacking the truck and getting both of our cars to Virginia.

While we considered this option my Dad called to tell us that he was going to be visiting Oklahoma. Since he was flying in, he said he would be willing to drive one of our cars back to Virginia for us. We didn't want him to have to do this but it would give us more flexibility for moving. If he drove one car, we could pull the other car behind our moving truck and drive together in the truck to Virginia. This was a greater blessing than we knew.

We still hadn't found a place to live so we also had to go with our backup plan for living arrangements and move in with Sheila. In the absence of any supernatural actions on God's part, we decided that the backup plan must be the way to go on both fronts. I was disappointed that these were our only options but at least we had these options. We had a way of moving to Virginia and we could stay with family until we got settled. We weren't where we wanted to be, but enough things were in place for us to finally move to Virginia.

Chapter Fourteen

Surviving The Journey

Moving Day

I woke up on our moving day and went to get the truck. In my opinion, this company's prices have always been close to the competition but their trucks and intangibles were usually better. Yet, I was a little disappointed that the attendant wouldn't help me attach the car to the hitch or let me pick the hitch up later that morning after I had finished packing the truck. I remember thinking that customer service wasn't one of their strong points. I signed the paperwork and left with a 24′ truck and a trailer hitch.

When I got back home, one of the movers we hired had arrived but the other was nowhere to be found. He finally showed up late and had the audacity to try to negotiate a higher rate of pay. All kinds of violent thoughts crept into my head, but thank God I didn't act on them. I simply told him that I was only going to pay the agreed upon rate and that he could leave whenever he wanted to. I would rather load all of the boxes myself then put up with his attitude for the next three hours. I guess I called his bluff because he backed down and slowly got to work. I had put out a small fire but the day wasn't starting off as I had hoped.

The rest of the loading and packing was uneventful. I didn't trust the late worker so I watched him most of the move. He moved really slowly but he was better than nothing. The mover that arrived early was great. He took three loads to the truck for every one load the lazy guy took. And he smiled the whole way through. I think I actually saw a halo over his head at one point.

After everything was packed onto the truck, we went to my sister's house to say goodbye and leave the second car for my Dad to drive. I drove the first mile of the trip with the emergency brake on in the car we were pulling. There was smoke coming from the rear of the truck but I didn't see it. Robin, who was following me in the other car, tried to get my attention. She flashed her lights and even got out of the car at a stoplight but I didn't notice anything. Finally, she reached me on my wireless phone to tell me to stop.

It's hard to believe that I didn't notice that the emergency brake was on. I was so concerned about chaining the car properly that I put the brakes on to hold it steady and forgot to take them off. Normally, I don't forget little details like that. My mind was just so preoccupied with the significance of what we were doing that I wasn't myself. I almost stripped the brakes off of our car and we hadn't even left Tulsa yet.

Dangerous Highways

We made it to my sister's house and after a thousand hugs and kisses we were on our way. Robin and I and everything we owned were in a rental truck and heading east. The magnitude of what we were doing was really great. When we got married and moved to Tulsa, we did it in a two-door car with a storage pack on the roof. Now, we had 24′ of stuff and a lot to lose if something went wrong. And a million things could go wrong.

I was silent at the beginning of the trip as I thought about the risks we were taking. Robin sensed that something was wrong and asked me how I was doing. She knows I'm quiet in public but I'm never quiet when I'm alone with her unless something is wrong. Before I could form my words, I thought about how great it was to be with someone who knows you so well. Robin knows my quirks, my habits, my dreams and my fears. She loved me enough to move to Oklahoma and she loves me enough to move back to Virginia in a rented moving van. I realized that I wasn't really risking anything. My most valuable possession was right in the next seat and nothing else mattered.

As we drove out of Oklahoma, our moving day turned into a regular road trip. We almost forgot that we were in a huge truck with no horsepower and started having fun. We had good discussions, we ate our travel snacks and we played lots of games. I remember making a deal with Robin to receive a massage if I could name 45 of the 50 states. After a long period of racking my brain I came up with all 50 of the states but she wasn't in position to massage my shoulders so I took a rain check.

We drove for several hours without any problems until it was time to find a hotel. We weren't sure how far we would make it so we didn't have a hotel room reserved. This always worked with our other road trips but we usually don't travel in a 24′ truck pulling a car. We needed to find a safe hotel with a large parking lot and good rates in the middle of the night. Also, before we could retire for the night we had to find some gas.

If you've never driven a truck with a diesel engine then you're in for a surprise. It's fairly easy to find diesel gas during the day when you're on a major highway, but it's pretty difficult at midnight when you're between major cities. Even when you find a place, it's quite a trick to maneuver in a tight space while pulling another car that prevents you from going in reverse. This was our mission and, so far, we weren't successful.

We were riding close to empty and couldn't find a station that was open. We would see a diesel sign from the highway then realize that it was closed. We finally found an open station that also sold diesel gas but, after spending 15 minutes trying to get close to the gas pump, the station had closed. We persisted through the back roads and finally found an open station. After three attempts to park, and a small fortune in gas, we were on our way.

Soon after we filled up on gas, we found a hotel with a huge parking lot. There was another rental truck in the parking lot so we figured we were with kindred spirits. We tried to get a deal on the room but the attendant told us that it was counterproductive for him to give deals after people showed up to the hotel. He did tell us that we might find a coupon in one of those road map coupon books. We went to the truck to look through our stash of maps and found a coupon we could use. Frugality pays off sometimes.

The Rolling Hills of West Virginia

The second day of our trip was more of the same. We did the usual tricky gas stops and found a hotel pretty easily. Things began to change, however, as we approached West Virginia. I had heard about the rolling hills of West Virginia but I never paid much attention to the reasoning behind the nickname. I thought it referred to the beautiful scenery or the farmland. I soon realized that the statement wasn't just a plug for tourism; for me, it referred to the very real and very steep inclines and declines that existed throughout the state's highways.

At first, the hills seemed mild. I had to give the truck some extra gas to maintain my speed but nothing serious. Then I started to notice that a little gas wasn't helping anymore. I was putting the pedal to the floor and we were still losing speed. The experienced tractor-trailers were zipping past me like I was standing still. The truck was just struggling to climb these large hills.

The inclines got pretty serious but we finally made it through. Then we hit a series of declines. I saw a sign that warned about a 5% grade decline coming up but I didn't have an appreciation for what that meant. I didn't start slowing down until I saw an emergency exit for tractor-trailers that was filled with sand. I wondered how many drivers actually ran off the road into the sandbags, but it must have been a serious enough problem for them to go through the trouble of building those special exits. I began to get a little scared and started slowing down. I was traveling at a safe speed but the reality of the situation made me nervous.

After we finally made it through the hills in West Virginia I started to calm down. I guess the stress of the whole move had just crept up on me. Just as we started to relax, I saw a rental truck sitting on the other side of the road. It looked like ours but it was split in two as if another truck had run into it. The people on the side of the road looked all right but the scene was scary. It made us realize how serious it was to travel across the country in just a truck. We prayed for God's protection even more fervently than before.

When we finally recovered from our West Virginia driving experiences, I noticed that the engine warning light came on in the truck. I wasn't sure what was wrong so I turned off on the next exit and pulled into a restaurant. As we looked for the manual to decode the warning signal, I started to think of all the possible things that could be wrong with the truck. I let my mind run for a while then I found my faith again and started to think clearly. The car wasn't smoking or anything. I just needed to call the rental company to see what they wanted me to do.

Robin and I went into the restaurant-slash-convenience store and instantly noticed that no one in the place looked like us. There was someone using the only pay phone they had so we waited. While the guy on the phone was sweet-talking his girlfriend, people started staring at us. As they stared, my mind began to wander again. We were in a small-town hangout and no one knew exactly where we were. We couldn't go anywhere because our truck was about to fall apart. We could be killed and no one would miss us for a day or two. I could see the headline now "Couple killed beside a pay phone while holding 50-cents. In a related story, there's a sale on household items in a rental truck in the parking lot."

The sweet-talker finally got off the phone and I called the rental company's emergency service number. The service representative asked me whether I noticed anything strange about the truck. She asked a few more basic questions and then deduced that everything was all right. The engine probably was overworked from the hills but would be fine to keep going. I figured she must know what she was talking about (she worked for the rental company didn't she?) so we got back in the truck and headed for Virginia.

THE ~~BEVERLY~~ HAMPTON HILLBILLIES

We arrived at the home of Sheila and her husband around 8 o'clock on Friday night. Sheila was excited to see us and we were glad to be there. Her husband was happy to see us but he was even more amused at how we looked when we arrived. We were coming into town with all of our belongings on one truck. He said we looked like the Beverly Hillbillies and he was right. I just wished we had also found some crude oil and were moving into a mansion like Granny and Uncle Jed.

I was still a little uneasy about living with them. We always had fun while staying there on vacation but this wasn't vacation. We were living there until we could find a place of our own and that couldn't happen soon enough for me. I desperately wanted to get going with my life and have some good things happen for us. I didn't want to live in the spare bedroom, I didn't want to ask for permission to use things and I didn't want to be a burden to anyone. I wanted God to do something to help us get our life back.

God had brought us safely to Hampton, Virginia but I was still questioning Him. Things just weren't going the way that I begged and prayed that they would. I had such high expectations for my life and career and I was so disappointed by what was happening. I felt like God was only doing half of what He could do to help us. At the same time, I was still praying to God for His blessings and His help. I'm sure God was irritated by the contradiction in my thoughts but I didn't know what else to do. God knew how I felt so there was no reason to deny my feelings. I just had to keep holding on as long as I could and wait for God to intervene with a miraculous change in my life.

In the meantime, Sheila and her husband were excellent hosts. They coordinated for us to use the neighbor's driveway while they were on vacation. They introduced us to their other neighbor who was an employment consultant. They gave us free reign of their home and treated us as if we were paying half of the mortgage. I really didn't understand their hospitality but I really appreciated it. I needed some encouragement to spark my faith again and they were demonstrating the unreserved love of Christ.

Chapter Fifteen

Finding Our Home

Home Search

We had fun with our hosts immediately upon our arrival. We watched movies, talked and ate good food just like we always did when we visited them on vacation. As far as couples go, we were pretty compatible. Sheila and I had a lot in common due to our mutual love for business. And her husband is as practical and straightforward as Robin. When we were together we had a great time and enjoyed each other far beyond the normal tolerance that is reserved for family. Things were feeling good and we were recovering well from our trip.

After a good night of rest, we began looking for homes on Saturday. We only found one prospect but we wouldn't be able to gain access for several more days and that just wasn't going to work. All of our things were still in the rental truck and we only had a few days to either move into a place or move into storage. We really didn't want to move our things twice so there was desperation in our home search. We spent Sunday doing research and strategizing so that we could hit the ground running and visit as many places as possible on Monday.

Our brother-in-law had given us the address of a house to check out so we looked at it first. As we approached it I noticed that it looked a bit run down. The closer I got to it, the worse it looked. I really appreciated the referral but that house was not the clean, new dwelling I had imagined. As I approached the door, I started to wonder if this was the type of home we would see all day. Before I reached the door, I passed a guy who was leaving the house. He told me that the place had already been rented so I turned away. I wasn't sure if he was telling the truth or not but I was relieved to have an excuse to keep going.

We looked at a few other properties but we didn't get much accomplished during the day. The search on Monday evening went much better with our fantastic brother-in-law at the wheel. The main difference was that he was a Hampton native and a truck driver who knew every road like the back of his hand. He really blessed us with his knowledge and we got a great overview of the city while we were with him. Even more important, we discovered many of the intangibles of a home search like which areas we could raise our children in and which areas would require extra security.

Even with "our wonderful tour guide" at our disposal, the home hunt was tiring and inefficient. Part of the problem was the confusing way the property descriptions were written. Many ads were even more liberal with their property descriptions than I had been with my resumes – evidently "cozy" means that there is only room for one person in each room and "quaint" is a French word that means "beware the hungry cockroach". Even the properties that were accurately described had at least one glaring error. Either it was already rented or it didn't have a designated parking spot or the yard was bare or the neighborhood was run down. No one place fit all of our wants and very few of them fit our needs.

The longer we looked, the more I appreciated that we didn't move into a place sight unseen. We really didn't know enough about these areas to sign a lease, much less buy a house. I wanted God to miraculously find a place for us while we were still in Tulsa but that was simply impossible. Even if He found the perfect place for us, we wouldn't have appreciated it without going through this looking experience for ourselves. Once again, God was right and my impetuousness almost caused us years of displeasure. Thank God for His grace.

Seek and You Will Find

One of the pleasant surprises about our current home search was that people were so willing to help now that we were physically present in Virginia. The apathetic agents we spoke to from Tulsa were now attentive and eager to assist. I wasn't sure if it was just our change of location, but I was glad that we were finally being embraced by the housing professionals.

On Tuesday, day four of our search, we decided to revisit a property that we had driven to on the previous Sunday. According to the description in the newspaper, this was a 2 bedroom, 2 ½ bath townhouse in Newport News. We couldn't meet with the agent on Sunday so we just went to see it ourselves. It was tucked away on the west corner of the city, but our personal tour guide, found it with no problem.

The main street was kind of modest (i.e. run down) but then it opened up into a nice neighborhood. The first section was filled with very nice single-family houses about the size of the one we hoped to buy soon. In the section behind the houses were the townhouses. They were fairly new, generous yards, and many had garages. The area was pretty quiet and we were optimistic about the unit we were going to see.

We finally found the unit in the back of the neighborhood. It had a one car garage and additional space for me to park my car. We couldn't get into the unit without the agent so we peaked into the windows to view the rooms. When we went around the back of the townhouse, we found a huge two-story window that gave us a great view of the living room, balcony and part of the entranceway. From our viewpoint, the unit was very spacious, new and, best of all, there was a great view of the lake from the rear deck.

We called the agent and made arrangements to see the inside of the townhouse. It actually looked better from the inside than it did from the outside. The only real problem was that it didn't have three bedrooms (one for an office) but there was a formal dining room. Since we didn't have any formal dining room furniture, this worked out well for us. I loved how new and clean the place was. It was really a step up from the condition of our home in Tulsa. And the master bedroom was huge. Robin's eyes doubled in size when she saw it and I immediately knew this was the place we wanted.

"Forget the Former Things; do not Dwell on the Past." (Isaiah 43:18 – NIV)

The leasing agent gave us an application and we filled it out on the spot. Due to my past credit issues, I always got shaky when I filled out applications like this one. I knew the Lord had forgiven me for my past credit problems but I always had a thought about being turned down or rejected in some way. I also thought about the fact that I was back in Virginia where my bad credit started. I had bounced checks, maxed out my credit cards and mishandled my utility payments here. I had a great record and reputation in Oklahoma but I wasn't sure it would matter in the Commonwealth of Virginia.

I finished my part of the application and let Robin fill out her part. I was happy to be able to write down that I had a job and was getting paid but I was still humbled by the application process. It was just so weird to be applying to rent a place when you've already owned a home. I reasoned that if we could own a 3 bedroom, 2 bath house then surely we could handle a rented townhouse. Shouldn't they have just given us the keys immediately and thanked us for living there?

Unfortunately, the leasing agent didn't see things the way I did. She was eager to rent the place but she still had to process the application and check our credit. If she looked at Robin's credit and my job then things would be great. But if she looked at things the opposite way then we were going to have to find another place to live.

About 20 minutes after we left the townhouse we got a call from the leasing agent. In my experience, quick decisions were bad ones so I prepared for the worse. As it turned out, she told us that we were approved and could move in as soon as we signed the lease. I was overcome with joy and wanted to sign the lease before she changed her mind. I figured she had checked someone else's credit by mistake and I didn't want to give her any time to fix her error. So, later that day, we signed our lease, paid our rent, paid our deposit and made plans to move into our new home.

Finding our home was a great blessing! We were 25 minutes from Sheila, an hour from my Dad and 15 minutes from our alma mater. It was a great place and it was in a quiet, relaxed part of town. Although we were renting a townhouse, it was almost as big as our previous home. The fixtures and appliances seemed brand new and the yard was being maintained by the housing association. The rental life definitely had its advantages.

Moving Day 2

The best part about finding our place was the timing. We left Tulsa on a Wednesday, arrived in Hampton on Friday, found our home on Sunday, viewed it on Tuesday and moved in on Wednesday. God created the world in a week and, for an encore, He created our new Hampton world in about the same amount of time.

I wanted to stop and celebrate but we had to return the truck that same Wednesday. We had just enough time to avoid moving our belongings into a storage facility or paying a late fee for the rental truck. Since we were moving in the middle of the day, and we didn't know many people in the area, we had to hire movers again. This was a small price to pay to get settled in our new home.

We awoke bright and early and drove our big rental truck to our new home. I took off a few things from the truck then waited for the movers to come. We had to pay for a minimum of four hours so I figured I would leave as many things on the truck for me to get my money's worth. While we waited for the movers, I helped Robin put contact paper in the kitchen. After that, we did a bunch of other little housekeeping things that my wife wanted to do, but usually I don't care about.

After waiting for an hour, we called the moving company to see where they were. We couldn't reach anyone at the office so we left a message. No one called us back and I started to get worried. We needed to get the truck back in a few hours and it was still full. I started to unload the boxes but I wasn't going to be able to move any of the big items by myself. Instead of worrying, I tried to preoccupy myself by unloading as much as I could unload alone. Before long, I had gotten the truck down to just a few big items and the movers still weren't there.

We kept calling the moving agency but no one answered. Ironically, we chose this agency because their advertisement in the phone book and their customer service person seemed so professional. Now they were missing in action and I was going to have to pay another day's rental for our truck. We finally reached someone at the main office but all they could tell us was that the movers were on their way. This was no help at all but we didn't have any choice but to wait.

After two full hours of waiting, the movers finally arrived. Evidently, they were held up in the tunnel coming from Virginia Beach. I know that traffic in the tunnel gets bad at midday but that wasn't my problem. Why didn't they leave earlier? I didn't have time to be mad but I did call the main office to complain. Complaining didn't make me feel much better but I got a minor discount on my rate and the movers got to work. After an hour of moving, a few scratches and some dropped pieces, they were finished.

The day had been frustrating but I didn't have time for my customary pity party. I still had to clean the truck and return it in order to get my deposit and avoid a late fee. As I drove the truck back, I started to take in the fact that the move was over. As bad as things had gotten between moving day in Tulsa and moving day in Virginia, it was finally over. I breathed a long, slow sigh of relief and thanked God for the opportunity to just relax.

Settling In

Once we moved our furniture in and set everything up, we were really happy with our home. Our furniture fit the townhouse as well as expected and we were finally settled in. The only thing left to do was to get the utilities turned on. The electricity was already on, but we needed cable, phone and trash service to make it complete.

I called the utilities to get everything setup for our home. You would think this would be an easy process but things got confusing pretty quickly. In Oklahoma, you just paid one water bill and that was it. In Newport News you paid for water service and then you paid for water treatment. What kind of a rip off was that? I could buy water from one company but I had to pay another if I wanted it to be clean. And the phone service wasn't much better. In addition to regular service, I had to choose a long distance carrier and a regional long distance carrier. The choice would be pretty basic if the prices didn't change based on what zip code you were calling and the time of day that you actually dialed the numbers.

Aside from the confusing array of service packages, I also ran into a problem with the deposits. One of the utilities must have remembered me from my former life because they wanted me to give them a $180 deposit for a $50 a month service. The representative said that this was typical of people setting up new service but they must have changed their policy by the time Robin called. I'm not sure if it was her warm voice or her perfect credit, but somehow they didn't require a deposit from her.

Setting up the cable service was actually fun. We always got the basic service, which only included the major networks and a few other channels for a low monthly rate. I still liked to ask about the specials in the hope that we could get free premium channels for a few months. We didn't get any specials, but since my job required that I have computer access over the Internet, I could justify getting a cable modem for high-speed Internet access. I had wanted a high speed Internet connection for a while. Thankfully, I could surf the Internet again at blazing fast speeds.

The installation was set up for the next day, the utilities were on and everything was in place. I had my office set up in the former dining room and was ready to get to work. It took a while but we were finally in Virginia. After eight years in the Midwest, we were home.

Chapter Sixteen

Our New Life

Quick and Easy

Several years ago, the pastor of our church in Tulsa preached a message titled "Quick and Easy". He preached it during the New Year's Eve service and it became the mantra for the entire year. Since that time, I had been looking for a "Quick and Easy" miracle but to no avail. It just didn't seem to exist. Things could be quick or easy but never both. And with respect to my current situation, neither was true.

Although it was a long and hard road to Virginia, our new life was shaping up well. We had a home, my Dad drove up our second car and I was working every day from our dining room/office. All we needed now was to find a church and find Robin a job. Our former pastor recommended a church in Norfolk so we were on the right path there. Norfolk was an hour away but we had traveled that far to go to church while in college. So for the first few Sundays, we headed to Norfolk.

Although Robin's job was a more immediate need, I also needed to find a place to work. My job with DMI was only guaranteed for a month. We both needed some professional help finding jobs so we connected with a headhunter. He had a lot of contacts but Robin didn't use any of them. She found an opening and applied for a job with one of the local housing agencies. The job was Manager of Human Resources (a promotion that she really deserved) and she would be working in the same building with Sheila.

While Robin waited to hear from the organization she applied to, Sheila had a conversation with her boss regarding the position. I'm not sure what was said but I knew that Sheila could be pretty persuasive. The end result of the conversation was that Sheila's boss intervened on Robin's behalf and helped secure an interview. And after two interviews with a team of executives, Robin became the Manager of Human Resources. Only a month after relocating to Virginia, Robin had found a great position and we were really excited about it. Things were looking good for us.

SLOW AND HARD

I was really excited for Robin and her new opportunity. She was just such an excellent employee that deserves to have a great job. She comes in early, leaves late and gives 100% while she's there. In my opinion, there was no one better qualified to do the job.

As Robin got situated in her new position, I continued to work from our home. It was really fun at first but I knew it wasn't what I was going to be doing long term. I was running out of time on my guaranteed month and I really wanted to find a more purposeful position. I called the headhunter again for his expertise.

This headhunter was the type of guy that was busy all the time. If you could manage to get him on the phone, you could expect him to be interrupted at least twice before you told him why you were calling. And if you tried to meet him at his office you would end up waiting while he put out fires and juggled multiple appointments. Still, he was a very sincere person who really wanted to help. After our meeting, he managed to connect me with a handful of business leads and I left his office feeling like I had been with a master networker.

I immediately called the contacts to see how they could help me in my search. They were all more polite than they had to be and they made me aware of some jobs in the area. I took their advice and applied for the job openings. None of the jobs were really what I wanted but I just needed a local job. I kept on the job trail in between my daily duties and hoped for the best.

As I continued looking for jobs, days turned into weeks and I hadn't gotten anywhere. My job with DMI had been extended on a weekly basis, but I was getting more desperate to find something permanent. At the same time, I was getting disappointed with the job opportunities that were available to me. Since there were several military bases in this area, all of the technology jobs were with defense contractors. I quickly found out that these contractors favored those who had military backgrounds and that didn't include me. Besides, I was only applying for technology jobs because that was the bulk of my work experience. I was actually getting tired of programming and technology. I wanted to do something in line with my purpose – to help God's people obtain wealth using the talents and abilities that He had given them.

COFFEE FOR CHRIST

In my search for purposeful jobs, I found a business incubator that was affiliated with one of the local universities. The incubator worked with the city to help entrepreneurs build businesses and that was very interesting to me. My research didn't uncover any job opportunities there but I thought I might be able to volunteer my time in order to be in an entrepreneurial environment. I spoke with the Assistant Director about my desires and made an appointment to visit with the Director the next day.

I was early for my appointment so I stopped off at a coffee shop that Sheila had recommended. The coffee shop was closed and I noticed a For Sale sign in the window. There was a number to call and a reference to a web site for additional information. Immediately I got excited about the possibilities of this business. In the five minutes I spent peaking through the window, I applied each of my coffee shop business plans to this location. I saw myself behind the counter serving a packed crowd of college students and downtown employees while Gospel jazz played in the background. This was going to be a great opportunity and I had to check it out.

Before we left Tulsa, I made the decision to give up on business until we got settled and saved some money. I barely had enough cash for the Café Mocha that I was going to buy but now I wanted to buy the whole coffee shop. I didn't want to borrow money to buy the business so I didn't have a realistic way of purchasing it. But all of my entrepreneurial urges had resurfaced in full force and I couldn't stop them. I had to at least check into the business and give God the opportunity to work. I had just enough time to run into the library down the street and view the sale listing before my appointment.

I arrived for my appointment with a minute to spare. The door to the main office was open but no one was there. The place was like a ghost town. I said "Hello" in a loud voice. I repeated it louder and then knocked on the door that led to the back offices. I waited, then proceeded through the door. I wandered through the back offices and looked around for about 15 minutes. This was getting spooky so I left. I called the offices later and never got an answer. I chose to believe that volunteering was not in my immediate future. God wanted me to pursue the coffee shop.

I made an appointment, via email, to meet with the owners of the coffee shop. They were a young Christian couple who had started the business as a ministry a few years prior. They were successful at getting people in the door but the huge initial investment prevented them from making the profit they expected. The husband recently got a job opportunity in another state and they had to sell it in a month. They only wanted to pay off their existing loan and trust that it would go to a good owner.

In subsequent meetings, I got more and more excited about the opportunity. The business was barely profitable, but I could fix that rather quickly. They were going to train me to run the shop before leaving town and everything was already in place. I wouldn't have to do anything except switch the utilities into my name and open for business. And, best of all, they were willing to finance the entire purchase price by allowing me to pay them without getting another loan.

Robin and I talked the idea over and she was less excited than I was. She was concerned about the unstable revenues. They were only projections and they weren't high enough to support us and have children in the near future. The other problem was the financing. They were willing to let us assume their loan, which would allow us to buy the business without accumulating any debt. But we would be assuming the risk of running a business that we didn't fully own. And we still didn't have any money for working capital to get the business going.

We were trying to make this decision using the sound financial judgment found in the Bible. We reviewed our financial Bible study materials and came across the scripture in Proverbs 15:22, "Plans fail for lack of counsel, but with many advisers they succeed." At the prompting of that scripture, I called the

CFO (Chief Financial Officer) of our former church in Tulsa and another friend whom I respected. After talking to both men, my fear had been confirmed. It became clear to me that this was a risky proposition. I would owe the couple and the couple would owe the bank. It's not that the current owners were shady in any way, they just were not in a position to guarantee what the debt holders would do.

After acknowledging the risk of the purchase structure, I also saw the cash problem. Without an infusion of cash, I would never get off of the ground. I prayed that if God wanted me to have this business then He would give me the cash to purchase it outright or, at least, the working capital necessary to lessen the burden. He answered my prayer by not making any financial change in my life. I was disappointed but not really sad this time. I had lost out on another opportunity to own a coffee shop but I had done everything I could to get it. I knew I wanted God's will to be done and this was clearly not His will. I put aside my business desires (again) and continued searching for jobs.

Déjà vu All Over Again

My job search wasn't going anywhere and I was getting increasingly frustrated with my current programming position. The job was supposed to be over and I was hanging on like a dying man. I felt confident that the Lord would find an opportunity for me to pursue my purpose but I didn't know when. I thought that maybe I was holding myself back by hanging onto this job. When I made the decision to leave the first time, God met my faith with a 'ram in the bush'. He had done that many times throughout this season I was in, so I believed that He would do it again. I just needed to move in faith. So, after two months of long distance employment, I made the decision to end my job at DMI and spend my time seeking God's true purpose for me.

When I made the decision to end my job, I felt really free. This time, I didn't have to be kicked out of a company, I moved out in faith and I was eager to see the rest of His plan. Robin and I were in a good place but He had promised us so many more blessings. He had also spoken many blessings to me personally through dreams, visions and prophecies. Now, I had broken free from the last vestige of bondage and I was in position to be used by God. I was debt free, living in Virginia and focused on purpose. Surely God was going to move in my life.

I remained focused on the great things I expected God to do for me. My faith was strong but my situation remained the same. In fact, I was having déjà vu from being laid off from TaxOn. I was unemployed and forced to spend my days looking for work. The difference now was that I was looking for jobs in the areas of education, marketing and training. I had limited experience in these fields and everyone interpreted my resume as belonging to a programmer. To counter this impression, I reworked my resume and drafted new cover letters. I was determined to seek purpose and, this time, I wouldn't settle for less.

HIGHER, HIGHER EDUCATION

During my pursuit of purpose, I received an invitation to participate in an annual conference for prospective doctoral candidates. The sponsoring organization was an alliance of corporations and educational institutions that sought to improve workforce diversity by recruiting more minorities to become business school professors. I was accepted to their conference last year but couldn't go. This year, I knew I had to go to find out if this was God's plan for me.

Becoming a business professor was not a new idea to me. I had thought about this off and on since I graduated from college. The lifestyle of a professor always appealed to me along with the opportunity to shape and influence young minds. The only problem was the large investment in time. I had already completed four years of undergraduate study and three years of graduate study. The idea of spending four more years of postgraduate study was not appealing. Of course the lack of opportunity I was facing caused me to rethink my priorities.

Before I arrived at the conference, I told myself that I needed to give it my full effort in order for it to be successful. My goal was to put aside the time investment and find out if I really wanted to do the work of a business school professor. When I arrived, I cast off my quiet demeanor and tried to talk to as many people as I could. This was a little awkward at first but I managed to get into some pretty interesting discussions. As it turned out, most prospective students had the same concerns I had. This was reassuring.

Each session was very enlightening. I learned how to choose a college and an area of specialization. I got tips on improving my score for the exam required for admission into postgraduate business study. I met lots of business professors and admissions counselors. The conference just surrounded me with kindred spirits. As my Dad would say, I was in hog heaven.

As the conference continued, I became more convinced that the four-year investment in time was a small price to pay for the lifestyle, respect and opportunity that came from being a professor. But I still really didn't know what a business professor did until my eyes were opened in some of the later sessions. I began to understand that professors only teach a third of their time. The majority of their efforts are focused on creating and presenting research on a specific area of study. I always knew that professors researched and wrote about their findings. I just never knew that it was their main focus.

Throughout my educational career, I assumed that professors were teachers at the pinnacle of their careers. In reality, teaching was only their secondary vocation. But I was drawn to being a professor because I wanted to teach. I thought there might be a way to de-emphasize the research and focus on teaching. As I asked more questions at the conference I found out that the research begins as a Ph.D. candidate and only intensifies. There is no way to get around it; teaching is only an interruption in the life of a researcher. If I wanted the lifestyle, respect and opportunity of a professor, I would have to commit to research.

Notwithstanding the research duties, I was sold on the benefits of life as a professor. It seemed so glamorous to spend a few days a week teaching students and the rest of my time reading and writing. But I didn't want that to be my final contribution to society. It just wouldn't be fulfilling to only influence the operations of businesses through working with students and writing articles. At some point, I wanted to have a direct influence on the world. I wasn't sure exactly how, but I wanted to lead by example and it seemed like being a professor wasn't the best way to accomplish this. So, before leaving the conference, I made the decision not to pursue a Ph.D.

Vast Nothingness

When I came home from the conference, I reevaluated my thoughts regarding a Ph.D. I knew it wasn't what I wanted to do but it had certain benefits that couldn't be denied. Aside from the prestige and salary of a professor, I was also attracted to the predictable nature of the Ph.D. process. Most programs require a rigorous four years of study (without salary) that includes oral exams, written exams and a final dissertation. But, at least there was a plan and its success was dependent on my efforts. If I were accepted into a Ph.D. program then I could be assured of a job in four years and the respect of everyone during that time.

Trusting in God for a purposeful job didn't seem to hold any guarantees. I had done it before and I ended up with a temporary job. It served a good purpose for a time but I wanted so much more. I knew that being a professor wasn't my ultimate destiny but that wasn't very comforting. Now that I had found another item that I didn't want to do, I needed to find out what God wanted me to do with my life.

I kept searching for jobs as intently as ever. For the first several hours of the day I would look through job listings and apply to positions. In the middle of the day, I would exercise to have some human interaction and protect my body from atrophy. Later in the day, I would return to my search until Robin came home.

My daily schedule was filling my time but wasn't yielding any fruit. I had a few job interviews but nothing became of them. I seemed to only get interviews for the jobs that I didn't want. These jobs offered the potential for employment, which is why I applied to them, but they didn't offer anything in the area of fulfillment. In truth, I was as glad not to get these jobs as I was that I didn't waste time becoming a professor. I wanted purpose, purpose, purpose!

Unfortunately, purpose didn't come. Instead, I fell back into the trap of depression. I maintained my job search but, periodically, I would get emotional and frustrated like I did before. At times I would literally cry out to God for immediate help. I was hurting and I didn't want to be in this situation. I didn't want to be unemployed and I didn't want to feel useless. God helped Robin find a job at the first company she applied to. Why wouldn't he use His omnipotence and supernatural ability to help me?

I yelled, "Help Me!!!" several times one day. I waited to hear a response from God but nothing happened. God responded with a loud silence. I had called on His name and, for whatever reason, He chose not to answer me. I was legitimately hurting and my Savior wasn't doing anything to help. When I did this during my first period of unemployment, I continued to get madder. This time, however, I just stopped. I wasn't getting anywhere with my outbursts. I realized that God was not only omnipotent but He was also omniscient and omnipresent. He knew exactly what I felt and He could see me in pain. Reminding Him of the pain wasn't going to help.

My failure to get God's attention left me with two options. I could choose to keep calling Him or I could accept what His silence was saying. I chose to accept His silence as a way of saying that the best thing for me was not for Him to swoop down and rescue me. I wasn't sure what I needed but I believed that if I just kept pressing on then things would eventually get clear. By faith, I believed that God would reveal Himself to me in the best possible way and at the best possible time. I just needed to stop complaining, get up, and keep looking for God's plan.

Ill-Gotten Gains

The realization that I was in a period of waiting helped me a lot. No one likes to wait, but it helps to know that you're waiting on God. I heard someone say that God is never late, but He's never early either. I laughed when I heard it but now I was actually living it. The motivating part was that waiting on God assures you of a good end. It may take a while and it may not be what you want, but it will be good.

With the frustration and pressure subsiding, I was able to be more social and interact with the world. Robin's job had a holiday party that we enjoyed and Sheila had invited us to a Christmas party. It was weird being around people that neither Robin nor I knew, but you can't go wrong with free food and entertainment. Sheila even offered to pay for the gift that we were supposed to bring to the party.

Sheila's party started with a great meal cooked by two grandmothers. They had pork barbecue, sweet potatoes, greens and an array of southern desserts that made me happy I was back in Virginia. After the meal, we played the "Yankee Exchange" game. We called it White Elephant in Tulsa but the theory was the same. You chose numbers to determine the order of play, and then took turns either selecting gifts from a table or stealing gifts that had already been chosen. It was loads of fun and didn't cost me any money.

When it was my turn to choose, I picked a small bag that surprisingly had lottery tickets inside. I have never played the lottery so I thought a lot about the irony of getting tickets at a Christmas party game. I convinced myself that there was something special about this so I held my tickets close until the end of the night.

Later that night, I realized how silly it was to put hope in lottery tickets. When I worked in a convenience store I watched hundreds of people buy scratch tickets daily and walk away without winning anything. Millions of people bought the lottery tickets that I had won from the party and millions lost everyday. Reality finally took over and I stopped hoping for the impossible. I would find out whether I won when they picked the winning numbers in two days. Until then, I wouldn't think about it.

While my enthusiasm for the lottery dissipated, Robin's excitement grew. She had never bought a lottery ticket either but we had been praying for a miracle harvest for years. She figured that if God could allow a random gambler to win $10 million dollars then He could just as easily give it to us. Her logic made sense to me so we eagerly waited for the winning numbers to be revealed.

We had received five tickets so we had five chances to win. As the numbers were selected, I remembered some of them from our tickets. We scanned the lottery tickets slowly and then SURPRISE we had five losing tickets! We checked them again and again with the same result – no $10 million dollars for us, at least not now. It almost seemed like a sick joke someone was playing on us. But since we put our hope in God we needed to continue believing that God was in control. Instead of being upset that we didn't win, we laughed and continued to believe for our harvest.

Chapter Seventeen

Finding Peace, Finding Purpose

Sunday is the Lord's Day

While I searched for a job, Robin and I continued our search for a local church. We were careful not to look for an exact replica of our former church in Tulsa. We went into our church search with open expectations. We knew there was a lot we liked from our former church, but we also knew that God had moved us to Virginia for a reason. So, as we visited churches, we prayed that God would reveal His will to us. And with each visit, our criteria changed to include new things that we didn't want in a church.

First we went to the church in Norfolk that was recommended by our pastor. The church was an hour drive from our home, but it offered lots of the things that our former church offered. It had a large congregation, a TV ministry that impacted the community and lots of events in addition to regular Sunday service. We enjoyed praise and worship but the compactness of the audience (i.e. people stuffed like sardines) made it hard to participate freely.

We were still interested in joining but we found out that it would take 16 weeks before we became members. This gave us reason to pause and make sure we were making the right decision. As we sought more information about the ministry, I started to feel some frustration from dealing with a mega church. It didn't seem like it was going to be easy to volunteer, especially driving an hour each way. In addition, we didn't feel like this big church needed us since most things were already in place and just needed to be maintained. After a few weeks of attendance, we decided to move on.

After this experience, we realized that we wanted a smaller church with a mission to impact the community. We also hoped to find a church that would allow us to establish finance and purpose programs at some point. We asked for suggestions from the few people we knew and I listened to advertisements on the TV and radio. I thought about going to the library to use its business directory to search for a church but I figured that was overkill. We took a small sample of the churches we found and started visiting.

During the discussions for buying the coffee shop, the owners recommended a church to us. They raved over the praise and worship and the involvement of the members. I thought that the reason I met them might have been to find a church instead of buying a business so we decided to visit. When we arrived, we noticed that the congregation was only slightly diverse. The praise and worship wasn't as vibrant or as expressive as we expected, and, at one point, the pastor had the choir sing the same song four times. By the third time we heard that song, we were ready to go but the pastor hadn't even preached yet.

The pastor's message was biblical but, in our opinion, showed a rigid interpretation of the gospel. It seemed more like condemnation than good news. I couldn't imagine hearing that type of a message every Sunday so we left immediately after service. They had a small reception for visitors after service but no amount of free food was going to convince us to come back. We were through with that church.

The next series of churches offered more of the same. They were small, up and coming churches with a charismatic pastor and an excited congregation. We decided to attend each one for two Sunday services and a Bible Study in order to get a good feel. Regrettably, the good feeling we were anticipating never came. Sometimes the messages were good but most times they were either uninspiring, depressing or both. At one church, the message always started nicely but the pastor could only speak for 15 minutes before the congregation erupted into shouting and dancing. Not that shouting was bad, but eventually I would need some actual information of content that I could use throughout the week.

It Was Right There All the Time

We had been in Virginia for about five months without a

church home. Our anxiety brought us close to just picking the best one out of all the churches. We came very close to joining one in particular but we backed out at the last minute. We just couldn't make our bodies say "yes" when our hearts were saying "no".

One day, while Robin and I were in the office together, I remembered my idea of using the library's business database to select a church. I had copied a list of churches onto a disk and brought it home a few weeks previously. We looked through the listing and filtered it down by various categories. We wanted a nondenominational church, located in Newport News, more than 5 employees on staff and a website. We wanted to use the website to gain additional information about a church instead of spending an entire Sunday service in disappointment.

After a couple of dead ends, we found the website of a church that had a lot of promise. In addition to our initial criteria, the church's mission and vision closely matched what we believed and carried from our former church in Tulsa. They had just hosted a leadership conference (just like in Tulsa) and were in the process of a January fast (just like in Tulsa). They were temporarily meeting in a middle school right around the corner from us until they finished renovating their church and community center. Based on the website, this church had it all; great values, community focus, active congregation and convenience to our home. We decided to attend the next Sunday service.

When we arrived at the school, service had already started. There was a pre-church warm up that they did to get people ready to praise God. Robin and I were both impressed. We really enjoyed the praise and worship and felt genuine love from the congregation. We were disappointed to find out that a guest pastor was speaking but he gave us an idea of the quality of messages we could expect. Most importantly, we felt the presence of the Lord. By the time we left, Robin was ready to join. I suggested we wait until we had actually heard the pastor but I was excited about the possibilities.

After another visit, we heard the pastor and he confirmed our expectations. This wasn't just the best church we had visited; it was possibly better than our former church. Robin wanted to join at the end of service when the pastor gave the opening, but I was a little apprehensive. My hesitation didn't have any basis, I was mainly just afraid of commitment. We had almost joined the other church we visited and I realized that would have been a huge mistake. I guess I just lost confidence in my own decision-making ability.

While I thought about our decision, the pastor continued to speak. I asked the Lord to use the pastor to give me a sign if this was the Sunday we should join. I felt like Gideon in the book of Judges as he put out a fleece to make sure he was hearing from God. I knew this was unusual but later in the message the pastor spoke directly to my lost confidence regarding joining a church. It was as if the pastor had heard the conversation in my head and was talking to me about it over the pulpit. I realized that God was encouraging me to shun my fear and step out in faith. So, at the end of the service, we joined.

GILGAL REVISITED

We were both happy and relieved to have found a church. I was even more amazed at the way we found it. I originally obtained the database from the library to use it to create a Christian business directory on the web. After the website never materialized, the Lord reminded me that I could use it to find churches. I originally dismissed this God-idea because it didn't seem feasible to my human intellect. Eventually it was the only option we had, and of course, it was the one that worked.

The more I thought about the process, the more I realized how my delay caused our church search to extend much longer than necessary. If I had simply put aside my own doubts and obeyed the still small voice of God then we could have found our church a few weeks earlier. We would have already been finished with our New Member's courses and been able to start serving in the church that we had come to love. The timing of our success hinged on obedience.

Since I was still waiting on God to open up the right job opportunity, I began to wonder how my disobedience might be delaying this search. I started to pray and ask God to remind me of those things that He had told me but that I had failed to do. Before long, I remembered that God told me to write down my thoughts and dreams. I had been journaling throughout the unemployment process and started turning my journal into a book a while ago. I soon stopped because it didn't make sense to formally write my personal feelings since I knew I wasn't going to ever show anyone. Just like the business directory, I had taken one step in God's direction then stopped because it didn't make sense to me.

At this point, I was out of options for finding a purposeful job so I decided to go back and pick up my journal. This was the last thing that I remembered God telling me to do and I needed to finish it. I thought it might make a good book or just help me to release my frustrations in a productive way. I tried to make sense out of writing a book. I wanted to figure a way to justify the time it would take away from my job search but these thoughts missed the point. I didn't need to know why I was writing in a journal, I just needed to do it because God told me to do it. This was a radical change for me but, being without other options, I did it anyway.

I had stopped my journal around the time of the conference in Texas. In order to remember what was going on, I looked in my planner for the original notes on the conference. I noticed that I had taken a lot of notes on the message about the Israelites stopping at Gilgal before they made their way to Jericho. I remembered the story but it seemed to resonate with me on a deeper level this time.

> *When the whole nation had finished crossing the Jordan, the LORD said to Joshua, "Choose twelve men from among the people, one from each tribe, and tell them to take up twelve stones from the middle*

> *of the Jordan from right where the priests stood and to carry them over with you and put them down at the place where you stay tonight." So Joshua called together the twelve men he had appointed from the Israelites, one from each tribe, and said to them, "Go over before the ark of the LORD your God into the middle of the Jordan. Each of you is to take up a stone on his shoulder, according to the number of the tribes of the Israelites, to serve as a sign among you. In the future, when your children ask you, 'What do these stones mean?' tell them that the flow of the Jordan was cut off before the Ark of the Covenant of the LORD. When it crossed the Jordan, the waters of the Jordan were cut off. These stones are to be a memorial to the people of Israel forever."*
>
> Joshua 4:1-7 (NIV)

At the conference, I answered an altar call to make Dallas, Texas my Gilgal. In the heat of the moment and in my desperation for victory, I thought that it was my place of rest or remembrance. But after leaving there, I didn't feel rested or remember it as a place of victory. My declaration of the conference as my Gilgal was premature. It wasn't the end of my season in the wilderness; it was a single, important step near the beginning.

After reading the story again, I was drawn to the meticulous detail that was involved in making the memorial at Gilgal. It wasn't as simple as a conference or an altar call; it was a detailed, physical representation of both the struggles in the wilderness and the miracles that brought them out. The twelve stones seemed to denote chapters in the lives of the Israelites where each tribe was given a chance to add their own personal interpretation. The whole memorial was more like the memoirs of a group of people. It was the early day equivalent of a book.

Writing What I'm Writing

That was when it hit me. God wanted me to write a book about my season of unemployment. Instead of just a journal, I was to write a formal book of my experiences in the hope of helping someone else that may be in the same situation. I wasn't sure if that was the real reason, but I had to be obedient despite the potential outcome. And if I proceeded with the thought of helping someone make it through the pain and agony that I experienced, then I would be more inclined to follow through with the book and be honest about my entire situation.

To help sooth my doubts about taking the time to write a book, I believe the Lord confirmed my decision in two ways. First, He confirmed it through Robin. My main concern was that she would think I was just jumping onto another idea that wouldn't produce any fruit. I can usually tell when I have a bad idea because Robin either doesn't understand it or doesn't respond to it. But when I told her about the book, the idea made as much sense to her as it did to me. This was extremely important since my delay in employment impacted her as much as it impacted me.

Secondly, the Lord confirmed my understanding of His will through my sister-in-law. Robin and I accompanied Sheila to a conference ball where many of the state's leaders and politicians were present. In one conversation, we were noticing how strange it was to be in the room with so many powerful and influential leaders. Out of the blue, Sheila looked at me and said, "When you write your book, you'll have to mention me in it." I thought her comment was strange because it didn't fit our conversation and I hadn't told her about my book. After the event, I asked Robin about it and she said that she hadn't mentioned the book either. I took this as another sign from God to get busy writing, so I did.

As you probably realize, the book that I was referring to is the one you are reading now. It has taken a long time to come together but you can see the fruits of my work in each of the previous chapters. As I wrote it, I gave up on the idea of publishing it for big bucks. That would be a great end to this season of unemployment but I don't think that was God's intention. I simply think that God was giving me an outlet to write my memoirs and review where I've been. During the review, I have had a wonderful opportunity to take note of the awesome blessings that God has bestowed upon me. No matter what happens, I have written proof that I have been blessed. And I can honestly say that God's blessing is enough for me.

THE POWER OF PURPOSE

You may be thinking that this book is coming to an end and there hasn't been a climax. Well, I can only say that I am as disappointed as you are. I really wanted to end this book by saying that I won a million dollars or that 5,000 people finally paid me for the software that I wrote last year. But none of those things happened.

However, I hope it helps to say that I am not deterred or dejected by the course of my life. I suffered through failed businesses, failed business negotiations and failed job opportunities but God was there to bring out a blessing in every circumstance. I felt like crap at times, but I emerged victorious over the situation because I'm still here and I'm still standing. And I still have much more than I've lost. I am debt free, I am back in Virginia, I know how to live a budgeted lifestyle, I have resolve and longsuffering, I have faith that has been tried and tested and many other things that have been made known through this book. And if you take a serious look at your life you can probably say the same thing.

I must say that the most interesting thing I learned while writing this book is my own personal purpose in Christ. As I continue in life, I trust that God will use it to give me strength and direction. My purpose statement has always been accurate but I haven't sufficiently interpreted it. Now, I feel like my actions are guided by God's purpose for me rather than my own desires for wealth and fortune. This makes all the difference in the world. With the hope of encouraging others to pursue their purpose, I've put an explanation of my purpose statement below.

My Purpose: *"To train God's people to obtain wealth according to the talents and abilities that He has given them"*.

To train – God has given me the unique ability to study and research information. I am fascinated about a wide range of topics and enjoy disseminating information about them. In addition to just delivering information, I believe that training suggests that I will help people to use the information in a productive way.

God's people – This refers to everyone. I am not called just to Christians or to unbelievers. I believe that my talents and abilities can be used by God in any situation.

To obtain wealth – The notion of obtaining wealth does not refer only to money. I believe that the Lord has given me specific interest in business but not just for business sake. Business represents God's calling for each of us to produce a profit in everything we do. Whether the profit is in saved lives, healed hearts or some other form, we must produce fruit from our gifts or we are simply making noise and wasting God's resources.

Talents and abilities He has given them – I believe that God has given each of us a set of unique talents and abilities. My purpose is to work with others to release that ability. In most cases, I expect God to use me to show others how to express their talents in a business or organization. But the main goal is that it be released in the way that God intended.

Chapter Eighteen

A New Beginning

It Ain't Over Till We Win

When I wrote the previous chapter, I was writing events as they were happening. I actually slowed down the writing in order to give God time to work. I know that God doesn't need me to stall for Him, but I didn't want to end the book without a successful conclusion. I am truly excited about my new understanding of purpose but my current prayer is to live my purpose through some activity that gives me a source of fulfillment and income.

I tried to stretch the ending as long as I could but you can only fool yourself for so long. So, on Friday, February 21st 2003, I ended the book and finished out the rest of my day. I was still disappointed but I felt good about my obedience to God. I was actually in a position to say that I did what God told me to do. This made me feel like my pastor in Tulsa. When he ran for public office and didn't win, he still had a smile on his face and joy in his heart because he had done what God told him to do. This was my time to take joy in obedience to the Father.

Since I had plenty of time on my hands, I cleaned the house until Robin came home. It made me feel useful and that meant a lot. When Robin came home she told me about her day as usual. Then she told me that her boss wanted me to call him on Saturday. I had never met her boss so I thought that was strange. Evidently, he had a job opportunity he wanted to talk about. Robin had mentioned the opportunity a few days ago but I didn't pay much attention to it. Actually, I intentionally put it off in order to finish my book. I didn't want it to distract me from obedience.

My feelings were mixed as I thought about what may happen. I knew that there was a job opening at Robin's company but I didn't qualify for it. Normally I wouldn't let a small thing like inexperience stop me from applying. In this case, however, the Human Resources Manager was my wife. And even if I did qualify, it seemed like it would create a conflict of interest to pursue it. Besides, the last candidate had the right credentials for the job but he didn't last a month in that position. I couldn't figure out what was going to happen so I just prayed that God's will would be done. That is my "catch all" prayer when I don't know what else to do.

When Saturday came, I was still uneasy about the call. I wasn't scared or nervous; I just wanted to see a clear path to my destiny. Unfortunately, that almost never happens. After four months of unemployment, God didn't seem to think it was necessary to give me a road map and He probably wasn't going to start now. Realizing that I was delaying the inevitable, I finally decided to call him at noon and get it over with. I figured I wouldn't get a job immediately but God could use this to open up a door of employment somewhere else. I was calling the Executive Director of a fairly large organization and I was sure he knew some pretty powerful people.

The Call

Noon finally came and I called him at his home. The conversation started off with the usual pleasantries. I remember thinking it was strange that I had never spoken to him before. Normally, I meet all of Robin's coworkers but I kept missing him when I went into the office. Maybe if I had met him I would have scared him off and we wouldn't be talking now. Anyway, we kept shooting the breeze and then finally started talking about the position that was open.

The position he was hiring for was different from the one that I had seen advertised. I guess he figured the original position wasn't going to work. Judging by the brief tenure of the previous applicant, I would guess that some changes were necessary. The current position revolved around one specific project that needed to be completed pretty soon. There was government money available and they needed to use it or lose it. Time was of the essence and, since he had heard that I was in between jobs, he thought of me.

The more we talked, the less nervous I became. I enjoyed the conversation and thought the job sounded interesting. The goal of the job didn't exactly match my purpose but I would get a chance to be useful and productive again. I wasn't excited at this point but I realized that it was a good opportunity. More importantly, it had God's signature on it.

We talked for about a half hour before he asked me whether I had heard enough. I told him I was interested in the position and he told me to come by on Monday. Except, he didn't mention anything about an interview. Instead, he asked me what the salary range was that I desired. I hate that question because I never know what to say. I just told him the truth about the salary range I wanted. (I was trying to watch my words. The last time I told someone my range, I ended up with an offer for much less.)

Robin's boss didn't gasp at the salary range I gave him but he let me know that it was high for the position. The position didn't sound too complicated to me so I figured his counter offer was fair. We agreed on a loose amount and I was ready to go into the interview on Monday. Then he said to just come in on Monday and be ready to get started. He also asked for my resume so he could get an idea of what my job skills were. I said "OK" and then said goodbye. I had just been hired.

THE END OF A SEASON

After my telephone conversation, I didn't really acknowledge that I had just been hired. Robin wasn't at home so I just went to the community center to exercise. As I was on the treadmill the fact that I was going to be working on Monday started to sink in. Tons of questions started to come into my mind about my new job. Was it the right job? (Who cares, it was a job.) But did I do the right thing? (Who cares, it's going to pay more than you were making while you were at home.) The questions kept coming and I felt like the Lord kept knocking them down.

My thoughts continued in this pattern until the end of my exercise routine. By this time I was getting happy about my situation and I drove home in a joyful daze. Even though I was happy, I still couldn't grasp the fact that I had been hired. After four months of searching I had finally been hired. And the job sounded like one that I actually wanted. It was project driven and I would be managing something. No more "worker bee" stuff for me, I was going to have responsibility and control of something. I was going to be purposeful.

By the time I got home, Robin had come back from her morning activities. Her boss, and my new employer, had called back while she was there and told her what happened. When I walked in the door she was overjoyed. There was no joyful daze for Robin, she fully understood the blessing that we just received and she was ready to rejoice. She loves to see God work and, to her, this was purely God. And for this to happen the day after I finished my book was the icing on the cake for her. As we talked about it, her enthusiasm became contagious and I started to celebrate too.

It was hard to put into words how great this was. It was just such an awesome blessing that I had to look at God in awe. When I thought of the tears I shed and the frustration I felt, I actually got embarrassed. God was there all along; He just wasn't doing what I wanted Him to do. And when I doubted His love for me, He just kept right on working on my behalf. He is just so awesome that I still can't express it.

The blessing of this job came into perspective when I thought of the effort I put into my job search. I had been submitting resumes everyday for months and nothing became of them. I had five resumes on three different Internet job sites. I was checking about 10 employment sites daily and sending customized resumes with cover letters to several employers a week. None of my sophisticated, Internet based job searching worked. But, in 30 minutes, God set me up to be hired over the phone without the employer ever seeing my resume or even my face. When I asked my new boss about his level of comfort in hiring me over the phone, his exact words were "You keep good company." He was referring to Robin but I knew that it was my relationship with God that caused this to happen.

MY FIRST DAY

When Monday came I was a little nervous about work. Robin and I had planned to ride together but then she told me that she had to go to a class after work. That meant that we needed to drive separate cars. Not only would I have to overcome my nervousness alone, I would have to defrost my car since it was parked outside.

Although my rear window defroster didn't work, the car finally thawed out and I drove to work. After about 15 minutes of driving, I ran into bumper-to-bumper traffic. The traffic was extremely heavy so I moved at a very slow pace. Most times I wasn't moving at all. I couldn't turn off of the highway and I couldn't go anywhere. The lane reserved for High Occupancy Vehicles (HOV) was free and clear but I couldn't get in it while riding in a car by myself. I couldn't do anything but pray.

I pray a lot of times but this was probably the most serious praying I had done in a while. The music was off and I was praying out loud for the Lord to move the traffic. I needed to get to work and I needed to be on time. Robin told me that my boss had a fascination for timeliness so I gave myself a 15-minute time cushion. But it was quickly being eaten up by this stupid traffic jam.

As I moved along at bicycle speeds, I thought about getting in the HOV lane. There were several lone drivers who had illegally jumped in the lane and they were all passing me. I thought that God would surely forgive me for breaking a minor traffic law but I wasn't sure that the Virginia State Police would. It just wasn't worth getting a ticket to get to work on time. Aside from the ticket, it wasn't worth risking my integrity to get to work on time. I decided that I was going to just keep praying and do the best I could. God would make a way for me somehow.

The traffic delay continued and I kept praying. At times, I

felt like I was actually moving the traffic with my prayer. It just wasn't moving fast enough. Finally, the traffic broke and I started moving at regular speeds again. About this time, I saw two cops pulling over those drivers who were illegally in the HOV lane. I wanted to gloat but I needed to get to work. I only had 10 minutes of time and 15 minutes of road.

At 7:55 am, I accepted that I was going to be late. I stopped praying that God would stop time and prayed that He would just get me through this. I had done everything I could to get there on time but it wasn't going to work out. When I walked in the office, my boss was there and made a joke about my tardiness. I laughed with the joke and then thought about the situation. I realized that I wasn't mad and I wasn't screaming at God about why He allowed this. I accepted that things didn't go my way and kept going.

This seemed like such a small thing but it really was a giant leap in my spiritual walk. While I was unemployed, I constantly tried to use prayer and scripture to get my way. When it didn't work out, I got mad at God for letting me down. Now, I realize that God can't let me down. His way is ALWAYS going to work out. My only decision is whether to accept it or to be mad about it. This time, I was mature enough to accept it and I had a great first day from that point on.

The Blessings Go On and On

Saying that I had a great first day is an understatement. I had a fantastic first day that just confirmed that this was God's perfect plan for me. Among other things, I had a real office with a nice view for the first time in my life. I also found out that I was going to make more money than I had initially agreed upon. And the project was more interesting than I thought it would be. I was actually excited about working on it. The best thing about it was, at the end, I would have helped families move from public assistance into their own homes. You can't get more purposeful than that.

As the week progressed, the blessings continued. I can't list all the details but everything was going well. I started to realize more blessings when I looked at our finances. While we were dependent on a single income, we were just barely getting by. The income didn't cover our minimum expenses so God always did something to make up the difference. We sold our spare washer and dryer. We cashed out a bad investment in order to get the tax loss before the year ended. God just kept holding our heads above water and, when we had gotten to the very bottom, He gave me a job in His own phenomenal way.

This job marked the end of a horrible and miraculous season. I could finally say, "Life is Good!" But this time, life was really good. My job search was over and I was poised for greatness. Best of all, I had learned the meaning of Philippians 4:19 "I have learned in all things…." In addition to teaching me the greatest lesson of life, God also gave me an ending for my book. Just like in all great stories, I learned a lot through my struggles and I will live happily ever after.

My final hope is for every reader to relate this story to himself or herself in a personal way. Don't discount it and don't pass it off as just someone else's tale. There are many lessons to be learned here and you'll either learn them through me or learn them for yourself. I hope that, among other things, you will realize that you can get up again. It may take a while to do it. And you may cry a lot in the process. But if you trust in God and allow Him to guide you through the painful steps of life, you will indeed Get Up Again!

Notes

Chapter 1

Major League Baseball is a registered trademark owned by Major League Baseball Properties, Inc.

Jerry Maguire. By Cameron Crowe. Dir. Cameron Crowe. Perf. Tom Cruise, Cuba Gooding, Jr. 1996. Gracie Films.

Chapter 5

National Basketball Association and NBA are registered trademarks owned by NBA Properties, Inc.

Chapter 10

Fred Hammond. "Yes, He Will". Purpose by design. CD. Zomba Recording Corporation, 2000.

Chapter 14

The Beverly Hillbillies. By Filmways, Inc. Perf. Buddy Ebsen (Jed Clampett), Irene Ryan (Granny Daisy Moses), Donna Douglas (Elly May Clampett), Max Baer, Jr. (Jethro Bodine) 1962 – 1971. CBS Television.

A Note From the Publisher, Kingdom Living Day by Day, LLC

Thank you for taking the time to read *Getting Up Again*. We hope that you were able to relate to the story in some way and trust that it was encouraging to you. If you have your own story to share, or if you just want to send any thoughts or questions, please contact us by visiting our website: www.kingdomlivingdbd.com. Furthermore, you can order additional copies of *Getting Up Again* for family or friends who you think would benefit from it. We look forward to hearing from you.

In addition to publishing, Kingdom Living Day by Day, LLC is an organization created to help people live their lives in a way that reflects kingdom principles. Our goal is to positively impact people by assisting them with their personal relationships, careers, finances and more. For information on how we can help you or your organization, please visit the website or send correspondence to the address below.

Kingdom Living Day by Day, LLC
P.O. Box 9003
Hampton, VA 23670-0003

Introduction

Manipulation is a form of social influence which uses indirect, underhanded, and deceptive tactics to change people's perceptions and their resultant behaviour. Usually, the end goal is to advance the interests of the person who initiates the manipulation. In many cases, manipulation happens at the expense of the person that is being manipulated; they may be emotionally, mentally, or physically harmed, or they may end up taking actions that are against their own best interests.

It's important to note that social influence is not inherently wrong; one person can use manipulation techniques for the good of the person he or she is manipulating. For example, your family members or friends can use social influence and manipulation to get you to do something for your good. The people who mean you well might manipulate you as a way of helping you deal with certain challenges or to help you make the right decisions.

However, in this book, we won't focus on the garden-variety harmless forms of social influence. We are more interested in the kind of manipulation that is done with malicious intentions. This is the kind of manipulation that

disregards a person's right to accept or reject influence. It is coercive in nature; when the person being targeted tries to push against it, this kind of manipulation gets more sophisticated, and the end goal is to negate the person's will to assert for themselves.

Historical Background

Manipulation has existed with man since the earliest civilizations. An ever-present yet background behaviour that people will use to benefit themselves. Usually for the pettiest of reasons. But some have used manipulation for the attainment of great power such as the Roman Emperors who manipulated for the power over millions, to politicians today saying what we want to hear. All the way down to the lover quarrelling in their relationship.

This begs the question of why, why someone would use social subterfuge for anything. Well, look at the people I mentioned prior they all have one thing in common. Power. They manipulated for the sake of power, and that power helped them accomplish many great things. Consider the modern corporate world. If you want to get ahead easily, you're going to do what is called by many individuals as "Playing the Game." Simply put, you'll act the way your superiors want to act; you'll go out of your

way to endear yourself to them. While at the same you prove that you are a more qualified employee for that opening you want to attain. Manipulation can have its roots in the earliest of human civilizations. This is simply because it works. You yourself manipulate and do not even realize it. Let's take this theoretical, for example, your good friends with someone and have helped them with difficult tasks before.

Can Manipulation be a Good Thing?

Well, now you need help moving, your most likely to go and try to call a close friend or family member because you know rather it be subconsciously or consciously that they will almost certainly help you. Simply by virtue of prior interactions you have had with them, interactions where you have helped them. So, as a result of this setup, you'll both be amicable to helping one another. Well, simply put that is manipulation because you recognize that the individuals you have asked for help from have asked you for help in the past. Hence this arrangement appears natural within the confines of this friendship, but it is still a form of manipulation, nonetheless.

This is also the odd part of manipulation; we use it so often in our daily lives to get things in what we think is a friendly way that benefits both parties in that they both feel good in the end. We end up becoming oblivious to the insidious side of manipulation to where the people using these tactics on us don't have anything for us to gain. They just want us to be manipulated into believing what they are offering counts as some kind of gain.

All of these behaviours are used in politics still today.

Concluding this point I would also like to point out the fact that some individuals who engage in manipulation are simply just mentally ill, and as a result of that, their manipulative behaviour is stemming from a place of hurt, because in a place of hurt you are incapable of thinking rationally of your actions and the consequences that they may have on other people.

These people who use emotional manipulation as a defines mechanism oftentimes, do it because it is the only mechanism of psychological defines; they grew up knowing. These individuals with mental illness, for the most part, intend no malicious intent or are even mean at heart, but their behaviour and activity they engage in can create that appearance. That still means don't go out

of your way to try to help people like this, such as boyfriends or girlfriends.

Romantic manipulation is by far the worst form that occurs and yet most common. Due to how it shatters trust barriers and bonds. So, in future encounters with manipulators, it is important for you to remember these things as they will help guide you in future encounters with manipulators since you now understand some of their storied histories.

We can begin to look at manipulation as it occurs now in the 21st century. Most of today's manipulation honestly occurs in something as simple as social media. What I am saying by this is people can manipulate and covertly trick us into thinking they live these blessed lives when, in reality, they don't. They show us only what looks good and what gets like. In a way, manipulation has gone from the background to the foreground. It has moved into our everyday lives with things like "fake news" and internet links that are designed to sound enticing yet simply accomplish nothing more than selling an ad.

This why it is important as ever to understand manipulation, given how often it occurs in this fast-paced world of ours. This may sound devious, but manipulation

can also be used to accomplish great things that benefit everyone, such as Gandhi's hunger strikes and other forms of peaceful negotiation. Concluding on the history of manipulation, just remember it has always been with us and always will be with us. It will just change forms over time.

Knowledge is the power

Knowledge is power, and you the reader knowing how people manipulate, the background on it, and why it happens, are now much better equipped to deal with manipulation when you encounter it in your day to life. But heed these last words because when looking at the history of manipulation do not always focus on the negative sometimes manipulation has accomplished great things and even saved lives.

As has been the case in things such as diplomacy. Think of it this way when you are arguing with a potential foe. It makes more sense to lie to them and tell them what they want to hear. Because if there are potentially millions of lives at stake, then why would you want to risk anything but an absolute success.

This may sound malevolent, but the fact of the matter is that sometimes, a bit of dishonesty needs to be used to allow honest virtues to thrive.

Finally, manipulation can also be used for good if you are a salesperson. The kind of manipulation used in sales as you will read further into this book. Tends to not be overt, it leans more on the subtle side of things as a result of how it functions and what the end goal of it is. To simply sell things, so remember while manipulation can look bad on the surface, it is what the end goal is that truly matters.

Types of Manipulation

Many of us are aware that manipulation is a form of deceit. Manipulators are the people who use deceptive tactics to achieve what they want, but this is regardless of the consequences to those around them, particularly to the victims of their tactics.

Manipulators are not worried about how their manipulation will affect you personally or psychological damage that they inflict; all they care about is getting the results that they want. These results could be anything from getting to pick the restaurant to gain

access to the funds or gifts needed to perpetuate a particular social standing.

Knowing the warning signs is a start but knowing the type of emotional manipulator you are dealing with can also help you in defending yourself against them and their deceptive tactics. So, let's talk about the various types of manipulators out in the world, thus gaining a more complete understanding of how they operate to achieve their ends.

- Indifferent

First up is the indifferent manipulator, which is the one that acts like they don't care. These manipulators often seem indifferent towards anything you are doing or saying. This indifference is not just toward your actions, but any circumstances in your life, including difficulties or even celebrations.

In acting indifferent, these individuals have actually caught your attention. You spend time and energy attempting to achieve that breakthrough to capture their attention, thus hoping to achieve a deeper connection. However, they have already singled you out for some specific reason, so they will provide just enough interest

to keep you hooked without really breaking out of the indifferent cycle.

In fact, the more indifferent they act, the more questions you are going to ask because you genuinely care. However, when you start asking questions that is when the manipulation starts in an earnest fashion because now a manipulator can use that they have information provided through those conversations to dig their hooks in ever deeper. Without them having to do or say anything directly, they have begun to play on your heartstrings, thus achieving the goal of your personal emotional investment into their lives.

As the victim, you are now in a position that allows them to use your sympathy to "make them feel better", but in reality, the manipulator is now just starting their sting to take from their victims whatever they want, from the emotional to the material. But when the victim has nothing left, then the manipulator moves on to their upcoming victim, typically without any real remorse.

Still at this moment, you are still a goose to be fleeced, so the indifferent manipulator may also take advantage of another type of manipulator, which is the one that is always in distress or poor me.

- Poor Me

This particular type of manipulator may be the easiest to spot, but in combination with other traits, makes them easy to fall for over and over again. So, what do the poor me manipulators do so effectively when dealing with their victims?

The poor me manipulators use sympathy and guilt, appealing to their victims need to try to help another human being in trouble or assist someone out of a sense of charity or faith. Appealing to their victim's better nature is one consistent way that a manipulator will attempt to get into someone's head. Often it is this goodness that a manipulator can turn on their victim.

It is merely part of our human nature to feel for people who are struggling through something or who are facing various challenges different from the ones that we are facing. We react by doing what we can to help them out, so we tend to cater to their demands without realizing we are being manipulated.

The demands can at first appear reasonable, but over time, will simply grow in complexity. These requests quickly turn into commands and ones that often prove to be real-time suckers. Thus, your whole world suddenly

becomes completely focused on the manipulator. So, the isolation can begin, making it harder for you or loved ones to observe the manipulation and point it out to you.

- Critic

As with other manipulators, this particular type is a bit more aggressive than the first two types. They will actively focus on their victim's habits and emotional cues. After finding areas of sensitivity or weakness, the manipulator will begin to focus on them, subtlety at first, and then gradually growing bolder over time.

While it might be easy to spot what a manipulator is doing, many of us who fall victim to manipulators are helpless to stop it, unless we work on improving our mindset. Other ways to help avoid being a victim or getting out of a manipulative situation involve using anti-manipulation techniques.

The critic uses criticism as a way to get what they want because the victim is trying to please, although the critical manipulator will set a bar for their standards, which the victim will find impossible to meet. The constant criticism for their victim contributes to neither making them feel like they are not good enough nor will

they ever be good enough. Through manipulation, the critic makes you feel like you are worthless, and they are better than you.

Thus, to achieve a better sense of your own self-worth, the victim will attempt to be more like the critic or to do things just the way the critic prefers them. Personality changes may also occur because the victim just wants to gain the affection and praise of the critic. However, the victim does not know this goal is simply unachievable. The critic is able to use a carrot versus stick approach to keep their victim within their grasp and easily influenced.

Still as bad as these types of manipulators can prove to be, there is one that can be far worse. Why? Because they are willing to go much further than any of the others to achieve their goals, including using fear and violence.

- Intimidators

When this particular manipulator comes into play, the victim can be in a very dangerous place. These manipulators are the worst of the worst; they are even more aggressive than the critic. In fact, the intimidator is not just critical, but they use fear and violence to make their victims cower.

These manipulators are more familiar with the stick than using a more carrot-like approach. Once their victim is afraid, these manipulators can easily have their demands met. In abusive relationships with intimidators, the tactic of using anger comes out frequently, along with the need to punish. Both of these tactics play into the fear aspect of the intimidator.

Let's face it, when we are afraid of someone, as individuals, we tend to give in much quicker than if we felt in a position of power or a defendable position. These manipulators are all about stripping away any sense of being able to defend yourself, physically or psychologically.

Nobody dares stand up to a person who uses fear to manipulate them because they are literally afraid of what that person might physically do. This is where the manipulator uses violence or the threat of violence to complete their hold on the victim. Abusive spousal relationships often demonstrate this type of intimidation manipulation with a mix of violence all too well.

So now that we have a greater understanding of the manipulator, their types, and tactics, it's time to get a better understanding of the victim. However, you might

be the one displaying those traits. Let's see how those traits play into a manipulator's hands, and then after, we will explore ways that you can defend against a manipulator or make the right moves to remove yourself from their grasp.

So, what specifically about your personality or way of carrying yourself is sending up flags for a manipulator to zero in on?

Chapter 1. When to Use Manipulation?

Motivation

Imagine that you are faced with a very tight deadline at work, but you are under a lot of pressure to get the project done on time. Perhaps a major contract is riding on your actions over the following few hours. Maybe your job is riding on it. How would you feel? Most of us would feel particularly anxious, especially if our livelihood was in the balance. As a result of that anxiety, you would be more likely to put in extra hours, start the project early, even get help from co-workers. You had an emotional response, anxiety, and you took action to get the job done and alleviate that anxiety. On the positive side, your love for your girlfriend could make you feel pressured to propose marriage. You could also seek out activities and experiences that induce positive emotions like happiness or excitement and avoid those that induce feelings of sadness or boredom.

Survival

Charles Darwin, the author of On the Origin of Species, held that emotions were evolutionary adaptations that fostered survival and reproduction in both humans and

animals. They motivate us to act quickly and take actions that will maximize our chances of survival and success. Anger leads us to confrontation, while fear induces us to flee a threat. Lust makes us seek out a mate; love makes us take care of the people close to us.

Decision-making

Emotions play a major role in the decisions we make; from what movie we watch after work to what we have for dinner to who we vote for at election time. Each one has an emotional component that informs the choices we make, even those that we truly believe are purely rational and logical. In fact, research shows that brain damage affecting the areas of the brain that control emotions is linked to a markedly decreased ability to make good decisions.

Communication

Emotions help us to understand others and to be understood. Our emotions offer important clues to those communicating with us as to how we are feeling. Sometimes this is done with facial expressions, sometimes with body language, and sometimes with explicit statements. This provides a point of

understanding and an opportunity to take action in response to a given situation.

Understanding Emotions in Others

Reading emotions in others is a function of your emotional intelligence. If you are going to be persuasive, influential, or even manipulative, improving your emotional intelligence will go a long way toward helping you reach your goals.

Universal Human Emotions

The first thing to do is to be able to recognize that there are two positive emotions and four negative ones. The positive ones are happiness and surprise. They reduce stress and improve mood. They also improve memory and awareness. The negative emotions are anger, fear, sadness, and disgust. They each increase stress, but they also help us to recognize and deal with threats and difficult situations. Each of these emotions is associated with a distinct set of behaviours, and to identify them in other people you need to learn to recognize those behaviours.

Facial Expressions

Now you are ready to start learning to read emotions. We will begin with facial expressions as they are an extremely important part of nonverbal communication. Just hearing a person's words without the benefit of seeing their facial expressions only gives you part of the message because words frequently do not match the emotions. You need to read the facial expression to know what the person you are speaking with is really feeling. It will help guide you through the conversation. Just remember that if you nail the emotion someone is feeling, you still do not know why they feel that way. If you are speaking with someone who seems upset or bored, they could be feeling that way for any number of reasons that have nothing to do with you.

Facial Expressions and Universal Emotions

There are seven facial expressions: surprise, fear, disgust, contempt, anger, sadness, and happiness. These expressions are universal across all cultures and are the same regardless of race, sex, country of origin. You could be from Paris trying to communicate with someone from the Amazon rainforest, and both of you would recognize these expressions. Get in front of a mirror and put in

some time practising each of them. Take your time and really explore them, and you will soon get much better at recognizing each of them in others.

Reading the Face

Once you have an idea about your own expressions, it is time to look at other people. Just remember, however, that these expressions are not necessarily automatic. As you can see in your own exercises, it is easy to manipulate your expression to appear one way when, in reality, you are feeling something very different. That is why you have to look at the whole person and listen to their voice. Here are some things to look for:

•A genuine smile. Fake smiles you very few facial muscles, primarily those just around the mouth, while the genuine smile encompasses far more of the face with the corners of the mouth as well as the cheeks raised and the area around the eyes tightened into "crow's feet." These characteristics together point to a genuine smile.

•Know the difference between happiness and sadness. People will often try to cover-up sadness by smiling. Again, look at the entire face. While a frown is a dead giveaway for sadness, look for a raising of the inner corners of the eyebrows and loose, drooping eyelids.

•Know the difference between anger and disgust. Anger and disgust are easily confused because they are associated with similar facial expressions. For example, people tend to wrinkle their noses when they are disgusted, angry, or simply annoyed, so you need to look for other clues. Anger is usually expressed by pulling down the eyebrows, bulging the eyes and pursing the lips. On the other hand, emotions like disgust, disdain or dislike can be seen in the raising of the upper lip and a simultaneous loosening of the lower lip, as well as furrowing of the brow, but not to the same extent as anger.

•Recognize the difference between fear and surprise. Fear and surprise can be thought of as two sides of the same coin in that each of them activates an instinctual "fight or flight" response, whether or not it is a true threat. In both cases, the eyes go wide, which allows us to better see a threat coming. The difference is in the eyebrows, which rise in surprise as the jaw drops, and furrow in fear, with dilated pupils. Also, fear makes us open our mouths and tense our facial muscles.

Micro-expressions

Facial expressions that pass quickly are referred to as micro-expressions. Have you ever had a feeling about someone that you just could not pin down? If so, you could be picking up on a micro-expression. Here are a few things to look for:

•Eyebrows. Watching the eyebrows will tell you a great deal about what a person is feeling. Eyebrows can be:

•Raised and arched, which shows surprise.

•Lowered and knit together in anger.

•Angled, with the inner corners drawn up, which shows sadness.

•Eyes. As expressive as eyebrows are, they can't hold a candle to the eyes themselves. They can be:

•Open wide to show surprise,

•Intense and staring in a way that screams anger, or

•Framed by wrinkles (crow's feet), a sign of happiness.

Note: Dilated pupils are an indication of either fear or lust, while rapid blinking is a definite sign of either a stress reaction or lying.

•Mouth. Then, to the eyes, the mouth is the most expressive part of the face. There are a number of things you should look for, including:

•An open mouth with a lowered jaw, which signals surprise.

•A tense open mouth, which shows fear.

•A sneer with a single corner of the mouth raised to show hatred.

•Both corners raised in a smile of happiness.

•Both corners are drawn down in a frown of sadness.

The mouth can signal other things as well, including:

•Anxiety through lip biting.

•Distaste through pursed lips.

•Deceit by covering the mouth.

Vocal Tone

Then, the vocal tone. While it does come into play as an emotional expression, it is not fool proof. This is because not all emotions are strongly expressed in the voice. Some of the weaker ones include happiness, sadness, fear, and friendliness. More than that, different emotions

can be expressed with very similar tones. A tense voice can mean anger, for example, but it can also mean excitement.

Depending on the intensity, a whispery or soft tone is concordant with a number of positive emotions including lust, relaxation, contentment, and friendship; but it also could indicate either sadness or boredom. If the tone is breathier, the more likely it is to indicate fear, shyness, or nervousness.

General Behaviour and Demeanour

Emotional displays often happen with the person being completely unaware of what they are doing. In fact, a person's general behaviour and demeanour often speak volumes about how they are feeling. When you look at the person, to they seem open and friendly, or are they closed off, and reserved? Again, you do not know why they might be feeling the way they do, but these signs will give you a clue as to how to proceed.

•Look for nonverbal cues. These will help you read emotion but do not rely solely upon them as there is often a cultural, physical, or psychological component involved. You are looking for body movements, posture, and eye contact. Notice whether or not the person

appears to be relaxed and animated, maintaining good eye contact and posture, and moving easily. If so, great; but a tense, stiff posture, especially if they stoop, fidget, or make other displays of irritation or nervousness all indicate negative emotions. A relaxed, straight posture with easy movement shows comfort and openness, but too much movement, especially combined with a loud voice, indicates excitement or anger. On the other hand, stooped shoulders and crossed arms indicate things like extreme discomfort or defensiveness, while a refusal to make eye contact can indicate upset or guilt.

•Remember that body language is heavily influenced by culture, personality, and social situations. Italians, for example, use gestures when they speak, while in Japan, such gesturing could be considered rude. Another example is eye contact. In the United States and Europe, eye contact denotes attention and respect, but some Asian and African cultures see it as rude or aggressive.

•Notice body movement and posture. Posture and body movement will show both the emotion as well as its intensity. Hunched shoulders combined with a forward-leaning posture denotes intense anger, while a more backwards-leaning stance indicates panic or fear. We see

an air of confidence in a straight posture with the shoulders back and head held high, but hunched shoulders or a pronounced forward slump indicates boredom, nervousness, or a need for sympathy. Hands at the side or in the pockets tend to indicate sadness, while annoyance or irritation is displayed with one arm at the side or hand on the hip, and the other hand gesturing, either pointing or with the palm flat. Hands behind the back indicate indifference. In regard to legs and feet, shaking legs or tapping toes can indicate anxiety, annoyance or impatience. They could also mean nothing at all.

•Notice signs of "fight or flight" reaction. When we are surprised or threatened, we experience a stress reaction that includes widened pupils, faster breathing, sweating, and heart palpitations. Sweaty palms or armpits, flushed complexion, and shaking hands all indicate stress, anxiety, or nervousness. Men react to stress and upset by becoming aggressive, angry, and/or frustrated, while women react by being more interactive, seeking help, and discussing their situation. That's not everyone, mind you, as there are those whose reaction to stress and upset is to withdraw, some describe it as "going underground."

Look to Your Own Reactions

Emotions are contagious, passing easily from one person to another. We have all experienced our mood changing as a result of someone else's emotion. You can use this to recognize emotions in others by taking note of your own reaction, the facial expression, tone, and body language you adopt in answer to someone else's emotions.

Emotion and Health

There is a direct connection between physical health and emotions. Stress and depression, for example, can leave you feeling sick and tired all the time with headaches, stomach issues, pain, and a host of other physical symptoms. They can also lead to alterations in eating habits as well as addictions to alcohol and/or drugs.

Improving Your Emotional Intelligence

You can develop and improve your emotional intelligence over time by observing your own emotions and, when looking at other people, applying what you have learned about your emotions to theirs. Begin by learning the four areas of emotional intelligence:

1. See and recognize your own emotions and the emotions of others.

2. Use what you have perceived in yourself and others as a basis to think about what is happening.

3. Learn the true importance of the role these emotions play and their meaning; and

4. Learn how to control your own emotional reactions and help others do likewise.

Since there is really no app for this, here are some strategies you can use to improve your emotional intelligence starting right now. They include:

- Work on your ability to read facial expressions and body language. It will require that you put the cell phone down and actually engage in verbal, in-person dialogue every day.

- Face your own uncomfortable or negative feelings, as well as those you see in others. Understand that these are valid feelings and that there is a reason you are experiencing them. You just need to figure out why and then counteract them with positive emotions.

- Consider your health and bodily reactions. Your emotions and your body are linked, so pay attention to

how it reacts when you are happy, sad, excited, and so on.

•Keep an Emotions Journal. Here you are to write down how you are feeling and record your activity at the time of the feeling as well as the thoughts you have that go along with those emotions. Include anything that you deem relevant. The key is to understand the connection between emotions, actions, and thoughts.

•Get an Emotion Reading from some close to you, a friend or family member that you trust. Having a distinct perspective is often quite useful and insightful, and the answers you get maybe both interesting and unexpected.

When All Else Fails, Just Ask

There is nothing wrong with simply asking someone how they are feeling. Try to speak to them alone; it will help them to open up to you, which may be difficult if they are in a group setting.

However, the other person might also lie and tell you that everything is fine when it really isn't. That is not uncommon, but it is also not the end of the world. Their response when you ask can tell you a lot by giving you a chance to examine their non-verbal expressions as well

as how they respond to you. Low tones and slow speech could indicate sadness, while higher tones and more rapid speech can indicate excitement or upset. Remember, context is important when trying to decipher the meanings behind these emotional expressions.

Gauging Your Influence

As you go through and practice these strategies of persuasion and influence, the most common question is this: How do I know it is working, and if it is working, by how much? One way is to simply count the number of times you get your way. That will not give you the whole story, though. You also need to consider the demeanour of the person you have influenced. Did they act or change willingly, or did they do it resentfully, just to get rid of you? If that is the case, then you cannot really count it as a win. When you convert someone to your way of thinking or get them to do something for you, they should do it willingly. Once you start getting that you know your efforts have risen above mere nagging.

Now, turn the tables and contemplate how you have affected the people around you all day. What sort of influence have you exerted on others? The more aware

you become of the influence you have, the quicker you will understand how effectively you influence them.

Chapter 2. Emotional manipulation

What is Emotional Manipulation?

Let me ask you a simple question—how would you feel if you realized that all along you have been acting out a script someone else has written for you? In simpler words, what would you feel like if you realized that you have not been in charge of your actions all this time? It certainly feels scary, as well as annoying. This is exactly what emotional manipulation is all about. Most people tend to use the phrase emotional manipulation in regular parlance, but not a lot of people know what they are talking about. So, it's time to set the record straight.

Emotional manipulation can be social as well as psychological, and the person using it does so to influence your behaviour or response to a situation in a manner that suits their needs. It is quite right to call it manipulation because you are merely acting out someone else's script while thinking that you are true to yourself. The approach to emotional manipulation isn't usually forceful, but it has more to do with preying on your emotions—or mind— to exploit you to suit their purpose.

It is hard to see anything good in manipulation. Manipulators use what belongs to someone else in a covert way to fuel their desires, without asking for the other's permission. The issue isn't with the secrecy; usually, manipulators tend to make others do things that they normally might not do and might have even objected to.

Why Understand about Emotional Manipulation Tactics?

If you aren't aware of the different methods or tactics that manipulators usually use on you, then you will never be able to break free of their hold on you. You will continue to deceive yourself into a false sense of security—that you are in control of your life when you actually aren't. Once you are aware of the common methods of manipulation, then you can identify them when someone tries to use them on you. Emotional manipulation is certainly not a desirable thing, but there might be times when you will need to apply them to attain what you want from those who refuse to cooperate with you, at least initially.

Essentially, an emotional manipulator tends to work with the weak points in the psychology of their victims.

Manipulators continuously try to look for a weak point in their victim's psyche that they can use to their advantage.

A primary characteristic trait that all emotional manipulators exhibit is secrecy. They always tend to work behind your back to achieve their goals, although they might start to blatantly exhibit their bravado once they have a firm grip on you. Manipulators tend to be great listeners naturally, and that's one of the reasons why they succeed—they pay great attention to all the details that you reveal to them in discussions, and they try to pick on those details and use them to their advantage.

Deception is an unalienable trait of a manipulator. When you think about it, that's all they do—deceive others. Armed with their cunningness, a manipulator can make you perceive something as black when it is in fact, white. If you think you have never been manipulated in your life, then you need to think again, or maybe you haven't come across a great manipulator until now. If you have been manipulated in the past, then you will notice that their personality was always domineering—at times, this is obvious.

Emotional Manipulation Tactics

You will learn about the different emotional tactics that manipulators use on others. These tactics aren't just limited to the ones that are mentioned however if you want to avoid being manipulated in your life, and you want to live your life on your terms, then you need to learn to recognize these common tactics.

Projection

Projection is one of the most prominent tactics that manipulators use.

Essentially, it is a diversionary tactic that emotional and psychological manipulators use to project all their deficiencies, as well as shortcomings, onto another person. Instead of stepping up and taking responsibility for their actions, they try to make someone else the scapegoat and take the blame for it all. Manipulators project their faults onto someone unsuspecting. It is a tactic of psychological abuse that essentially transfers the burden of guilt from them to someone else. They are trying to paint a clear picture of themselves by making someone else look rather unfortunate. In any lousy situation, the manipulator often skirts free of all blame.

You might have come across people who behave in this manner in your life. As soon as a problem is identified or a defect is found, they conveniently transfer it all onto their victim.

You might also have such a person as a partner in your relationship. Instead of simply coming clean about their need for some intimacy, they will try to make you feel like you are the one that's being clingy, and by obliging you, they are doing you a favour. They try to make you look weaker to make themselves appear stronger. If you take a moment and think about it, you will notice that they are the ones who are weak.

Look out for people who are always noticing the faults in others constantly. Such people are merely projecting their shortcomings onto others around them.

Gaslighting

What does gaslighting mean? It's when you cause someone to doubt themselves about whether something is real or not.

This technique is frequently used by emotional and psychological manipulators. They do this in a subtle manner that will make you question your beliefs, and

even make you think twice about all those things that are sacred to you.

For instance, let us assume that you've just graduated from college and received the trophy for showcasing great academic skills. In such a situation, an emotional manipulator will try to make you feel like such a thing didn't happen, or they will act in such a manner that you will feel unworthy of your achievement. Also, an emotional manipulator might make such statements that will make you feel like you aren't capable of achieving the feat that you did.

Now let's consider another situation where you are suspecting that your partner is using you or cheating on you. If the partner is a manipulator, then their go-to tactic will be to put such questions forward that will make you feel like all your doubts are nothing more than a figment of your imagination and aren't real. This is, perhaps, the most common reason why a lot of people stay trapped in an unhealthy relationship, in spite of seeing red flags all around them.

Denial

It can be quite difficult to distinguish between lying, denial, and the distortion of facts in any form of

emotional manipulation. A manipulator doesn't necessarily have to be opposed to the truth, but their "alleged" acceptance of it is only to serve the ulterior motive of manipulating you.

Denial is something that all emotional manipulators use—they might agree with something only to deny it.

This behaviour is not an accident.

From the get-go, they know that there will come a time when an issue will challenge their competence, and they are, therefore, prepared to deny that such an argument even took place!

For instance, a person might be asked to fill in for the position of a secretary at a company and could agree to it initially, but as soon as the demands of work started flowing in, he might deny that he ever even agreed to fill in for the post in the first place.

The same type of behaviour can be exhibited in a relationship—the manipulator might not define the relationship and might make the victim assume something that they know they didn't agree to. So, as soon as the problems start to creep in, the manipulator

will deny ever being in a relationship and will instead start to blame the victim.

Being in a relationship with an emotional manipulator is very unhealthy. They are the ones who make all the rules and change them to suit their needs, and it ends up leaving the victim feeling quite confused. When someone manipulates you emotionally, you might start to question yourself and even accept blame, regardless of whether you are at fault or not.

Intimidation

If an emotional manipulator perceives you to be a threat, then they often resort to intimidation to silence you. Part of this tactic is to stay close to you and talk to you in a manner that's a combination of aggressiveness and subtlety. They tend to look you in the eyes and have a strange body language so that you lose your train of thought in their hopes you stop arguing with them. They often use this tactic once they realize that it is easy to frighten or cajole you.

Don't forget that it is a basic trait of all manipulators to try and identify your weak points so that they can't use them against you. If a manipulator realizes that you get scared easily, then they will capitalize on this fear by

using intimidation and threats. A way to fix this situation is by overcoming your fears and standing up for yourself. There is a simple way in which you can prevent this from happening. If you have just met someone or you don't fully trust an individual yet, then it is a good idea to keep your fears, insecurities or weaknesses to yourself. If you reveal too much, too soon, then be aware that they can use it against you. You can ask for help as and when you need it, but don't let the manipulator feel that you are scared of anything—including them.

Magnify Their Problems

It is a part of a manipulator's tactics to magnify their problems and diminish yours. This is usually done subtly, and you will not even realize it when they do it.

Manipulators tend to pretend that they sympathize with you and what you are going through and might even express some empathy, but this is only temporary, and it shields their intentions. However, you will soon notice that they keep bringing up their problems and start magnifying their troubles to make yours seem insignificant.

A manipulator will always bring up their problems as soon as you mention yours. Instead of helping you find a

solution to your problems, they will bring up their allegedly bigger troubles to diminish the intensity of yours. This will, effectively, end any discussion that you were having about your problems. This unfair comparison tends to be quite annoying and frustrating since it doesn't give you the sympathy that you are looking for, and it will make you feel foolish for even bringing up your problems in the first place. They will make you feel like you are intolerant or that you don't have the willpower to deal with your problems and will make you feel bad about even thinking about your troubles when theirs are "much worse."

Intellectual Bullying

Another tactic that emotional manipulators use is intellectual bullying. They try to manipulate you by bombarding you with intellectual facts that can overwhelm you easily. Now, don't get me wrong—the manipulator might not quite accurate facts, but they are aware of the fact that you don't have the necessary access or the opportunity to verify and validate their claims. They try to portray themselves as an authority that you cannot dispute, allowing them to get their way with you.

This form of emotional manipulation is often used in financial institutions and while making sales. You don't have the opportunity to validate their alleged facts or claims, and since they are often sweet talkers, you will easily fall prey to their tactics without being aware of it. The only way to avoid this is by ensuring that you are well-informed before deciding. It doesn't mean that you must know everything about everything; it simply means that you need to have an idea of what they are talking about.

Intentional Digression

Digression is a tactic where the manipulator deviates from the usual course of discussion and moves onto a topic that is completely unrelated to the subject at hand. Manipulators play this card when they realize that you are holding them accountable for a certain act or deed of theirs. For instance, if you ask someone why the floor is a mess and it hasn't been cleaned yet and they promptly remind you of the UEFA Champions League match from the other day. Of course, the person realizes that football is your weakness and the only way to distract you from the issue at hand is by diverting the topic to something else that you enjoy.

Name-Calling

A common trait of an emotional manipulator is that they always have a rather exalted but often false opinion of themselves. They believe that they are correct, and others are wrong, always.

Most people who resort to any form of emotional manipulation tend to be narcissists. So, if you bring up a topic that challenges their ego by questioning their thoughts or opinions, then you must be prepared to get called more names than the one that's given to you at birth. Truth be told, if you aren't thick-skinned and are at all sensitive to criticism, then you will easily succumb to their manipulative tactics, even if it is out of sheer frustration. Being called a fanatic, a fascist, an extremist, a troublemaker or even an idiot, along with other choice adjectives, can make anyone feel annoyed, and even dejected. Once you feel any such negative emotion, you make it quite easy for the manipulator to prey on that vulnerability and make you feel bad about yourself.

So, every time you challenge a manipulator, be prepared for them to dirty your intentions to silence you.

Conditioning

Conditioning is a psychological technique used to train an animal or a human being towards a specific trait or taste that the trainer wants to inculcate in them. Of course, this would be done covertly and subtly so that the victim doesn't get suspicious—the victim wouldn't even realize that the manipulator is selling the idea to them and cornering them.

When it comes to emotional manipulation, the manipulator will think of the victim as a "pet project" that needs to be trained, and that they are the trainer. This is essentially a technique that will help them get rid of the victim's initial thoughts, encouraging them to embrace the manipulator's desires.

For instance, if you think that you are someone who values honesty, then the emotional manipulator will show you everything that you stand to gain, but only if you are dishonest. In this manner, the manipulator will slowly start to condition you to associate success with negative and undesirable values.

Gossiping and Stalking

The primary aim of any manipulator is to gain absolute control over you. However, when it seems like you are difficult to control or that it isn't going according to the

manipulator's plan, then the manipulator will quickly change their tactics to control how others see you.

They try to change others' opinions of you by spreading vile and vicious rumours about you behind your back. In some cases, they might even start stalking you.

Manipulators may also try to intimidate you and try to create a negative image about you. For instance, let us assume that you are dating someone who uses this tactic.

When you drop any hints about breaking up with her or ending the relationship due to her habits, she'll go around gossiping and spreading vile rumours about you. The point is that manipulators will prevent others from getting to know your version of facts and will start creating a story that inspires general dislike toward you.

Let me continue the example mentioned above and take it one step further. If your partner starts spreading a rumour amongst your circles of friends that you have been cheating on them, and that that's the reason why the relationship has come to an end, it will quickly turn the tables on you, even when you aren't at fault and it was nothing more than a rumour.

Love Smothering

Emotional manipulators tend to bombard their victims with a lot of love. Their sugar-coated words and behaviour can easily tempt anyone into thinking that they are a perfect match and that you are hopelessly in love with them. You need to pay close attention to the things they say about their ex and see how they tend to portray such people before you as being worthless. Remember, if you are dealing with a manipulator then sooner, you will be subjected to the same treatment as their ex is/was. As a rule of thumb, you need to stay away from all those who degrade their exes to make you seem good. A relationship involves two people, and if it does come to an end, then both parties are responsible, not just one.

An honest person will never try to ride on their past to make they're present seem great. Bringing down a person before you so that you sympathize with them is a technique of emotional manipulation. By trying to earn your sympathy, they try to manipulate you. They can quickly smother you with love so that you turn a blind eye toward everything else that they do.

Chapter 3. Manipulation in Relationship

A considerable proportion of manipulation occurs in close relationships, especially romantic ones. In fact, manipulation of all forms in romantic relationships has become almost like a pandemic. Many people find themselves stuck in relationships where they are controlled by their partners. Some even find themselves being controlled by their children.

The peculiar thing about manipulative relationships is how they are toxic to all parties involved. The victim of manipulation loses all self-esteem and finds their individual identity shattered in the long run, while the manipulator finds it impossible to keep relationships with loved ones or maintain friendships with co-workers and acquaintances.

Manipulators in manipulative relationships can have very twisted motivations. Some, chiefly due to psychopathic tendencies, see manipulations as merely gratifying activity. They manipulate others for recreation, almost as if it's a game. Some others are so fuelled by a quest for power that they are ready to destroy the other individual(s) just to feel superior. They are control-happy domination freaks who always like nothing other than to

feel on top. Some, as a result of their low self-esteem, manipulate others in their relationships because bringing someone else down helps them feel better about themselves, while others simply do so because they see no other way to advance their personal agendas.

One of the primary defences against manipulation in relationships, just like manipulation in other circumstances, is awareness. Most times, you may not need to know what techniques your manipulators are using before knowing that you've been a victim of manipulation. You just need to look at yourself. Still, because of the strong ties, you may have with your partner, you may feel some reluctance in ending a manipulative relationship even after deducing serious manipulative tendencies. It is up to you to determine if there is anything at all that's salvageable in the relationship. Experience has shown, though, that it is generally in the best interests of both parties to dissolve manipulative romantic relationships. If you realize that your partner or child or relative is manipulating you and you don't take concrete action, you're effectively enabling their poisonous behaviour, which is neither good for them nor you.

Even if you're lucky enough to be in a healthy relationship that's characterized by love, understanding, and open communication, you may realize that you're wondering why some people stay in relationships that hurt them. Why would anyone continue a relationship with someone who makes them frustrated, self-doubting, scared, depressed, or confused? Why would anyone punish themselves so?

One thing you must understand is that most manipulative relationships don't begin that way. He/she may be so sweet at first, it's like they are an angel sent from heaven to illuminate your life. You have the perfect honeymoon, and everything is absolutely amazing. Things go well for a bit, but then begin to turn sour. Because this manipulative partner has somehow sold you the idea that the downturn in the relationship is your fault, you blame yourself for the problems and persist, trying to regain your partner's love and loyalty for the wrong you have been made—through subtle techniques—to believe that you committed. Your efforts pay off, and you and your partner are back together and in love again, but only for a while. Then the vicious cycle begins all over again.

Also, you must be aware that manipulation in relationships evolves over time. In almost all cases, it starts slowly, building up until it escalates. The abuser in this instance grows more confident in their manipulation tactics over time, entrapping the victim in a mental loop perpetuated by uncertainty and doubt, wherein the victim is controlled through a series of promised benefits and threatened repercussions, almost as if they are about to get what they desire but could have it taken away at any time.

Warning Signs of Manipulation in a Relationship

If you are in a relationship, especially a romantic one, and you observe any of these, there's a large chance that you're being manipulated.

1. You don't feel as good about yourself now as you did when the relationship began. You feel less in control of yourself, less sane, less intelligent, less confident, less secure, or even less attractive.
2. Your partner seems to arbitrarily withdraw their affection at the slightest provocation. So, you police your words, careful not to trigger them into absolute withdrawal because of what you say.
3. Just to make your partner happy and keep the relationship intact, you begin to do things that go against your values and beliefs. You're constantly in ethical dilemmas, and you find yourself crossing boundaries that you ordinarily wouldn't have crossed.

4. You know you're unhappy with the relationship and filled with uncertainty, but somehow you can't bring yourself to call it quits, mostly because the other person makes you blissfully happy on some occasions.
5. You were filled with joy when this person came into your life. Now, this joy has become sadness and desperation.
6. Your mood depends heavily on the general state of the relationship, and these days you've been going through drastic highs and severe lows simultaneously.
7. You talk about your relationship every time and to everyone who cares to listen. It doesn't dissipate the weight in your chest. You become an analyst, scrutinizing every detail in hopes that at a point, it'll all make sense to you. Pondering about the relationship so much makes you obsessive and paranoid.
8. You don't understand why, but your relationship seems bizarre and difficult to explain. Each time you try to lay it out to someone, you find yourself concluding that they may be unable to reason certain aspects because it's all "so complicated".
9. The best thing that ever happened to you is ruined, and you feel strongly that you're responsible, though you don't know exactly what you did to mess it up.
10. You're always unsettled when your partner is not at home. You've developed an obsessive compulsion to know their exact whereabouts at any point in time because you don't have a clue where they might exactly be. You become a stalker, policing your partner's social media account, emails, texts, and browser history.

11. You frequently ask the person you are in a relationship with if something is wrong and they tell you that everything is fine, but inside of you, you're completely certain that something is amiss.
12. Your partner pulls away from you, and you blame yourself. You cannot understand why you keep sabotaging your relationship. You find yourself always apologizing and trying to repair the damage you believe you have caused.
13. You feel inadequate because regardless of your best efforts, you can't seem to make your partner happy. You used to be able to, but suddenly you lost the ability to bring a smile to their face. You cannot pinpoint the exact point where you began to get it wrong.
14. You find yourself feeling increasingly insecure, mistrustful, and filled with a strong fear of abandonment.
15. You always feel like you're falling short of your partner's expectations no matter what you do. This leads to you developing a problem with distrust, anger, insecurity, jealousy, and overreaction, which your partner points out to you from time to time.

If any of these is going on in your life, then you need to check yourself. Your partner is most likely manipulating you, and they may not even realize it. It is still up to you to decide on the following steps to take when manipulation his been diagnosed, but remember, under no circumstances will you ever have a social obligation to be victimized.

One of the most dangerous things about manipulators in relationships is how they generally do not care about the extent of psychological damage they inflict on you with their actions, as long as they achieve the results to which they're aiming. They will try to play dumb and feign ignorance when you accuse them of something wrong that they have done, they hate your honesty, and they may brandish anger or abandonment to keep you in check.

It helps to know their techniques and have an idea of the warning signs, but to truly protect yourself from manipulation in relationships, it helps to go further into determining the kind of manipulator you're dealing with and how best to tackle them.

1. The Intimidator

It's very easy to be broken by someone you're afraid of. When you operate from a place of strength and self-assurance, however, you can put up a stronger fight and are better protected.

The intimidator is chiefly found in abusive spousal relationships where he or she reinforces aggressive fearmongering with violence. What the manipulator here

does is strip away any sense of being able to defend yourself physically or psychologically, until you become putty in their hands. In such abusive relationships, anger is constantly used as a weapon, along with the threat of punishment, to instil significant fear in the victim.

2. The 'Pity Party'

This kind of manipulator is highly problematic because they are like a flu that keeps coming back over and over again. These 'pity party' manipulators twist the mind of their victims through guilt and sympathy, appealing to the natural sensibilities everyone has in which they feel the need to help others who are going through a rough patch.

Manipulators always look for ways to turn the sense of goodness that their victims have against them. They get into your head, painting such a pathetic scenario that your sense of charity is stirred. So, out of the kindness of your heart, you do what you can to help them out, meeting their every demand, and not realizing that you're being manipulated.

The worst part about 'pity party' manipulators is how their requests tend to increase in complexity and become more demanding, until they are practically issuing you

commands while you shut yourself off from the world, focusing all your attention on trying to fix a thing that was never broken.

3. The Indifferent

This category of manipulators always acts like they don't care. No matter what you do, even when you have a significant cause for celebration, the indifferent manipulator acts like they wouldn't give a hoot if you vanished from the earth's surface and were never seen again.

This type of manipulation may seem apparent and easy to avoid, but not at all. By acting so indifferent, these individuals seize your attention. You begin to wonder about what you have done, second-guessing your own actions, and trying to break through their shell. You spend time and energy trying to get their attention. Unbeknownst to you, they already singled you out. They will provide just enough interest to keep you hooked, but they won't break the cycle of indifference.

They make you become emotionally invested in them without as much a lifting a finger. At this point, they redirect your sympathy toward making them feel better with themselves.

4. The Critic

Manipulators in this category delight in destroying the confidence of their victims, especially when the victims seem to have an intrinsic need to please. They constantly criticize their victims, making them seem like they'll never be good enough, while simultaneously raising the bar of standards so high that the victim may never reach it. Through manipulation, critics make their victims feel worthless and establish that they are better than their victims.

This usually results in substantial personality changes, as the victim tries to be more like the critic, so they can feel better about themselves. The victim believes that if they walk and talk like the critic or develop the same preferences, they will develop a better sense of self-worth. This, however, is far from the truth, as they will only ever feel as good as the critic tells them that they are.

Tips for Handling Manipulation in Relationships

As has been established so far, manipulation in relationships is a serious ordeal that can severely damage both parties, but most especially the victim.

Below are important techniques through which you can employ to resist manipulators in your relationships:

1. Call Manipulation Out for What It Is

One of the quickest ways to solve the problem is to label it for what it is. Labelling it shows that you have carefully identified the problem, which sets you on the track to deal with it. Many folks who are in manipulative relationships continue to wallow there because they do not want to acknowledge that they are being manipulated. Admitting that you're a victim of manipulation isn't a weakness; it's a strength.

You will never stop feeling like the problem if you don't admit to yourself that it was never really you, that you were simply a pawn in another person's game of chess. The longer you stay quiet about manipulation, the longer it goes on, and the more damage you incur. Remember, in a manipulative relationship; you are never the problem.

2. Don't Explain Yourself

One famous method of entrapment used by manipulators is making the victim feel like they have to explain their choices or rationalize their actions to them. The moment you recognize a manipulator in your relationship,

instantly realize that you don't owe them any explanations.

It may be tempting but refrain from explaining to the manipulator why you need to take some time to think. They will act like it's their business, but you have to make them realize that it isn't. The moment you explain your need for space or, even worse, tell them what you intend to think about, you basically find yourself back in their clutches.

3. Give Yourself Some Time

Most manipulators are tactical. If you give them just a little space, they will fill up the entire room. When dealing with a manipulator, you need to take some time off. Manipulators will often make demands and expect instantaneous responses. Don't give it to them.

No matter how intensely they pressure you, stand your ground. You will only respond when you're ready after you've thought it all out properly. At the same time, never sound like you're asking for permission in any way, form, or shape, when you decide to take some time off. You don't want to put any power in their hands.

4. Remember That You Call the Shots

Never forget your right to the agency as an individual. When it comes to relationships, you have to be able to highlight your boundaries and stick with them. This will surely frustrate the manipulator, as they try to break through your boundaries, but you must stand your ground.

Set limits and be clear about them. If you do this, you will reclaim power over your life back from the manipulator.

Chapter 4. Mind Control Practices

Mind control involves using influence and persuasion to change the behaviours and beliefs in someone. That someone might be the person themselves, or it might be someone else. Mind control has also been referred to as brainwashing, thought reform, coercive persuasion, mental control, and manipulation, just to name a few. Some people feel that everything is done by manipulation. But if that is true to be believed, then important points about manipulation will be lost. Influence is much better thought of as a mental continuum with two extremes. One side has influences that are respectful, ethical, and work to improve the individual while showing respect for them and their basic human rights. The other side contains influences that are dark and destructive that work to remove basic human rights from a person, such as independence, the ability for rational thought, and sometimes their total identity.

When thinking of mind control, it is better to see it as a way to use influence on other people that will disrupt something in them, as their way of thinking or living. The influence works on the very basis of what makes people human, such as their behaviours, beliefs, and values. It can disrupt the very way they chose personal preferences

or make critical decisions. Mind control is nothing more than using words and ideas to convince someone to say or do something they might never have thought of saying or doing on their own.

There are scientifically proven methods that can be used to influence other people. Mind control has nothing to do with fakery, ancient arts, or even magical powers. Real mind control really is the basis of a word that many people hate to hear. That word is marketing. Many people hate to hear that word because of the negative connotations associated with it. When people hear "marketing," they automatically assume that it refers to those ideas taught in business school. But the basis of marketing is not about deciding which part of the market to target or deciding which customers will likely buy this product. The basis of marketing is one very simple word. That word is "YES."

If a salesperson asks a regular customer to write a brief endorsement of the product they buy, hopefully, they will say yes. If someone asks their significant other to take some of the business cards to pass out at work, hopefully, they will say yes. If you write any kind of blog and ask another blogger to provide a link to yours on

their blog, hopefully, they will say yes. When enough people say yes, the business or blog will begin to grow. With even more yesses, it will continue to grow and thrive. This is the very simple basis of marketing. Marketing is nothing more than using mind control to get other people to buy something or to do something beneficial for someone else. And the techniques can easily be learned.

The first technique in mind control is to tell people what you want them to want. Never tell people to think it over or take some time. That is a definite mind control killer. People already have too much going on in their minds. When they are told to think something over, they will not. It will be forgotten, and then it will never happen. This has nothing to do with being stupid or lazy and everything to do with just being way too busy.

So, the best strategy is to take the offensive and think for them. Everything must be explained in the beginning. Never assume that the other blogger will automatically understand the benefits of adding a link will be for them. Do not expect anyone to give a demonstration blindly. And merely asking for a testimonial, while it might garner an appositive response, probably will not garner a well-

formed testimonial to the product. Instead, be prepared to explain the blog, show examples, and offer compelling reasons why this merger will be a benefit to both parties. Have the demonstration laid out in great detail with notes on what to say when and visuals to go along with the notes, so all the other person has to do is present the information. Offer the customer a few variations of testimonials that have already been received and ask them to choose one and personalize it a bit. Always be specific in explaining what is desired. Explain why it is desired. Show how this will work. Tell the person how to do it and why they should do it. If done correctly, it will feel exactly like one friend advising another friend on which is the best path to take. And the answer will be yes simply because saying yes makes so much sense.

Think of the avalanche. Think of climbing all the way to the top of the highest mountain ever. Now, at the top, think of searching for the biggest heaviest boulder that exists on the mountain. Now, picture summoning up superhuman strength to push this boulder, dislodging it from the place it has rested for years and years. Once this boulder is loosened, it rolls easily over the edge of the cliff, crashing into thousands of other boulders on its way down the mountain, taking half of the mountain with

it in a beautiful cascade of rocks and dirt. Imagine sitting there, smiling cheerfully at the avalanche that was just created.

Marketing and mind control are very like creating an avalanche. Getting the first person to answer yes might be difficult. But each subsequent yes will be easier and easier. And always start at the top, never the bottom. Starting at the top is definitely more difficult, and it is more likely to come with more negative responses than positive responses in the beginning. But starting at the top also yields a much greater reward when the avalanche does begin. And the results will be far greater than beginning at the bottom of the mountain. Yes, the small rock is easier to push over. Then it can be built upon by pushing over another small rock, then another. This way can work, but it will take much longer than being successful at the top. No one ever went fishing for the smallest fish in the pond or auditioned for the secondary role just to be safe. Everyone wants that top prize. Do not be afraid to go for it.

On the other hand, never ask for the whole boulder the first time. Ask for part of it. This may seem directly contradictory, but it is not. Always start with a small

piece. Make the beginning easier for everyone to see. Let other people use their own insight to see the end result. When the first bit goes well, then gradually ask for more and more and more.

Think of writing a guest spot for someone else who has their own blog. By sending in the entire manuscript first, there is a greater risk of rejection. Begin small. Send them a paragraph or two discussing them the idea. Then make an outline of the idea and send that in an email. Then write the complete draft you would like them too to use and send it along. When asking a customer for a testimonial, start by asking for a few lines in an email. Then ask the customer to expand those few lines into a testimonial that covers at least half a typed page. Soon the customer will be ready for an hour-long webcast extolling the virtues of the product and your great customer service skills.

Everything must have a deadline that really exists. The important word here is the word 'real.' Everyone has heard the salesperson who said to decide quickly because the deal might not be available, or another customer was coming in, and they might get it. That is a total fabrication, and everyone knows it to be true. There are

no impending other customers, and the deal is not going to disappear. There is no real sense of urgency involved. But everyone does it. There are too many situations where people are given a totally fake deadline by someone who thinks it will instil a great sense of urgency for completion of the task. It is not only totally not effective but completely unneeded. It is a simple matter to create true urgency. Only leave free things available for a finite amount of time. When asking customers for testimonials, be certain to mention the last possible day for it to be received to be able to be used. Some people will be unable to assist but having people unable to participate is better than never being able to begin.

Always give before you receive. And do not ever think that giving is fifty-fifty. Always give much more than is expected in return. Before asking for a testimonial from a satisfied customer, be sure to make numerous acts of exceptional customer service. Before asking a blog writer for a link, link theirs to yours many times. This is not about helping someone out so they will help you. This is all about being so generous that the person who is asked for the favour cannot possibly say no. It might mean extra work, but that is how to influence other people.

Always stand up for something that is much bigger than average. Do not just write another blog on how to do something. Use an important issue to take a stand and defend the stance with unbeatable logic and fervent passion. Do not just write a how-to manual. Choose a particular idea and sell people on it, using examples of other people with the same idea living the philosophy.

Never feel shame. This does not mean being extremely extroverted to the point of silliness or having a total lack of conscience in business dealings. In the case of mind control shamelessness refers to a total complete belief that this course of action is the best possible course, and everyone will benefit greatly from it. This is about writing the best possible blog ever and believing that everyone needs to read it to be able to improve their lives. It is about believing in a particular product so deeply that the feeling is that everyone will benefit from using it. It knows deep inside that this belief is the correct belief ever, and everyone should believe it.

Mind control uses the idea that someone's decisions and emotions can be controlled using psychological means. It is using powers of negotiation or mental influence to ensure the outcome of the interaction is more favourable

to one person over the other. This is basically what marketing is: convincing someone to do something particular or buy something in particular. Being able to control someone else's mind merely means understanding the power of human emotion and being able to play upon those emotions. It is easier to have a mental impact on people if there is a basic understanding of human emotions. Angry people will back down when the subject of their anger is not afraid. Angry people feed upon the fear of others. Guilt is another great motivator. Making someone feel guilty for not thinking or feeling, in the same manner, is a wonderful way to get them to give in. Another way to use mind control over someone is to point out how valuable they are to the situation. Controlling the mind of another does not mean depriving them of free will and conscious thought. It means knowing what to say to impact the other person so profoundly they cannot see any other way to go but the one proposed.

Chapter 5. Protecting Oneself from Manipulation

Here are brilliant strategies to protect yourself from manipulation.

Ignore Their Words and Actions

Manipulators almost always go after shaking people's confidence and making them insecure about getting them to do what they (the manipulators) want. They will do their best to plant seeds of apprehension and self-doubt. There is a tendency to make the victim believe that the manipulator's opinion is actually the truth or fact. Rather than wanting to help you, they are more interested in trying to control you.

The best strategy to deal with these negative manipulators is to ignore them rather than trying to argue with them or correct them. This allows them to set an even deeper trap for you. Do not fall for their conflict or confrontation bet. Simply bypass them, without revealing your emotions. Do not let them see the emotions that make you tick. Once they gain a good understanding of your emotional triggers, they will sneakily use it for influencing your thoughts, behaviour, and decisions.

Some people are difficult to delete from our lives immediately. Think – boss, neighbour, family member, etc. Just pretend to listen to what they are saying, agree with it and eventually do exactly what you want.

Trust Your Judgment

Few people know what's good for you as well as you do. You do not have to ask everyone for their opinion and end up coming across as someone who is not sure of himself or herself. You are inviting manipulators into getting you to do what they want if you do not know what you want.

Do not look for definition and validation from other people. Trust your own judgment and feelings. Develop an inner voice that guides you through important decisions in life rather than relying on other people to do for you.

Tune in to your own values, beliefs, strengths, and interests. Hold on to what you believe in strongly. This way, you'll be less susceptible to let manipulators make inroads into your thought process and life. Your strong beliefs will prevent them from influencing or affecting you.

Do not Compromise

Guilt is one of the most insidious tools used by manipulators to get their victims to do what they want. Of course, it can be used positively to influence a person too, but in negative manipulation, its usage can spell disaster for the victim.

Manipulators induce a feeling of guilt in their victims for their past mistakes, choices, and failures. They will make your guilt about being self-assured and self-confident. Each time you experience happiness, they will make you feel bad about it. Their objective is to never make you feel good about yourself or happy.

They'll sow seeds of self-doubt about your true worth, persona, and abilities. Do not get knocked off balance or feel guilty; they start blaming you. Do not doubt your self-worth or abilities. Never believe that you do not deserve happiness or to feel wonderful about yourself. Take pride in who you are and your accomplishments. Build a strong sense of self-esteem and confidence. Do not compromise on your happiness or your feelings about yourself.

Do not Fit In, Stand Out

It isn't funny how many people make them susceptible to manipulation by trying hard to fit in. Manipulative people count on your desire to want to fit in to push their agenda. They lead you to believe that everyone does what they want you to do and that those who do not conform are abnormal. That is the only way to control your decisions and behaviour.

Give up the notion of trying to fit in and encourage the idea of standing out among the rest. Be different from other folks. Focus on reinventing yourself, laying your own rules (for what is good for you and others) and avoid cowing down to peer pressure.

Stop Seeking Permission

We've been conditioned to ask for permission since childhood, right from when we wanted to be fed as a baby to when we wanted to visit the bathroom in school to waiting for our turn to talk in the boardroom. The result of this conditioning is that people seldom do anything without seeking permission.

There is an excessive focus on being polite and making things comfortable for others. Manipulative people want

their victims to live by their own self-drafted, imaginary rules or values. The underlying idea is you are not free to take any decision without consultation. Be brave and give up this sense of confinement. You have the power to change your life without the need to live by someone else's self-fulfilling rules.

Do not be a Baby

If you are tricked once, it isn't your fault. However, if you are tricked 15 times, there's something wrong with you. Do not let people take advantage of you by being everyone's favourite punching bag. Have the courage to stand up to manipulators and say a firm no when you know they are taking advantage of you. Stop whining about other people are taking advantage of you and take complete control of your life.

Victims of manipulation almost always complain about how people use them. No one can take advantage of or you without your consent. You are indeed responsible for your own actions and their outcome. If someone has used sneaky tricks to outwit you, it is your fault. Learn from past blunders and stop trusting slippery people again and again. Move away from them. Focus on surrounding yourself with positive, constructive,

inspiring, and like-minded folks who make you feel good about yourself.

Have a Clear Sense of Purpose?

When you do not know what you want, you'll be more prone to do whatever everyone else wants. You'll be easily tricked into doing what other people want you to do without a firm goal or objective in life. People who lack a clear purpose or aim tend to function or go through life more mechanically. There is little logic in their actions or decisions. They will be more prone to experiencing a growing sense of emptiness in them that will craftily be filled by a manipulator.

This lack of objective or constructive activities makes the manipulator feel empowered enough to easily distract you or draw you to their agenda.

Have a higher purpose in life. It can be anything from taking up a cause for the betterment of the community to travelling around the world to rising in your professional life. Do not allow manipulators an opportunity to prey on your sense of purposelessness. When you are absolutely clear about where you are headed, it is difficult to stop you or get you to change tracks.

Chapter 6. Mental Manipulation Techniques

Mental Manipulation is perhaps one of the most common forms of manipulation people will try to use on you. As a result of how often it occurs, it can be somewhat challenging to know when a behaviour should be considered mental manipulation or not.

Simply put, think of mental manipulation as mind games, mind games that people will try and play with you. Some people will try to play these games at any chance they have no matter who you are and no matter the consequences they may face as a result of their behaviour, especially in the workforce we all know someone who will try and kiss up to the boss or put you down to make themselves look more appealing.

People will be better able to take advantage of you and use these tricks if you are not aware of what you should look for. That is why it is important that you pay attention to the subtleties of mental manipulation and what to look for these little stages people put themselves on when they are trying to get what they want. Your number one defines against all of these manipulation subtypes knows what to look for in individuals who use them, more

important understanding mental manipulation, and all the techniques that encompass it.

Mind Manipulation Techniques

Knowing how to use some of these mind manipulation techniques make it much easier to make money if you work in the corporate world. With the knowledge you will learn, you are now equipped with Armor to use against anyone or any institution that would intend to manipulate you for their own nefarious purposes, and you are in a position to do the same should the time or opportunity necessitate it.

Lying, is perhaps the simplest tactic mental manipulators like to use on their prey. The simple reason is that lying is fairly easy to accomplish and does not require much skill. Truthfully, their real reason for lying tends to be to hide information that would damage them or become a barrier to their goals. Because if they did something bad. Well, they're not going to want you to know about it. As while manipulators love to be charming. The thing they love above all else is maintaining appearances. So, if they can keep the appearance that they are a good person through deceit, then they most certainly will. We encounter liars every day in our life but, more often than

not, fail to realize they are telling us falsehoods. Detecting a liar can be difficult, as some people have mastered the craft of spewing falsehoods, so you're not going to be looking for overt signs like nervousness, scratching their nose, etc.

You want to look for patterns of untruthful behaviour that you can notice, and from there, you're able to slowly build up this pattern as a log in your mind, use that to your advantage. Sadly, the truth is that you have a very high likelihood of detecting a liar in a romantic relationship than you do say the nine to five workplaces.

This is because, during a romantic relationship, emotion is high. Therefore, this places the emotional stakes higher. This, in turn, means that someone who would do something that crosses these emotional stakes is willing to do whatever required to not get caught. A liar in a relationship will probably take the form of a partner who is never home but always has some elaborate excuse for why they're absent. In addition, they may try to quickly divert the conversation from the matter at hand when asked where or what they're doing. Defusing a liar thought is easy enough, but you must be persistent and firm in your belief of the truth.

Do not falter. The manipulator will try and get you to become convinced that it is, in fact, you who is wrong and not them, that your version of the truth is the real lie. Remember, though, if someone is innocent, they will not protest their innocence and will trust you. Simply put, think of the old saying that if you have nothing to hide, then you have nothing to fear.

Tying well into lying as a manipulation tactic, there are people who will spin the truth to make themselves look like the victim or to allow blame to be placed on you. This kind of manipulation tends to just be called playing the victim and spin.

Most of us commonly associate the idea of spinning the truth with news and politics. But the truth is covert manipulators will do that whenever they can. Take the example I used of the partner who is always absent and always seems to have a convenient explanation for them not being present. At times when confronted with this information, they will try and pin it on you by claiming you must be insecure in the relationship and how it has to be you who is jealous since you're so suspicious of them. This covert manipulation tactic works by preying on our own emotions and getting us to question them.

Getting us to look at our own feelings and actions with distrust allows the manipulator to convince us that we must be the crazy ones, we ourselves must be the manipulators. In simple terms spinning the truth works by trying to downplay whatever someone is being accused of in hopes that you will believe and trust them.

Flattery will Get You Everywhere

Moving on from lying and deceit, I would like to discuss one of the more effective methods of manipulation, and that is flattery. Flattery is an idea we think of when the thought of relationships come to mind. The spouses out to dinner are joyfully juking and jiving with each other. Or someone at a bar, trying to pick up a girl. On the surface that is technically flattery as in its simplest terms, flattery just defines a behaviour where someone goes out of their way to give platitudes to you regardless if their truthful or not. Because of how flattery can make us feel good about ourselves, it can be challenging to view it as something manipulative or bad. And the strange truth is that flattery or outright being a kiss-up is not always a bad thing if you want to get ahead in something. As mentioned, prior, this is especially true if you are trying to woo a girl.

To be honest, flattery, in its milder form, is one of the integral parts of our whole courting process as humans. Flattery used well in the workforce; for example, can be extremely advantageous for the person doing it as it allows them to try and endear themselves to their boss or other co-workers. In doing this, they will gain those individuals trust allowing them more upward movement within the company.

The issue with flattery is that it can be used to create relationships on false pretences, i.e., it lures someone into a false sense of security about how someone views them. Trust like this that is easily generated is always something you should be cautious about. For example, you start dating a man, and he is overly flirtatious and goes seemingly too far to make you feel good then perhaps consider that maybe his intentions are not quite pure. The line between flattery and genuine true compliments lies first in you knowing yourself and your own self-worth if you are a strong, confident person than you will know if someone is trying to compliment you in a way that seems to both tries too hard and also be untrue.

So, remember, general flattery is not always a bad thing, but it can be a segue for someone into getting you to give them a false sense of trust, which is not always the best—remembering this and what kind of behaviour to look for will help you avoid being the victim of a manipulator in the future. As the line between simple flattery to be friendly and flattery for malice has a fine line, just as anything does.

Remember – Manipulation isn't Necessarily Bad

Not all manipulation has to be used for bad purposes. Some forms of manipulation we regularly encounter, such as advertising and mass media. It can be used for good, so much so that they can make someone a profit. Or they can be used in the corporate world to climb up the ladder of hierarchy. In simple terms, at times, it can be required that you grease some palms and perhaps act a certain way to get ahead.

Using manipulation techniques such as bending the truth or flattery may be required here to give you an advantage over the competition. In this case, it could be argued that it can be morally permitted due to the honest fact that if you don't try to push your way into these positions, someone else will. At this point, you are only

playing the game that everyone else is playing by going out of your way to being friendly to your boss or bending the truth in how you present your accomplishments. Yes, you are using manipulation by giving your boss the impression an assignment you just completed may be better than it really might be.

Is that form of manipulation so bad? All you are doing is simply levelling the playing field. This type of behaviour is less manipulation and more in line with the idea of being persuasive or charismatic.

The difference here is you are using charm and ingratiation to convince someone further toward your line of thinking regardless of what that may be. It is still them making the decision in the end. All your doing is guiding and influencing them. This is far different from coercion, where you are using subtle threats and fear to get what you want. An example of this type of coercion would be lying to your boss about the performance of another co-worker to put them down and allow you to get a position that they currently hold.

Now that you understand manipulation from a moral aspect, let me explain how you can use it yourself. I am sure we have all been at home watching the television

when a flashy add with cool music comes on, and it catches our attention. But did you ever stop to realize that those ads are designed purposely like that to draw and suck you in? Pay attention when you walk down the supermarket at how so many different items have such colourful and unique packaging. It's all done on purpose to draw you in and make the item you may or may not purchase all the more enticing.

Marketing and Manipulation

For simplicity's sake, think of the mass marketing campaign for popular consumer electronics like the I-phone. Apple, the company that produces the I-phone, will release a new one every year that is not all that different from the one they released a year prior. The way they do this is first by hosting these big insider conferences and then allowing in only a few select journalists.

On the surface, this may just seem like perfectly normal industry practice done to perhaps protect job secrets. But the opposite is, in fact, true, by making access to this new product seem exclusive and hidden, they are then able to get people interested in it simply because people will always gravitate to what is mysterious and new.

Speaking of new, the main tactic most companies like to rely on for sales is a psychological phenomenon called the "fear of missing out" simply put, all this means is that you, a potential customer, are more likely to purchase a product because it is new. In your mind if you do not purchase the new fancy phone you have somehow fallen behind the social curve and are now missing out on something exclusive that all the cool people own.

This form of manipulation relies heavily on spinning the truth by virtue of the fact, that while, yes, the new product they are selling is slightly more advanced than the prior it really is not all that new, and the accompanying excitement around it is somewhat synthetic and not perhaps a natural occurrence.

So how can you use this tactic for yourself, well the best place this kind of covert manipulation works is the business world. Especially if you are in a sales-driven business, when trying to sell a service or good, people tend to only focus on what said service or good offers, not so much ring home how much it can benefit a potential customer.

This may sound like common sense, but in plain terms play up and ingratiate yourself to your customer base, let

them know how lucky they are for looking into your product and how if they purchase the product, they will be amongst some exclusive group. In these kinds of instances, you are not really harming the customer as you are persuading them to your side of the aisle. By making them feel good about this potential purchase, they, in turn, leave feeling validating and like they have perhaps earned something useful in their life.

While you, the salesperson, have just sold the said product to the customer, therefore, increasing your profit and meeting your requirements. Moving away from the idea of selling something, you can use this type of manipulation in your personal life to meet new and interesting people. Put on an air that you are someone unique, cool, or special when you are acting with someone. They will pick up on this, and it will translate into the appearance of confidence, in short sell yourself, why should they be friends with you, what do you bring to the table.

These are all the things you can covertly show by how you make yourself appear to them. By using flattery and charm while also being integral, you make both you and the people your meeting feel good, something that is

almost never a bad thing. Some people will call this charm the truth is that this really a form of manipulation.

Now that you are aware of these kinds of sales tricks, you are now armed to defend against them. But how do you defeat something that prays on basic instinct?

Manipulation and Basic Instinct

Well, the answer lies in your own basic instinct. As I said, confidence brings with it the appearance of charm by putting on a confident mask; you are able to get a potential manipulator into thinking that you are a hard target to hit. Think of the common image of the used car salesperson, an individual who will try to sweet talk an individual into an overpriced purchase even though they know the person can't afford it.

They prey on people they can tell are not going to call them out on their behaviour. This stereotype exists for a reason. It is because it is somewhat true if you present yourself as weak and powerless people will pick up on that. Recognizing that confidence is needed is only one step in the battle against manipulation.

The second is using a bit of common sense and taking a step back and thinking. If something someone is telling

you seems too good to be true, then do not just take it at face value. Start by considering the context of the situation and what could possibly motivate someone to be untruthful or manipulative in a situation. What if someone is cheating in a relationship? They may be willing to lie and be dishonest to keep that relationship going. Or, if someone is trying to sell you something, then they have the incentive to lie in that context, due to the fact that their livelihood most likely depends on how many of a good or service they can sell someone. Knowing this context allows you to look at what you're being told as a piece of a much larger picture instead of just an isolated occurrence.

Manipulators Try to Wear You Down

Moving ahead a little bit and diverging from lying. I would like to bring up one of the most common tricks that manipulators like to try and use on you. That trick would be wearing you down. We have all probably other seen in person or on the internet videos of children throwing temper tantrums when they don't get their way. And the parents after a long period of their child screaming and yelling finally giving in to their kid's demands.

Well, the same fact goes for covert manipulators they love to waste time and try and get you to wear the hell down. Take an example of a friend trying to get you to give them a ride, and you say no I am busy right now at work and as a result, cannot come and pick you up. Well then, this friend may begin, and excuse my language here "bitching and moaning." In short, they will begin to complain about how you are unfair to them, and they are your friend and would do the same for you.

Chapter 7. Dark Psychology Manipulation Techniques

Love Bombing

If you have heard of the term *stink bomb* and know what it is, then you probably have an idea of what love bombing might be. In the simplest terms, love bombing is a form of manipulation that involves showing someone a lot of affection and adoration with the intention of influencing their behaviour. The origin of the term love bombing can be traced to the 1970s when members of the Unification Church of the United States purportedly coined it to refer to the intense affection showered upon each other and visitors. Back then, love bombing was used as a positive phrase. Over the years, critics of the group and psychologists alike have painted a different picture of love bombing, even labelling it as the secret weapon of many narcissists and abusive partners.

So, how does love bombing work?

Just like a bomb goes off unexpectedly and instantly, love bombing works in the very same way. A person who is trying to manipulate you through love bombing will shower you with lots and lots of affection and attention

soon after you meet, or as soon as they need something for you. Love bombers will often come across as the perfect partners, especially when the relationship is young and new. A manipulative person who is looking to love to bomb, you will call you and text you all day and every day, or as much as they think you want them to. They will complement everything about you and will pay attention to all your needs. Expect to receive gifts and surprise visits left, right and centre. You might find yourself wondering how you got so lucky. Or you might find yourself feeling overwhelmed because you are not used to this much attention. Whatever the case may be, you should not get used to this affection and attention because it will not last very long. Your manipulator is only using it to hook you.

The following stage in love bombing is where your manipulator does the exact opposite of what they were initially doing. Instead of showers of praise, you will now be subjected to unending torrents of criticism. Where once you felt like the most valuable person in the individual's life, you begin to question your own self-worth. Essentially, the person has pulled the rug from under your feet and now you are left confused and wondering where to go. What's likely to happen if you are

unaware of what is happening (manipulation through love bombing) is that you will start to seek validation from your manipulator. You will constantly be seeking their approval in the big and small decisions and events of your life. Gradually, you hand power over to the manipulator and allow them to influence your behaviour and decisions. This is a process that happens unknowingly because you have been tricked into this situation. Perhaps the most tragic part of love bombing is that the final stage is where your manipulator discards you after you have outlived your value in their life.

You're probably wondering whether you are being love-bombed by someone in your life right now. Here are some signs that should tell you whether you are being manipulated through the love bombing tactic:

Everything is happening too quickly

While there's such a thing as love at first sight, it's also true that more often than not rational people require sufficient time to develop real and deep love. If you are on a second meeting and your date is already talking about being hopelessly in love with you, you might want to proceed with caution. Yes, you are an amazing human,

and you deserve the very best that life has to offer. However, you should be careful of anyone who tries to paint you as the perfect human ever to exist, especially if they have not known you long enough to make such a conclusion. Love bombers will want to inflate your ego and self-image to the point where you are high on the belief that you are perfect. Once you are addicted to this high, the manipulator knows that they are in control and can make you do whatever they please.

They want to be the superheroes in your story

The people in our lives come in handy in different ways. At the most fundamental level, they provide companionship. Human beings are social animals, and a good friend or two will go a long way in alleviating your loneliness and providing some much-needed warmth in your life. When you are in trouble, it is natural to turn to the people in your life to provide solutions for these troubles. Your genuine friends will provide solutions and go on their merry way because they know you'd have done the same for them is the situations were reversed. A manipulator who wants to control you through love bombing will help you because they want to have some control in your life. They want to be the person that loved

you so much that they came to your help. You're the damsel in distress, and they are the knight in shining Armor. What the damsel does not know is that they are racking up a debt in the eye of the manipulator and very soon the manipulator will come to collect.

Watch out for relationships--be they casual, intimate or formal--where one individual seems to always be running to the rescue and bringing up the fact long after the matter has been resolved. You should also be keen to identify the individuals who seem to always be looking out for ways to assist by asking about the things that make you sad. They are bringing up the bad parts of your life so that they can get a chance to make you happy and be the hero of the story. This is what love bombing is all about.

You are constantly receiving gifts

Most people love getting gifts. It is not for no reason that gift-giving ranks as one of the love languages of the world. Getting a thoughtful gift from a loved one can brighten up anyone's day. In many cases, gifts are just that: gifts. In the world of love, bombing manipulators, gifts are debts. Every time you receive a gift, you owe

them something in return. If the new guy you met at the bar two weeks ago has started sending gifts your way every day of the week, you might want to put an end to it before he comes to collect. You can be sure he will not be nice about it, and he will likely guilt trip you by suggesting that you should not have accepted the gifts if you were not willing to give in to his demands.

It is important to note that love bombing does not just apply to romantic encounters. Any situation where someone you barely know is doing too much to show you how valuable you are qualifying as love bombing. Granted, there are some socially awkward people who do not understand that relationships require sufficient time to fully unfold, but those are few and far between. The majority of people who rush to show you unprecedented adoration are typically manipulators who are very well aware of exactly what they are doing.

How to successfully love bomb anyone before they love to bomb you

Now that you understand what love bombing is, you're probably wondering how to do it to someone before they do it on you. While it is always better to pursue genuine relationships that are mutually beneficial, you'll find that these are often few and far between. Most people are

friends with other people because they get something out of it. When you finally meet that person, who thinks they can love to bomb you into gaining control over your life, you need to be one step ahead of them.

When dealing with someone who is manipulative, the key is to always mirror their actions. When they complement you, compliment them back? When they buy you gifts, buy them something in return. Before long, you will be dancing the love bomb tango, and you will be well on your way to getting what you want. It is important that you determine whether what you want is worth the effort you will be putting into love bombing this person. Manipulation requires concerted time and effort. Manipulation does not occur overnight. You have to make sure that the benefits outweigh the cost. Otherwise, you are investing too much for nothing in return. Once you figure out what you stand to gain by love-bombing a particular person, you are free to go all out in your bid to showcase how important, perfect and loved that person is, at least from where you stand.

You will learn about the process of brainwashing and the various continents involved. The media portray the way brainwashing, and in the movies, it makes a lot of people believe it is an evil practise professed by those who are trying to influence, corrupt or gain undue power over others. The entire process of brainwashing seldom involves any harmful practices, and it usually occurs quite subtly.

Since we're talking about human psychology, the term brainwashing can be described as a method of reforming one's thoughts using social influence. This type of social impact is present everywhere, and it occurs all day long regardless of whether an individual realizes this or not. Social influence is the summation of methods that are used to change the other person's beliefs, attitudes, or even behaviour. For instance, any process of compliance used in the workplace can technically be referred to as a form of brainwashing since it requires the employees to act and think in a specific way whenever at work. Brainwashing tends to become a social issue in its most severe form since this method radically changes the way someone feels without their realization or prior consent.

For brainwashing to be effective, the subject is required to go through a phase of complete isolation and dependency because of its invasive effect. This is perhaps one of the main reasons why plenty of known cases related to brainwashing occur in prison camps or even cults. The brainwasher is referred to as the agent, and the target is known as the subject. The aim of brainwashing is for the agent to gain complete and total control over the issue. It means that the agent must be able to control and regulate the subject's physical, emotional, and mental patterns. During the process of brainwashing, the agent will strategically and systematically work on breaking down the subject's identity and then rebuild it to suit his needs. Once the subject's identity is broken, the agent can start replacing it with other desirable beliefs, thoughts, attitudes, and even behaviour.

Steps in Brainwashing

The concept of brainwashing is not new and has been around since time began. However, it was documented for the first time by Robert Jay Lifton, a psychologist during the 1950s. He studied the behavioural and thinking patterns of the prisoners of the Chinese war

camps and the Korean War. After carefully examining them, he concluded that brainwashing is a technique that starts with an attack on one's sense of self and ends when said person's beliefs have entirely changed. He identifies that there are ten steps involved in the process of brainwashing in all the cases he studied, and they are as follows.

Attack on identity

The statement- "You are not who you think you are," forms the basis of this stage of brainwashing. You must launch a direct and strategic assault on your target's identity, sense of self, or even ego. By attacking his core values and beliefs, you can cripple your target's sense of self. As an agent, you must deny everything that essentially is a part of your target identity. If you keep at it for a significant time, then your target will be in a state of confusion and will experience an identity crisis. In such a state, he's more susceptible to manipulation and external events. The strategic assault you launch doesn't have to be anything extreme. You can make someone question their sense of self by contradicting their core values.

The guilt

This stage is about making the target feel that he is terrible. As your target starts experiencing an identity crisis, you must try to make him feel guilty. The overwhelming sense of guilt experienced by him, along with uncertainty about who he is, makes your target compliant and fully susceptible to manipulation. In this stage, the agent can try to make his target feel wrong about anything from how slowly he eats to the invalidity of his beliefs. By doing this, the agent is essentially making the target feel inadequate and ashamed about everything.

Self-betrayal

This stage is about making the target admit that he is terrible. The target starts to feel confused, and disoriented; the agent can quickly force him to denounce his fundamental beliefs and all those people who share his so-called wrong ideas. The force used by the agent at this stage can be real or even imaginary. The agent is merely preying on the emotions of his victim to manipulate him. Once the subject starts to betray his own beliefs, the loss of identity he experiences will become severe. If he promises to sever all ties with his

loved ones, he will lose a part of himself. Well, this is one of the tricks commonly employed by cults.

Breaking point

At this stage, the subject is in the midst of a severe identity crisis. The subject matter experiences shame for denouncing his beliefs and guilt for betraying his values. Don't be surprised if your subject starts having a nervous breakdown at this point. A nervous breakdown is not a technical concept, and it mostly is an amalgamation of various symptoms that indicate a variety of psychological disturbances the subject is experiencing. It can be in the form of overall disorientation coupled with depression and an uncontrollable urge to cry are all signs of a nervous breakdown. A subset might even start losing his grip on reality and feel like he is completely alone and lost in this universe. When the subject reaches this breaking point, he has no sense of self, and now, the agent has full power to start moulding him. The subject's personality is pretty much like play-doh at this point, and the manipulator can easily manipulate him.

Lenient

In this stage, the agent needs to provide or show certain leniency to the subject. The subject is clearly in the midst

of an identity crisis, and a little indulgence or help given at this stage will have a significant effect on the subject's mind. Something as simple as having a heart to heart conversation with a subject will do. When the subject is in a miserable state, even the smallest act of kindness can generate a sense of gratitude in the matter toward the agent.

Confession

In this stage, the agent makes the subject believe that he can help himself. Perhaps, for the first time, the subject experiences a drastic difference between the guilt combined with the loss of identity and the sudden burst of relief due to leniency. Now, the subject might feel like he must reciprocate the kindness shown to him at this point. So, he might even be inclined to confess to something merely because of the little generosity he was taught.

Channel the guilt

After the continuous emotional and mental assault, the subject's guilt tends to lose a little meaning. He might not be aware of the mistakes he made, but he knows he is wrong. This tends to create a clean blank slate, which is the void of all opinions, expectations, and dreams. The

agent has complete control to fill up this blank slate the way he wants to. So, he can attach the feeling of guilt or a sense of wrongdoing to anything he wants. The agent might connect the feeling of shame or guilt with the belief system he is working on replacing. By doing this, the subject concludes that all the pain he experienced was because of his belief systems and will try to change it. In his mind, the old belief system is associated with agony, whereas the new one with relief.

Let go of the guilt

In this stage, the subject comes to understand that he is not inherently wrong and that it was his belief system that was wrong. So, by changing his belief system, he can escape the guilt he was experiencing. He will start to denounce all the institutions and people he helped the early in the past. The target now has the power to release himself from the agony of any wrongness by merely confessing to all those acts that were associated with his old belief system. Once the subject comes to this conclusion, it signifies complete detachment with his old belief system.

Progress

Now, the agent starts introducing the subject to a new and better belief system. At this stage, all the abuse and assaults stop, and the subject gets to experience some physical and mental peace after a harrowing experience. All this enables the subject to form a positive association with the new belief system and the negative one with the past belief system. The target now feels like he has an option to choose between his past and the future.

Now, the cycle of brainwashing comes to an end, and the subject is essentially putty in the hands of the agent. The subject might not realize this yet, but every action of his is according to the agent's plan.

Chapter 8. Mental manipulation techniques used by the mass media how to recognize and protect them

Marketing and its strategy: THE POWER OF THE BRAND

Archaeologists have found the remains of some advertisements dating back to 3,000 years ago, but at that time, even in urban areas, exposure to advertisements was minimal. Posters and graffiti announcing events, displaying goods, or promoting political candidates were concentrated in the highly trafficked areas of the city.

Today advertisements are practically impossible to avoid experts estimate that in borderline cases, we are exposed to 5 thousand advertisements per day. Of course, we are unable to process all this information, and a large part of it we do not even notice. But Edwards says that even non-consciously recorded ads have equally impact: "The brain is extraordinary: it absorbs everything" and "a good part [of the advertising, ed.] Acts subliminally, often it is not known to have been

influenced by what we have seen: we hear and listen until this influence is tangibly manifested ».

A 2007 study from University College London showed that subliminal images actually attract brain attention at a subconscious level; the results of this study led to a ban on subliminal advertising in the UK. Advertisers are perfectly aware that these messages have an impact on the brain, and some innovative techniques in the field of neuro-marketing use smartphones and other 'wearable technology' to measure the subconscious reaction to certain products or messages.

This is just one of the many tools used to understand how to better capture our attention: with so many advertisements that saturate the market, the struggle to be visible has never been so fierce.

And that's why companies devote so much effort into building an indelible brand. In the past, the term 'branding' referred to using a hot iron to imprint a mark on people, animals or objects that indicated the owner. Today the term 'branding' is used figuratively, to describe the process of impressing a message in mind: «We know that it must be displayed several times (6 or 7) before

the concept or brand becomes fixed in the mind of a person", explains Isha Edwards.

A good branding policy can convince you to make a purchase, but the ultimate goal of branding is to forge a lasting relationship with consumers. If the emotional connection persists, the consumer will be forever devoted to the product.

The branding that worked for our parents or grandparents appears crude and outdated if assessed by current standards: today, advertisements to impress themselves must be more fun, sexually winked and easily recognizable, to be noticed in the midst of the growing tide of messages that they compete to capture the consumer's attention.

The current commercials often have bizarre content that has no relation to the advertised product. It may sound stupid, but marketing is effective if it is able to make the brand remember. An emblematic case is that of the hybrid puppy-monkey-child character used by Mountain Dew in the Super Bowl 2016 commercial, which currently has over 28 million views on YouTube.

Advertising is vital for companies, as it is necessary to receive their message to consumers, but Edwards nuts

that could be done better: she is a supporter of 'responsible marketing', and believes that advertisers, instead of resort to mental games and hide their intentions, commit to describe the products honestly and accurately; and which is particularly important in marketing for children.

But it is not exclusively about advertising in the strict sense: other forms of media can also use persuasive tactics because when a message is enclosed in media forms to dedicate all the entertainment, it is easier for the public to accept it. "American cinema is the largest and most unconscious propaganda vehicle in the world," wrote Edward Louis Bernays, the father of modern advertising tactics.

Until the media changes for the better, Edwards suggests everyone become more aware of the impressions they leave in their mind. The most effective method is limited by the content you consume, and regularly respects what you truly believe in; in short, a sort of media notification, in which the more you become aware of the hypnotic message that stimulates my desires, the easier it is to break the spell.

Edwards calls it "protecting the mind": "You can make the rather extreme choice of not having a television or of subscribing exclusively to channels that consider themselves honest, quality and described".

Other examples of protection of the mind are sporting events, videos or music that praise violence, misogyny or other unhealthy tendencies, just as they choose the brands that support the community and promote the positive image of themselves: "It's about protecting what happens in one's psyche.

What is fuelling this growing campaign to capture our hearts, minds, and wallets? History reveals that the whole work is more than just market forces. In the old days, advertisements were quite essential: a simple description of goods and services. But in 1920 everything changed: Edward Bernays, inspired by the research of his uncle Sigmund Freud (YES, HIM), dealt with psychology to develop a new marketing strategy that aimed to influence the subconscious; he called this strategy "consensus engineering": in essence, a form of mass hypnosis. Meanwhile, mass consumption was also born, an economic model in which people buy things not only

out of necessity, but out of pleasure, prestige, or even out of rebellion.

Bernays made his first strategic advertising campaign in 1929: the owners of the Lucky Strike cigarette brand try to find time to conquer the female market, but at the time it was considered a taboo for a respectable woman; so they asked Bernays for help, who hired young women and gave them cigarettes to blatantly light during the 1929 Easter parade in New York. And he informed the press in advance, presenting the event as a courageous demonstration of female emancipation, referring to the cigarettes such as "Torches of Liberty". The following day the news arrived published nationally, and from that moment, the number of smokers grew steadily. Today we could consider it a publicity stunt, but at the time it caused a profound cultural change. It is no coincidence that Life magazine included Bernays on the list of the 100 most influential American men of the twentieth century.

And now tell me, how did you feel the first time you saw the advertisement for the new iPhone? Or when you saw the Nike advertisement when the first thing you thought was you running and reaching your training goals? How were your feelings, what were your feelings?

All sellers know the importance of emotions, but there is a fundamental difference. Normal sellers focus on letting customers experience emotions. Sellers who know effective mental manipulation techniques are able to create the emotions necessary to sell a product or service.

For this reason, we can say with extreme certainty that the real seller is the one who is capable of creating the right emotions that will lead the customer to buy the product or service sold.

STRATEGIES AND TECHNIQUES OF SOCIAL MANIPULATION

1. A diversion tactic

The key feature of social regulation is the tactic of diversion, which consists of deviating popular interest from the major problems and mutations determined by the political and economic classes by the technique of flooding or the constant inundation of disturbances and irrelevant details.

A diversion technique is similarly important to keep the public from being involved in critical expertise in the

areas of research, finance, psychology, neurology, and cybernetics.

"To hold general interest occupied, the actual societal issues emerge, captivated by topics of no particular significance. To keep the people occupied, occupied, without any opportunity to think, to go back to the farm with the other animals. "

2. Develop challenges, and propose answers to them

This approach is often referred to as "problem-reaction-solution." It generates an issue, a perceived "situation," in order to cause a certain response in the population, in order to make it the compelling power of the steps that are to be adopted. For example: to encourage urban crime to grow and intensify, or to mobilize bloodthirsty terrorist attempts in order for the public to threaten protection or police rules to the detriment of democracy. Or: to establish an economic recession and make the downward erosion of civil justice tolerated and the elimination of public infrastructure a required evil.

3. Degradation policy

To order to make an unreasonable rule appropriate, it is necessary to implement it slowly, in a "degraded" way, over a span of 10 years. It is in this sense that fundamentally different socio-economic structures were introduced in the years 1980 to 1990. Massive unemployment, loss of opportunity, displacement, wages that no longer have a reasonable livelihood, too many reforms that might have caused unrest if they were implemented unexpectedly.

4. The technique is special

Another approach to make a controversial action approved is to portray it as "painful yet important" and to gain public approval at the time of the proposed proposal. A potential compromise is harder to consider than an imminent one. Second, the initiative is not automatically implemented. Second, as the country, the citizens still have a propensity to naively believe that "things will be better tomorrow" and that the sacrifice requested can be prevented. In any scenario, this gives sufficient room for the people to get used to the notion and embrace it with acceptance when the time comes. A recent example: the changeover to the euro and the lack

of their economic and monetary autonomy were agreed by the European countries from 1994 to 1995 for their implementation in 2001. Another example is the multilateral ALCA (or FTAA) arrangements that the United States placed in 2001 on the countries of the whole American continent (Central and South America) following their refusal to approve an invitation and to come into effect in 2005.

5. To view the population as children of the younger generation

Much of the advertising "spots" are presented to the general audience through the usage of rhetoric, statements, personalities, and a language that is especially infantile, sometimes similar to the vulnerable, as though the viewer is a smaller child or a mentally handicapped adult. The most probable it is to try the illusion of the viewer or audience, the more probable it is to assume a childish language. Why? Why? If it is presented to a child as if he or she is 12 years of age, otherwise, on the basis of a comment, he or she will, therefore, have, with a reasonable possibility, an answer or reaction that lacks the same essential sense as that of an individual 12 years of age.

6. To have a subjective dimension rather than a description

Use the emotional dimension is a classic strategy for creating a short-circuit to logical thought, and therefore to the vital meaning of the person. In fact, the usage of the mental register enables one to unlock an entry door for the unconscious of injecting or introducing thoughts, desires, worries or anxieties, pulsations, or behaviours.

7. To hold the country in denial and foolishness

To do it in a manner where the public is unwilling to grasp the techniques and strategies used to regulate and enslave them. "The standard of education offered to the lower classes of society must be as weak or as inferior as practicable, in such a manner that the break of indifference that distinguishes the lower classes from the upper classes of society exists and will remain incomprehensible to the lower classes of society."

8. Promote complacency of mediocrity in the press

Promoting in the society the belief that being dumb, filthy, and uneducated is "sweet."

9. Replacing the uprising with remorse

To have the person feel that he or she is the only one accountable for his or her failure, the source of the inadequacy of his or her intellect, ability, or actions. Thus, instead of rebelling against the economic environment, the person self-depreciates and self-blames that give rise to a depressed condition, inhibiting behaviour is one of its consequences. And there is no revolt without practice!

10. To know people better than they know themselves

In the last 50 years, exponential developments in research have contributed to an increasing gap between the awareness of the public and that of the leading leaders. Thanks to physiology, neurology, and behavioural psychology, the "machine" has gained an extensive understanding of the human person, both biologically and mentally. The program has become more trained to learn the average citizen than the person does about himself. This implies that, in most situations, the program has more influence and more authority over people than people have over themselves.

Chapter 9. How to Eliminate Manipulative People?

Know the Signs

The most important way you can eliminate manipulation in your life is to make sure you are aware of the signs. You can check that off of the list. Remember, the methods that manipulators use are oftentimes incredibly insidious and are meant to be harmful. The manipulator wants you to give in and do whatever the manipulator wants without you realizing that you are being manipulated in the first place. However, if you know the signs, you can notice when a red flag goes up, and when that flag does, in fact, fly, you are able to act. If you notice that the manipulator is attempting to coerce you or guilt you, if you are aware that those are techniques manipulators favour, you are able to then avoid falling for it simply because you know it is there. Knowing the warning signs is your first defines against manipulation.

Be Assertive

Remember, the manipulator is counting on your remaining cooperative. In fact, you were likely selected to be manipulated because you are not combative in

general. However, that complacency, that desire to remain silent and put up with the manipulation, does not have to define you any longer. If you are able to stop and become assertive about your wants and needs, the manipulator may decide you are no longer worthwhile. For example, if you know what you want to get a chance to pick out a restaurant once and a while on a date night, assert that and refuse to back down. If you want to make sure you are no longer called names or told you are worthless, assert that, and refuse to back down.

This can be a particularly difficult skill to master, but you can do it. There are seven key points to remember when being assertive, and if you can do so, you will be able to make your points clearly and concisely, though the manipulator will likely try to find some way to spin things to be your own fault. These are the seven steps to becoming a more assertive, and therefore less easily manipulated individual:

- Make sure you are clear: The most important thing when being assertive is ensuring you express yourself clearly. Use direct, clear, and calm language.

- Maintain eye contact: As you assert yourself, make sure you face the individual and make eye contact as you do. This shows that you are not willing to back down.
- Open, positive posture: Remember, there is a difference between assertive and aggressive—you are aiming for assertive here. Make sure that you are upright, relaxed, and facing the other person. Make sure your arms are not crossed, and your jaw is not tense. You do not want to come across as aggressive or unwilling to communicate.
- Plan your point in advance: Make sure you have a general plan for what you are asserting. Back it up with facts, if necessary. This keeps you from getting flustered, which can quickly become defensive and negative.
- Do not be afraid to call a time out: If you need it, it is okay to take a time out from the situation. If emotions begin to run to high, you are well within your rights to call for a break to regather your thoughts and recollect yourself before continuing.
- Avoid any attacks or accusations: Make sure your language is as non-aggressive as possible. Statements should always begin with "I" instead of

"You" in order to avoid confrontational language. Instead of saying, "You hurt my feelings," you would word it as, "I'm feeling bad."

- Remain calm: When you are asserting yourself, ensure that you do manage to keep yourself calm and under control. Doing so ensures that you cannot be made the aggressor in the argument. It also makes sure the manipulator cannot attempt to manipulate your emotions in order to get a rise out of you.

Avoid Suspected Manipulators

Ultimately, the most effective way to escape the grasp of a manipulator is by separating yourself from manipulators altogether. You cannot be manipulated if you have no contact with the manipulator, after all. For this reason, if you suspect that someone in your general vicinity is a manipulator, you should probably make it a point to end the relationship or keep your space. Of course, a manipulator who has targeted you is going to do one of two things in this instance: Pursue you more, or let you go because you have proven that you are not an easy target. After all, most manipulators would prefer

an easy target over one who is going to constantly put up a fight.

Never Give Up Values

Manipulators always want to force you to give. However, no matter how much a manipulator guilts you, you should have a set of values that you refuse to back down on. These values are likely your innermost beliefs; they could be religious or moral in nature, and they likely define your own behaviours. Do not let the manipulator erode at those values. In making it clear that you will stick to your convictions and refuse to back down, you are telling the manipulator that there is no way you are willing to give in. You ensure that you are honouring values and beliefs in a way that you will never give up on, and the manipulator has to either accept that or move on to someone else that will give up on those beliefs.

Always Take Time to Consider Options

No matter how much the manipulator may try to pressure you into making a decision right at that moment, remember that it is entirely acceptable to push off most major decisions a day. For example, if the manipulator

wants you to take out a car loan for him or her and is pressuring you to do so that night, you are well within your rights to stop, tell the manipulator that you would prefer to take the night to consider it, and actually follow through with weighing the pros and cons. After all, something like that is a major purchase that will take years to pay off, and you will be responsible for the car if the manipulator does anything or decides to no longer pay for it.

While the manipulator may wish that you would be willing to give in right that second, remember that you can make these decisions for yourself. You need to make decisions that are right for you, even if you are married to the manipulator in the example. All major decisions should always be slept on and considered before they are impulsively followed. After all, something that seems like a good idea at the moment may not actually be that good of an idea when you have time to research and reconsider when emotions are not pressuring you.

Learn to Say No

This one goes hand-in-hand with the skill of assertiveness. Considering you were targeted for

manipulation; you were likely afraid of confrontation. This, of course, entails saying no to someone. People who hate confrontation hate having to say no to other people. After all, saying no is inherently displeasing, and if you are a people-pleaser, you likely will not like the process. Nevertheless, the best way to avoid being manipulated if you cannot stay away from the manipulator is learning to say no to the manipulator, no matter what strings are being pulled.

When you are saying no to someone, there are three factors to consider—you want your no to be firm, clear, and without excuses. When you are firm, you avoid making too many apologies, and you are not defensive. You can be firm while still being polite, which tells the manipulator that while you recognize that you are not doing what was desired of you, you are not willing to change your mind. By being clear that what you are saying is a no, the manipulator is aware that your opinion and answer are not changing any time soon. If you make it seem as though you may reconsider in the future, you are going to create even more conflict in the future. Lastly, you want to avoid excuses when you are saying no. You do not have to have a reason to tell someone no; you do not owe anyone an explanation for your reasoning

behind declining, and your reason for declining does not invalidate the answer. You are not obligated to do anything that other people are asking of you, no matter how much the manipulator may try to convince you otherwise.

Beyond hitting the above criteria, there are three steps to effectively saying no. First, you must simply say it out loud. You simply say, "No, I'm sorry; I can't help you right now." That is, it. If you are not ready to say no at that moment, it is also acceptable to instead say that you want to take some time to reconsider. If even after reconsidering, you cannot think of a way to make it work, or you simply do not want to make it work, you can offer to say yes to something else instead. You can let the other person know that while you cannot do what they have requested, you can help in another way, and offer up that other way in return.

Ask if Request is Reasonable

The last technique you can use to at once challenge manipulation as it happens is to turn things back around on the manipulator. If the manipulator is really insisting that you do something and will not accept any of the other methods you have used to try to tell the

manipulator that you cannot help at that time, you can try turning things around by asking if the request seems reasonable. The manipulator will most likely confirm that it is, in fact, reasonable, at which point, you should ask the manipulator if it would be reasonable to make that same request back to you. The manipulator is now stuck between either doing what he wanted himself or admitting that the request was not actually reasonable in the first place.

For example, imagine that your manipulative partner has been insisting that you should spend an extra two hours that night preparing something for a potluck that he did not inform you about until that evening. He did not get any of the ingredients for the item he wants you to cook, nor did he give you any warning before you got home from your own job, exhausted after working full time. Your partner then assumes that you will have no problems going to the store to get the ingredients, come home, cook dinner, clean up dinner, then cook the potluck dish, clean up that mess, and somehow still get the kids finished with their homework and sent to bed on time. Of course, your partner will sit on the couch and complain about how tired he is after his long day at the

desk at work while you somehow attempt to juggle everything.

In this instance, you could stop and ask your partner if it is reasonable to expect all of that all at once. Chances are, your partner will say that, of course, it is reasonable and that you are better at cooking, and he has already told all of his co-workers that he is bringing in that particular dish cooked by you, which has been a huge hit at past potlucks before. Instead of asking how he could help, he assumes you will go along with everything. At this point, you could ask that he does it instead, and when he baulks, you tell him that you cannot do it for the same reasons he cannot—you are tired and busy after work, and you still have kids to get ready for bed and school.

Chapter 10. Manipulation Tips and Tricks

The first tip in manipulation is the change of environment.

More often than not, your environment can influence how people react and respond to what you're asking for. For example, if you are in the workplace or any other kind of business environment, people in that environment with you will most likely see you as a rival or as a competitor. This would make it difficult for them to give in to your request. So, if you want to get people to agree to what you're requesting for, especially your work colleagues, take them out for a drink or a lunch date. The drinking environment or the lunch environment helps them see you less as a colleague and more as a friend, and everyone easily agrees to what your friend is asking for, right?

The second tip you can try out when manipulating people is to make it all about the person you want to manipulate.

Yes, your aim is to learn manipulation techniques to use on people for your own good. However, nobody would like to answer your request if they find out you are doing it for your own good. This means you have to be as subtle

as possible, make your request all about the other person. How do you do this? When you render help to people, people will be willing to help you. So, if you want to manipulate someone, help the person out first, then they would be willing to help when you need it.

Another tip is to speak quickly.

Many great manipulators use this. The secret behind this is that when you speak very fast, people will find it difficult to understand what you're saying and when they don't know what you're saying, they will easily agree to what you're asking for.

How do you do this? Walk up briskly to someone that you want to manipulate, issue fast instructions, and leave immediately. This would not allow the person enough time to think upon what you said or react to what you said. Therefore, they would carry out your instructions even without understanding them. This especially works if you are in a position of authority. It will make your victim see you as an important person, and they will see you as someone who does not have the time to explain every detail. You can use this technique in car sales and various forms of a business closing.

This following tip goes without saying; you have to dress nicely.

Before I knew how powerful this was in manipulating people, I could care less about how I looked or dressed. However, when I saw that this was a powerful manipulation tip, I began to literally dress to kill. Remember the aim of manipulation is to get your own good, so spend money on clothing, read books and magazines on how to look good and well-groomed, spend well on jewellery, a nice wristwatch and buy expensive perfumes. Try this for the following week can see how people react to you.

You see that when people complain about what happened to them when they encountered a con artist, one thing many of them say is that the con artist looked responsible, so they fell for him or her. The dressing goes a long way in helping you manipulate people.

So, research on what people term as good dressing in your location, spend well on it and go-ahead to talk to people you will see how easily they will give into your requests. Who doesn't like a person that looks good and smells good?

This following tip means you're going to be tapping into the basic survival instinct of every human being. It's called scare tactics.

When I tell you that you have a lot to lose if you don't do what I want you to do, I am basically using scare tactics to manipulate you. That means if you want to manipulate someone using scare tactics, all you have to do is mention what the person might lose if the person doesn't do what you are asking for. Don't make it sound like a threat, just subtly do it.

When marketers or advertisers mention things like 'buy now', 'this offer will close in 3 days', 'get this now so that you'll be among the first ten people to get it' and so on, what these marketers do in such instances is to manipulate their listeners or potential buyers into getting what they want using scare tactics.

In scare tactics, you are tapping into the basic need to survive the unknown that all human beings have. This is what the insurance business uses. I come to you and tell you to pay an amount of money to protect yourself from unforeseen accidents that might happen in the future. All I just did was to scare you with what might happen. Since this has been proven to work in the insurance industry,

you can also use it as an expert manipulator. This is best used when you are manipulating someone to accept a solution that you want to give the person. Also, you can use it in relationships such as your work or personal relationships; you just have to get the right angle.

This following tip applies to every aspect of life. When you are consistent with something, you get results from it. So, if you're consistent with manipulation, you get results from it and get better at it. Now, how can you apply consistency to manipulation? This is easy; just stay in character. When you are acting like a nice person, be nice to everybody, the waiter, your work colleague, everybody. This will prevent people from seeing you as two different persons.

A master manipulator needs to be believed; people need to believe you. Now, if they need to believe you, you also need to stay faithful to the character you are trying to portray. Once they see a red flag in your character, once they see something conflicting in your character, they would notice it and not give in to your demands. Therefore, you need to be consistent in the way you speak and act to everybody. Speak in the same tone and manner to everybody, and that way, you will easily win

people over. This is especially true because a consistent person is seen as a person of integrity, and a person of integrity is easily believed. When they believe and trust you, you have them like putty in your palms.

This following tip is very easy to do. Why? This is because all you must do is to keep quiet; silence is Golden. When you are silent around people, they get uncomfortable, and their discomfort makes them give out information. How do you do this? Simple, just repeat the last two or three words of every statement that they make.

Let me show you an example:

Victim: I saw John in the morning.

Manipulator: John

Victim: Yes, John, I saw him at the phone store.

Manipulator: Phone store?

Victim: Yes, I went to buy a new phone for my daughter for her birthday.

Did you see what just happened now? The manipulator was able to get information from the victim by just keeping silent and asking just enough questions.

Wisdom, however, is not to do this too much. Else, you will begin to look awkward.

In this following tip, you would realize that it pays to be nice.

When you want to get someone to do what you want to do, you have to be as nice as possible even when internally, you are very angry. The reason for this is that people want to see how far you can go in staying nice, people want to see your breaking point. Therefore, you have to be positive always, begin your conversations on a happy note, stay in a happy tone, and with a positive note even when internally, you are angry, stay cool. Never let your anger show to the surface, rather, play nice.

The choice of words is very important in playing nice. You have to look at how best to say what you are about to say. Rather than make someone feel foolish with your words, you can make someone feel responsible and want to do the correct thing just by saying the right words. For example, you can say, "have you considered this option", rather than saying, "you must do this option."

In manipulation, nice words always work.

So far, I'm showing you tips on how to live as a good human being right? Well, you're not too far from the truth, human beings are born to be natural manipulators.

However, as we grow older, we begin to conform to society's rules, whims, and caprices. This makes us forget our natural manipulative tendencies.

In this following tip, what I am going to tell you is that you should basically be responsible. Own up to your actions. Carry your cross!

When you do some things, people will easily think that you are a good person, someone that they should trust. For example, when a Christian or a person wears a rosary or a cross necklace on his neck or her neck, people would easily think that you are a person with good morals or a Christian. Once they believe this about you, they lower their defences and attack instincts around you, and when they do this, you will find it easy to get them to do what you want.

So, what this means is that the accessories and items you carry along with you make you more agreeable to manipulate people. For example, if you are a man and you walk around with a cute dog, women would easily be attracted to you. This increases your appeal to women. Also, if you carry around a baby or your child, it will make you come up as a responsible man, and people would want to talk to you. Women would easily want to give

you their numbers, you can even ask them out on a date, and they would agree.

Of course, for this tip, you don't need to carry or force a child to come along with you or even borrow your nephews and nieces. What you are trying to achieve here is creating an illusion or picturing yourself in the mind of the person you want to manipulate as someone that is responsible.

In this following trick, I am going to be showing you how to get people to believe what you are trying to portray about yourself. You are going to learn how to talk the talk and walk the walk. For example, if you sound stupid, everyone will assume that you are stupid. However, when you sound smart, people around you are shame you're smart and therefore take you seriously.

So rather than use filler words and sound like a teenage girl that no one would want to take seriously, you can broaden your vocabulary by listening to authorities in various fields and industries, great speakers and read a lot of books. Also, you can listen to the news as well as watch various documentaries on a wide range of subjects. This would make you have a big bank of things to say to make you sound intelligent.

Also, learn to measure your intellect. People like to trust people that sound intelligent. When you sound intelligent, they would easily give in to what you want them to think and believe this will make it easy for people to agree to your terms.

For this following tip, all you need to do is to be a good storyteller. People are more agreeable to a good storyteller. Great manipulators are great storytellers. Of course, there are times where you might need to back up what you say with data, but more often than not, a good storyteller always has the ear of his or her listeners.

Therefore, you need to put the data aside sometimes and tell stories. In your stories, use anecdotes, they make the story more personal and more human. If you don't have any personal anecdotes, you could always borrow from someone's story somewhere, just be creative.

The number one rule for manipulation is that you should stand out in the mind of the person you want to manipulate; they should remember you but not suspect you. For you to achieve this, you should use terms people use every day, be easy-going, talk about topics that just anybody talks about, the aim is for you to be predictable in a way that people can relate.

Therefore, you need to learn how to blend with the crowd. This would help you receive protection from the crowd around you. So, you don't need to forcibly be unique. Rather, be predictable and still sound smart and charming.

For this following trick or tip, you can decide to help the newbie in your company. Everybody trusts the person who wants to help. So, if you want to manipulate a newcomer in your company or environment, just render him or her some help. This will make them trust you and then give in easily to your demands. Once they give in to your demands, you can manipulate them as you like.

The statement 'I need your help' when crafted in some ways can either help you achieve your manipulative goals or reduce your hopes of achieving your manipulative goals. For example, if you are the boss of a company and yew bark out orders to your staff, of course, they would go-ahead to do what you want because they do not want to get fired. But when you give the same instructions and say them as ‘I need your help’, you're getting your staff to put in more to help you achieve what you want. This is the best because they do not just see you as their boss; they now see you as their colleague, just with a better

office. Politicians do this a lot. They sit and eat with you so as to make you think that they are just one of your friends or neighbours who wants to make the community a better place. They do this for four years or five years and then cart away with the society's funds. So, you too can use this powerful trick to get people to do your whims and caprices.

One tip that works every time is food. It is a known fact that people are more agreeable when they have eaten. So, to win over the person you intend manipulating, ensure he or she is well fed. This would help them easily give in to what you want. A lot of business deals and contracts have been closed over dinners; there is a reason for this. You can try it out too.

So, which one out of these tips and tricks would you try out first? For me, I would definitely recommend starting with dressing and smelling good. This would go so well with offering help and looking responsible. Combining this would make you an expert manipulator anytime.

Conclusion

You will agree with the assessment that manipulation is everywhere in our daily lives. Even while you sleep, there is a brand somewhere that is looking to unleash their manipulative marketing campaign with the goal of making you spend your money. While you slave away at work at the mercy of your boss, there is often no guarantee that you will get a promotion. In your personal relationships, there is probably someone who is pretending to be your friend but is only looking out for themselves. It almost seems like whichever way you turn, there is someone waiting to influence your following move. This can be quite overwhelming.

Being manipulated does not feel good. Knowing that everything you thought was true was an altered reality created by a manipulative person makes you feel betrayed and, oftentimes, stupid. You wonder why you did not see the red flags and what you could have done differently. The truth of the matter is that however smart you think you are, there is always someone who believes they can outsmart you. Enter your new manipulation methods.

You do not have to sit back and watch other people take control and get what you want when you can do it yourself. Influencing other people into fulfilling your desires is well within your reach if you internalize and incorporate the teachings and methods of this book. It might seem like an uphill climb, especially if you are used to giving other people what they want and getting nothing in return, but it really is not. Learning how to manipulate people is not something that should overwhelm you. It only feels overwhelming now because you are learning all these new things all at once. With time and practice, the things you have learned will become second nature. You will find yourself smiling and flirting without even thinking about it.

Start the work from within--working on your body language, presentation, communication techniques--and then apply the outcome to the external environment. You will be surprised how much more you can gain from people and the world around you if you subtly manipulate them. Becoming an expert manipulator will take you longer than a few days, but it will be worth the work and the wait. Remember, as long as you are not hurting anyone who does not deserve to be hurt; you are well

within your rights to manipulate your way to the success that you have always envisioned for yourself!

CPSIA information can be obtained
at www.ICGtesting.com
Printed in the USA
LVHW021709011220
672997LV00006B/675

9 781801 200080

4166431

Made in the USA
Charleston, SC
08 December 2009

TABLE OF CONTENTS

MANIPULATION MASTERY

LEVEL UP

THE ULTIMATE GUIDE TO LEARN MENTAL MANIPULATION TECHNIQUES SUCH AS LOVE BOMBING, SOCIAL CONTROL, LABELING TACTICS OF DARK PSYCHOLOGY. LEARN TO DEFEND FROM EMOTIONAL ABUSE.

BY JOHN WILLS

INTRODUCTION

There I was, on August 13, 2010, on a hot summer day in the global capital of the world—New York City—at the NASDAQ trading desk. Just a couple of years earlier, I cofounded an international technology leadership network called HITEC (Hispanic IT Executive Council), and we had taken off like a rocket ship, gathering the support of corporate executives and many corporations, including Target, Cisco, Oracle, Disney, UBS, GM, and many others.

As I reflected on these rapid accomplishments, I looked over a sea of smiling, excited members, video cameras, photographers, and pictures up on the large NASDAQ Times Square digital billboard. I could not forget that this would have never happened if I had not put in the *work* behind NetWORKing. This work included leveraging years of readings, mentorship, networking events, taking action, and following up. In the end, it was one of the most memorable events in my life, highlighting the true joys of networking.

We live in a world that has become increasingly digital and a world that continues to thirst for more meaningful relationships. Networking continues to be vitally important for finding a job, progressing in a career, accomplishing goals, and maintaining long-term health.

From a career growth perspective, 80 percent of professionals consider networking important to career success. However, only 48 percent consistently keep in touch with their network (LinkedIn Corporate Communications 2017). When it comes to using networking to find jobs, 70 percent of jobs never publish publicly, and according to HubSpot, 85 percent of all jobs fill through networking (Fisher 2019; Apollo Technical 2022). Additionally, a study by LinkedIn in 2017 showed that 35 percent of participants said casual conversation through LinkedIn Messaging led to new opportunities (LinkedIn Corporate Communications 2017).

The problem with this is that if networking is so important for getting jobs, career advancement, accomplishing your goals, and living longer, why isn't it taught in schools? Why isn't more focus and emphasis put on this vital skill? I believe only 48 percent of professionals consistently stay connected with their network because they leverage the use of goals, daily rituals, and other easy tools and techniques (LinkedIn Corporate Communications 2017). The reason 52 percent of people do not consistently stay connected with their networks is that schools do not teach those tools, techniques, and best practices. Goals, daily rituals, tools, techniques, and tips from leading networking experts can help this 52 percent not only consistently keep in touch with their network but also help them accelerate the value of networking.

When I look at my life and career around networking, I built an amazing network, and I am fortunate to have accomplished many things I never thought I would be able to accomplish.

My disciplined approach to networking has helped me rise through the corporate ranks at leading technology companies, cofound leading nonprofits, obtain board of directors positions at leading technology companies, get invited to the White House across three different presidential administrations, open the NASDAQ, and receive an honorary doctorate from Bentley University, among many other accomplishments.

I have leveraged a methodology and approach to networking, which is an amalgamation of books, best practices, mentors, and observing and interviewing great networkers. This process and methodology have a foundational component around self-understanding and a focus on execution and optimization. It focuses on goals, rituals, and building networks to ensure mutual success. Lastly, many in my network have come up to me and said, "Wow, you know lots of people and are super connected." In the spirit of networking, this compliment inspired me to write down my approach and best practices to help others do the same.

Networking has allowed me to meet amazing people. The learnings, approach, and action around networking allowed me to meet and network with people who align with my life purpose and goals. This includes CEOs, Fortune 500 board members, presidents of countries, members of Congress, nonprofit leaders, investors, executives, professional athletes, connectors, and many other interesting people. The approach and actions described in this book can help you build deeper relationships with those focused on your life purpose and goals. Additionally, it makes life fun and rewarding.

Networking has helped accelerate my career and life goals. I delivered results in senior executive roles in some of the world's best companies, started nonprofits, some of which are the strongest leadership nonprofits in the world, served on the board of national nonprofits, received invitations to the White House by multiple presidential administrations, and opened the NASDAQ, among other memorable accomplishments. I attribute these networking accomplishments to the value-based networks I have built over time and the intentional way I go about adding value to my network. This book can help you accelerate your career and life goals, no matter what they are.

I learned about networking from many great people over the years by observing master networkers in action, watching how they work their networks in a room, and participating in various networks. I also learned a ton about networks from reading. I read dozens of books on networking, leadership, goal setting, relationships, and value/value creation. I also taught some of the world's leading sales professionals about value selling. Finally, and most importantly, I put all these learnings into *action* around a methodology (more detail within this book), which is a key differentiator.

To be excellent at networking requires discipline, an approach, and work. This book will discuss various ways to work to build, nurture, and grow relationships. There are foundational components to networking. You need to ensure that as part of this foundation, you are strong at the center, you network with the right people, and you use your time efficiently.

This book focuses on self-understanding within the foundation you can use to identify goals, rituals, and people to help you accomplish your goals. The magic happens as you begin to connect with and add value to this network. There are tips, techniques, and ways to optimize networking events better.

Reading the tips and stories from leaders who are excellent at networking will help you more efficiently approach events you attend. Finally, we are moving into an ever-increasingly digital world. World-class networkers will need to leverage digital tools and social media to stay connected and nurture a digital network to help them accelerate their goals.

This book is for business leaders, nonprofit leaders, public servants, entrepreneurs, sales leaders, or anybody who is looking to live a more meaningful life, more rapidly accomplish their goals, find tips and techniques to be a better networker, and better leverage digital and social media tools to fulfill their goals and help others accomplish theirs.

As I reflect on my life and my career, one of the many things that have made it enjoyable is networking with people and helping them succeed in their goals. I also look back fondly on those who have helped me and the various networks that have connected me to these people and enabled many of my own accomplishments.

Human survival has depended on people and relationships for thousands of years. Embedded in our DNA, this enables us to be social creatures and desire social interaction. By reading this book, you will grow as a human and develop more meaningful relationships. As proven in several studies around networking and relationships, you will also increase your chances of living a longer, more meaningful life. Finally, you will increase your chances of growing rapidly in your career and having more fun.

In the spirit of networking, I hope this book, the experiences, and the approach I share help you and others in your network achieve your goals.

FOUNDATION

What Is Networking and Why Is It Important?

Everything you want to achieve in life is going to be with and through other people.

—KEITH FERRAZZI

How do you define networking?

Whenever I am with a group discussing a new topic, I like to ensure we are on the same page about what it means. If you do not know what networking is, it is hard to improve or make it excellent. Many people talk about the importance of networking, but when you ask people what the definition is, you get many different answers. As I heard these definitions over the years, I learned there are some good ones and some bad ones.

Through reading the literature on networking, executing sales and leadership trainings across my career, watching many top leaders build relationships through networking, and seeing bad networking practices, I have been able to come up with the following definition. Networking is:

Creating and improving value-based relationships to facilitate mutual goal accomplishment

- **Creating and improving**—Networking is not just about creating connections. You should continuously improve your networking relationships.
- **Value-based relationships**—Networking focuses on an ongoing relationship of deeply understanding what the other person values, their goals, and how to help them.
- **Facilitate**—Make it easy to accomplish mutual goals. A good networker is always looking to help their peers accomplish its goals and help make it as easy as possible.
- **Mutual goals**—Networking is not about your goals. It is more about helping the other person and your network accomplish their goals.

The bad networking definitions include:

- Distributing your business cards at events to as many people as possible.
- Meeting people to accomplish your goals.
- Connecting with as many people as you can on LinkedIn.

- Working the entire room.

For this book, I interviewed Raymond Arroyo, a friend from whom I learned a lot about networking. We met in the early 2000s when he was the chief diversity officer at Aetna, and I am grateful for his continued friendship and perspectives on networking. For Raymond, networking is really about building authentic relationships.

Raymond said, "There is a hunger for authenticity in people's behavior. So, if you become somewhat vulnerable or exposed but authentic, people become attracted to you, creating its own charisma."

Raymond also mentions that you must be alert to people's intentions when networking. He discussed how bad intentions have put some skepticism into how he views networking. This derived from people feeling more attracted to his perceived power and influence versus him. This has had an impact on trust, which is a vital component of relationship building and networking.

Raymond's network has evolved throughout his life as he has moved out of his corporate leadership role and is now a managing director for the executive search firm Chapman Farrell Group. The benefits of networking are different for him at this point in his career and life. At this point, Raymond has narrowed his inner circle to a few he really trusts and is more self-aware of people's intentions as he is networking.

Keith Ferrazzi Value of Networking

In a YouTube video, Keith Ferrazzi, CEO of Ferrazzi Greenlight and an American author of several books on networking, mentions that about 70,000 years ago, we called networks tribes, and there were only about twelve of those tribes in Africa. If those groups didn't connect and come together, they wouldn't survive.

Keith said, "As a result, DNA hardwiring in our core is for connecting, serving, and helping each other succeed. If we didn't, we were thrown out and eaten by mountain lions." Therefore, networking and connections are deep within our DNA, and we long for them (Ferrazzi 2011).

David Wieland on the Value of Networking

In my interview with David Weiland, cofounder and managing partner at Motivate Venture Capital, David said, "Humans prefer to do business with and interact with humans. That is why networking is so powerful. We need to be deliberate about networking to realize this."

On the definition of networking, David said, "I look to connect with interesting and diverse people and try to be helpful, expecting nothing in return."

Settling on a common definition of networking and identifying actions and approaches has helped create the first piece of a foundation to build off. Additionally, taking into account misconceptions about networking and some of the actions that aren't networking will further help build a strong foundation for excellence.

Great Things Are Done through People and Networks

Throughout history, individuals have had very few great accomplishments on their own. Winning battles in war, growing companies, winning in team sports, landing a person on the moon, and countless other examples are great things accomplished with a group and would be impossible to achieve as an individual. It takes groups, teams, and networks to carry out big things. Networks provide efficiency, scale, and diverse views to improve outcomes.

Gale Wilkinson, managing partner at VITALIZE, an early stage VC (venture capital) plus angel platform investing in the *work revolution*, is a leading venture capitalist and has built networks across angel investing groups, venture capital firms, start-ups, and Fortune 500 corporations. In my interview with Gale about the value of networks, Gale mentions the research of Ron Burt, a professor at University of Chicago Booth School of Business, which showed that more than 50 percent of the value an individual created at work was due to their network of external connections. I have seen these external connections open up sales opportunities, form partnerships with new entities, and bring new innovative ideas into organizations as an example (@GaleforceVC 2021).

I look back at many memorable events in groups or teams, and I not only realized you need the team but also realized celebrating these events as a group was much more fun. Personally, I was a state champion in the 4x100 meter relay and football as a team. I remember winning proposals and hitting company milestones as a team. I have started nonprofits from scratch and watched them grow as a team. I also opened the NASDAQ with a team and celebrated the opening as a team. I also invested in unicorn start-ups as a group. All these great accomplishments in my life happened through people and networks.

Law of Reciprocity

The law of reciprocity is also known as the rule of reciprocation, or the norm of reciprocity. A simple definition is when someone does something nice for you, you will have a deep-rooted psychological urge to do something nice in return. An article from *Psychology Today* states, "This tendency has survived and been present throughout human history because it has survival value for the human species" (Bloom 2015).

Additionally, the nicer the action or the larger the deposit of value toward you, the larger your desire will be to do something nicer or larger in return. Reciprocal giving and receiving is a characteristic of all highly successful relationships.

Benefits of Having a Strong Network

There are many benefits to networking and having a strong network. Below are a sample of the benefits:

- **Scale and acceleration**—By having a network, you can reach out for advice on any problem you are trying to solve, gather different perspectives, receive counsel, and collect expertise you would not have if you did not have your network.

- **Leverage**—Leverage is finding additional resources you utilize to give you an accelerated advantage. On the popular website eToro, it states that leverage is to use something to maximum advantage. Your network of relationships gives you maximum advantage toward whatever you want to accomplish. (eToro, n.d.)

- **Support in tough times**—In my case, I have had many ups and downs. When there have been downtimes, I have reached out to my network for help, and in good times, I have reached out to my network to thank them.

- **Satisfaction from helping**—You can receive satisfaction from connecting with people within your network who don't know each other, and through this connection, they both win. This happened to me when I connected Adela Cepeda, a board member at BMO Harris Bank, to Luis Ubiñas, who serves on the board of directors of AT&T. Luis and Adela did not know each other, but through this connection, Luis Ubiñas got appointed to serve as a trustee of Mercer Funds.

- **Career success**—Your network can help you find better jobs and give you the relationships to accelerate promotions.

Networking Benefits: Health Improvements and Living Longer

In my interview with Raymond Arroyo, another benefit of building relationships and networking was health and living longer. He pointed me to a TEDx Talk by Susan Pinker titled, "The Secret to Living Longer May Be Your Social Life." You can find the talk here:

https://www.ted.com/talks/susan_pinker_the_secret_to_living_longer_may_be_your_social_life?language=en

The presentation goes to Sardinia, Italy, where there is six times the number of centenarians, those one hundred years or older, as on the Italian mainland. That is ten times the number in North America. Susan Pinker did research into why. One of the interesting parts of her research focused on the density of houses in Sardinia and how that enabled the people to intersect constantly. She highlights three centenarians and how they have lots of love, interactions, and family caring for them. She found them at kitchen parties, always surrounded by friends and the priest, and were never left to live solitary lives.

She then discusses the research of Julianne Holt-Lunstad, a BYU (Brigham Young University) professor of psychology and neuroscience who studied tens of thousands of middle-aged people. She looked at all aspects of their lifestyle (smile, diet, exercise, smoking, weight, marital status, doctors' visits, clean air). She recorded all of this, waited seven years, and asked, "Of those still alive, what reduced their chance of dying the most" (Pinker 2017)?

The top two answers:

1. **Social integration:** How much do you interact with people as you move through the day? How many people do you talk to? This includes your weak and strong bonds, not just your great friends. Do you talk to the person who makes your coffee, the mail carrier, or the person who walks their dog? Do you play bridge or poker?

2. **Close relationships:** These are the people you can call on for help. Who will take you to the hospital? They will sit with you when you are in despair (Pinker 2017).

For social integration and close relationships, there is a further study by Kelly Harding of Columbia University that concludes you can also increase life expectancy by being kind in these relationships and interactions (Harding, n.d.).

These are the strongest predictors of how much you will live. She also notes that face-to-face is better and healthier for us versus virtual.

NETWORKING BENEFITS: FROM *A MESSAGE FROM GARCIA*

Charles P. Garcia's *A Message from Garcia* was a foundational book for me as it relates to my knowledge and growth around networking. His book has various messages from Garcia that are insightful. Below is one around networking benefits:

> Being smart is good. Being smart and knowing a lot of smart people is better. Networking is essential to achieving great success. Successful people know and interact with other successful people. Successful people cultivate and nurture these relationships to enhance their personal and business lives. Try to meet others in your field who are above you. People who are well known and have excellent reputations. Meet people from outside your field. By interacting with people outside your immediate field, you increase your network of relationships. These people can bring

a fresh perspective to your personal and business life. And you can likewise offer the same to them. Be interesting, informative, and willing to help others without expecting to earn something in return.

By having a wide network of relationships, you can solicit the opinions of others to get their take on a problem or situation you might be facing. Third party impartial advice can be valuable when no one has a stake in a decision or an emotional connection to it. Their perspective can be clearer and often more valid when faced with a particularly demanding problem. Reach into your network for more than one opinion from people you respect by getting at least three opinions on any one matter. You should be able to decipher the correct course of action (Garcia 2003, 119).

Barriers to Networking

Networking does not always come easy for people. There might be many personal items, fears, and things going on in your life that make networking hard. There is a reason the word *work* is within *network*. Building a strong network and accomplishing mutual goals requires work.

Here are some of the networking barriers I typically hear or see from people.

FEAR OF GOING TO AN EVENT BY YOURSELF

Going to a networking event by yourself can be scary. Especially if it is with a group where you know minimal to zero people who will be there. It's common to feel anxious about conversing with people we don't know. I am very good at networking, but I sometimes feel scared about not connecting with anybody at an event, others seeing me alone, or others seeing me as not interesting, which could be self-fulfilling. Additionally, many of us feel that having a guaranteed conversational partner gives us a level of comfort and protection in these environments. This fear hinders us from meeting new people.

FEAR OF REJECTION

People do not like rejection. There are times while networking when people will not have an interest in you and reject you as well as what you say. Some people find this rejection intimidating.

LACK OF TIME

There are many demands on our time. Networking takes time and work, and other priorities can replace networking time. As a data point, 38 percent globally said they find it hard to stay in touch with their network. Nearly half (49 percent) globally say it's because they don't have enough time (LinkedIn Corporate Communications 2017).

COSTS

Networking is an investment of your time and can also have a direct cost depending on the event or group. These expenses can add up and hinder one's desire to network. Direct costs include meals, parking, membership fees, or donations.

I asked one of my past employers to fund my attendance at a Gartner IT Symposium, the premier event for IT executives across the nation. My employer said they did not have the budget. Many folks I know would not have gone. I did a quick cost-benefit analysis and decided it would be worth the investment from my personal budget for the conference and travel. On the second night of the conference, over dinner with a group of people within my network, I received a job offer due to personally funding a trip to the conference. I received the investment in this trip and registration ten times over in the salary increase. Even if I hadn't received the job offer, the relationships and knowledge from the conference were worth it.

This book will work to increase your confidence and approach to networking to minimize these barriers. It will provide many tools, techniques, and perspectives from those who are great at networking to help you.

Networking Principles to Consider

BUILD YOUR NETWORK BEFORE YOU NEED IT

With these value points of networking understood, focus on actions that help you proactively build your network. Enhancing a network and keeping connected to it requires work. Having the network in place before you need it is an easy way to show proactivity and reduce any barriers.

You do not want to reach out to people in a very cold way and make an ask without having built a relationship. For example, and I think many of us have experienced this, there are people in our network whom we have not heard from in years, and then suddenly, they reach out to you, sometimes not even saying hi or asking how one is doing, and go straight for the ask.

"Hi David, I'm at a point in my career at my current employer where I am looking for new opportunities. I was hoping you could connect me to people who can help me find a job."

This book will provide rituals, tools, exercises, frameworks, and examples of ways to proactively build your network before you need it.

SERVE AND HELP

Networking is about helping others achieve their goals and mutual success. Your intention should be about serving and helping.

CONNECT OTHERS

Look for and facilitate opportunities to connect others who have similar goals and can help and provide value to each other.

The true value of networking doesn't come from how many people we can meet but rather how many people we can introduce to others.

—SIMON SINEK

EXERCISE

- What is your definition of networking?

- What are the ways that networking will be valuable for you?

- How much time do you spend per week networking?

- What are some things holding you back from networking?

RESOURCES

- *The 7 Habits of Highly Effective People* by Steve Covey

- *Never Eat Alone* by Keith Ferrazzi

- *A Message from Garcia* by Charles P. Garcia

- *The Rabbit Effect* by Dr. Kelli Harding

Psychology Today:
https://www.psychologytoday.com/us/blog/stronger-the-broken-places/201510/honoring-the-rule-reciprocation

STEP 1

DEEPLY UNDERSTAND YOURSELF

I think self-awareness is the most important thing toward being a champion.

—BILLIE JEAN KING

Our sun is amazing. It gives us life and energy and helps us see. The center of our universe, holding things together; we can't imagine life without it. As somebody who is building toward networking excellence, you should view yourself like the sun, the center of your network, and the planets and stars as various connections you have. The more you understand about yourself, the brighter and more energy you will be able to provide to your relationships. Like the sun, a strong network needs strength from its center, which is you.

If you study great leaders and people with massive networks, one of the main characteristics you will find is their deep understanding of themselves. This knowledge of oneself provides the strength, endurance, and energy of your network.

Here are some examples of leaders who had their values and purpose and deeply understood themselves:

- Gandhi
  - Mohandas Karamchand Gandhi was an Indian lawyer, social activist, and politician who employed nonviolent resistance to lead the successful campaign for India's independence from British rule and inspire later movements for civil rights and freedom across the world (Nanda 2022).
  - Gandhi was a seeker, and his introspection was the method of his sadhana. He wrote, "I have gone through deep introspection, searched myself through and through, and examined and analyzed every psychological situation." The study of the *Gita* and the process of self-introspection brought him face-to-face with the true meaning of ahimsa—no violence in thought, speech, and act. He concluded that the realization of truth was impossible without adherence to the supreme conduct of man—ahimsa. In his opinion, truth and ahimsa were as intermingled as the two sides of a coin. For the achievement of one or the other, complete control over the senses of action (karmendriyas) and those of perception (jnanendriyas) is essential (Kumar 2018).
- Martin Luther King, Jr.
  - Martin Luther King, Jr. was an American Christian minister and social activist who became the most

visible spokesman and leader in the civil rights movement from 1955 until his assassination in 1968. His leadership was fundamental to that movement's success in ending the legal segregation of African Americans in the South and other parts of the United States. He received the Nobel Peace Prize in 1964 (Lewis 2022).

  - He had a dream (a vision), knew his role, and knew the strengths he had to enable that vision.

- Pope John Paul II

  - Pope John Paul II was the head of the Catholic Church and sovereign of the Vatican City State from 1978 until his death in 2005. The second papal conclave of 1978 elected him and named him after John Paul I, elected in August to succeed Pope Paul VI, who died after thirty-three days (Blakemore 2022).

  - He spent many hours in prayer and self-reflection.

  - He practiced what he preached and forgave Ali Agca, the person who shot him. He also asked for forgiveness for church sins, crusades, divisions within the church, persecution of Jews, inquisitions, racism, and social injustice (Blakemore 2022).

- Mother Teresa

  - Mother Teresa was the founder of the Order of the Missionaries of Charity, a Roman Catholic congregation of women dedicated to helping the poor. Many consider her one of the twentieth century's greatest humanitarians and canonized her as Saint Teresa of Calcutta in 2016 (Biography 2017).

- Her mission was to care for the hungry, the naked, the homeless, the crippled, the blind, the lepers, and all those who felt unwanted, unloved, and uncared for throughout society. To do this, she felt she had to live like them (Biography 2017).

- So moved was Mother Teresa by the plight of the people in this slum that she left her Loreto convent's serene and cloistered environment to live and work among the poorest of the poor.

- Dalai Lama

  - The fourteenth Dalai Lama, known as Gyalwa Rinpoche to the Tibetan people, is the highest spiritual leader and former head of the state of Tibet (The Nobel Prize 2022).

  - He authored the book *How to See Yourself as You Really Are*. According to His Holiness, the Dalai Lama, we each possess the ability to achieve happiness and a meaningful life, but the key to realizing that goal is self-knowledge. Through illuminating explanations and step-by-step exercises, His Holiness helps readers to see the world as it actually exists and explains how, through the interconnection of meditative

> concentration and love, true altruistic enlightenment is attained (Dalai Lama 2007).

These leaders had not only strong beliefs, a mission, and a purpose but also deep self-understanding of themselves. They were generous and sincerely cared about people. These are key attributes of leaders who have achieved networking excellence. Their beliefs, conviction, and leadership around those beliefs resonated with people and attracted them to these leaders. When you are generous and care about people, you attract people. The care and generosity of these leaders have millions of people in their relationship scope.

Below are areas of self-understanding that are vital for networking excellence. Some of these areas overlap, but by looking at them individually, you can strengthen your self-understanding. These areas include:

- Vision
- Mission
- Purpose
- Personal core values
- SWOT
- Value
- Happiness

YOUR VISION

"Begin with the end in mind" is one of the habits listed in *The 7 Habits of Highly Effective People* by author Steven Covey. It was a foundational book for me, which I read around 1995.

If you don't have a vision of where you are going, how will you get to your destination most efficiently? There are lots of distractions in this world. Having a clear vision of our lives can help us prioritize.

You can determine your vision in a nice quiet place. You can close your eyes and visualize. Our lives are often so busy that we don't have time to visualize, dream, and imagine.

Albert Einstein said, "Imagination is everything. It is the preview to life's coming attractions." Use this time to imagine those coming attractions!

After twenty to thirty minutes of closing your eyes and visualizing, begin to write things down. This can be words, paragraphs, or bullet points. There are multiple ways you can articulate this. Choose whatever is most comfortable for you and captures your vision. Don't aim for perfection, as this will shift over time.

This shifting over time will require you to visit it regularly. For example, I visit mine in-depth once a quarter and adjust if necessary.

Some questions that can help you are:

- What is your vision of yourself?
- Where do you see yourself in three, five, ten, and twenty years?
- Where do you see yourself across the many dimensions (professional, relationships, health, family, spiritual, giving, nonprofits, etc.) of life?

- Where are you physically at during each of these periods in the future?

- How are all your senses reacting in this vision?

Your answers to these questions should paint a mental picture of each phase in the future.

YOUR MISSION

A personal mission statement defines who you are as a person (or as a team member where you work) and identifies your purpose, whether that pertains to your career or simply to your life. It explains how you aim to pursue that purpose and why it matters so much to you. Unlike a vision statement, a mission is something you should do each day to achieve your dream (Ramsey Solutions 2021).

Career coach Dan Miller says a good mission statement includes the following items:

1. Your skills and abilities (what you like to do)
2. Your personality traits (how you operate)
3. Your values, dreams, and passions (why you want to excel)

It describes your convictions, what you stand for, and how you plan to create a life that embodies your values. In other words, it becomes your personal definition of success—one that is separate from the approval of others (Ramsey Solutions 2021).

It serves as a guidepost for where you want to go in life. Writing a mission statement requires minimal work, and it keeps you from wandering off track and helps you focus your time.

How to create a mission statement:

Think about your life principles and goals. Why did you set these goals? How do your goals make you a better person? The mission statement should answer these questions in fifty words or less, so try to get to the heart of who you are and exclude unnecessary details. Don't worry if your statement doesn't mirror someone else's—every statement is different because no two people are the same (Ramsey Solutions 2021).

Below are examples of mission statements:

To be a teacher. And to be known for inspiring my students to be more than they thought they could be.

—OPRAH WINFREY

To have fun in [my] journey through life and learn from [my] mistakes.

—SIR RICHARD BRANSON, FOUNDER OF THE VIRGIN GROUP

To create content that educates, informs, and inspires.

—PUBLIC BROADCASTING SYSTEM (PBS)

(Ramsey Solutions 2021).

YOUR PURPOSE

Your purpose incorporates elements of both a vision and a mission statement. Personal purpose statements encompass one's key values, major passions, and outstanding talents, as well as give a hint at the expected outcome.

Purpose statements should be concise, clear, realistic, and inspiring.

Here are some thought starter questions to help you create your purpose:

- Values: What do I believe? What do I value? What is important to me?

- Passions: What do I love to do? What am I passionate about?

- Talents: What are my superpowers? What am I best at doing or being?

- Results: How do I want to live my life? What will be my legacy?

Here are some examples of purpose statements (Hicks, n.d.):

Teacher: "To instill in students the joy of learning."

Teacher: "Broaden the possibility horizons of my students."

Chef: "Prepare food that is healthy, tasty, pleasing to the eye, and enjoyable."

Restaurant owner: "Create remarkable and memorable experiences for our customers."

Software engineer: "Develop software that makes planning for everyday tasks easier."

Financial planner: "Help people fulfill their financial promises."

Performance Coach: "Bring out the best in others."

Purpose: *Ikigai*

A great tool to help you find your purpose is the *ikigai.* Ikigai is your reason or purpose for life.

According to the Japanese, everyone has an ikigai. Some have found it, and others are still looking, though they carry it with them. Ikigai is a combination of the Japanese words *iki* (生き), which translates to "life," and *gai* (甲斐), which is useful in describing value or worth. Ikigai is all about finding joy in life through purpose. The origin of the word ikigai goes back to the Heian period (794 to 1185) (Mitsuhashi 2017).

Our ikigai is inside each of us, and finding it requires a patient and continuous search.

Some of the longest-living citizens in the world live in Japan. Author Dan Buettner believes ikigai plays a role in that longevity due to its focus on purpose in life, doing what you love, and the responsibility of what the world needs.

The ikigai focuses on the intersection of four main questions (Kenny 2019).

- What does the world need?
- What can you get paid for?
- What are you good at?
- What do you love?

The answer to these ikigai questions changes over time, so it requires periodic updates and reflection. You can view each of the four questions as concentric circles. You want to reflect and act such that you are either waking up and operating at the center of the four concentric circles or moving yourself closer to the center. This center is where you maximize all four areas and are at your *purpose.*

MY PERSONAL IKIGAI

In my personal journey, all these areas have changed over time.

From a love perspective, I love technology and its exponential impact on the world. I love investing in companies that are leveraging these technologies. I also love building relationships and networking,

From a paid perspective, I know I can get paid well for investing in companies leveraging disruptive technologies. I currently have invested in two unicorns. Unicorns are companies that made it to over one billion in valuation. In addition, I have ten unicorns in the stable. The stable is my term for start-up companies with $100 million in revenue and projected to double in revenue year over year for the next three to five years. I can also receive good income for services, speaking, and coaching I can provide around networking and technology disruption coaching.

From a good perspective, I am good at networking, investing in early stage companies, speaking, and teaching about networking.

From a needs perspective, the world needs innovation and technological advancement for good and needs more people building better relationships to accomplish their goals.

While reflecting on this over time, I decided I would retire from my managing director role at Accenture in January of 2023 to pursue this ikigai—my purpose. This book and sharing these experiences to help my readers are part of that.

PURPOSE: SIMON SINEK WHAT IS YOUR WHY

Another tool to help you find your purpose is from leading author Simon Sinek on finding your *why*.

He describes this story to find your why in a YouTube video. In the video, Simon recommends finding a friend, not a family member, and asking them, "Why are we friends?" He mentions that it is a difficult question because it is hard to put feelings into words. After listening intently to the answer, Simon mentions asking, "What specifically is it about me that makes me your friend?" This is also difficult to answer, and Simon recommends not helping them. By taking your friend through this line of questioning and listening to them, in Simon's words, "They will put into words the value you have in their life, and you will have the emotional reaction of either relative tears, or you will get goosebumps. This puts you in the ballpark. *This is where your Why lives.*"

If you do this with multiple friends, they will say similar things, which can help solidify and reinforce your why. Your why is the thing you give to the world, and among your closest and best friends is the space you fill in their lives (Sinek 2021).

YOUR PERSONAL CORE VALUES: CHARACTERISTICS

Dr. Tomi White Bryan is the leader behind Tomi Llama, which focuses on helping people find their purpose, personal values, and happiness. She is a systems thinker, using a systems perspective to guide individuals, teams, and organizations to a more balanced way of being. She helps people find their purpose and live it in meaningful ways. She shares lots of content, perspectives, and tools on personal core values on her website (TomiLlama.com).

On her website, it states: "Personal core values are personal ideals or principles that you use to live your life, make decisions, and focus your attention."

There are a couple of characteristics that define your core values. They should be things you:

- Consider important and essential;
- Feel are worth seeking; and
- Hold most dear in the world.

These personal core values are unique to you and not influenced by others or what is going on in the world. They help you live each day as your authentic self and help you live your purpose.

Some examples include family, freedom, authenticity, and health, among others. You can find a sample list of core values as well as a worksheet to more deeply understand your values and their impacts on her website, TomiLlama.com (Bryan, n.d.).

PERSONAL CORE VALUES: SEVEN RULES FOR SELF-DISCOVERY

Another leader who not only lives his personal values but shares them regularly on social media is Henri Pierre-Jacques, managing partner at Harlem Capital. Founded in 2015, Harlem Capital is one of the nation's fastest-growing venture capital firms. Via a tweet, he succinctly summarizes the self-discovery questions that will help you find your personal core values. These questions are:

1. What do we want most?

2. What do we think about most?

3. How do we use our money?

4. What do we do with our leisure time?

5. What company do we enjoy?

6. Who and what do we admire?

7. What do we laugh at?

Answer these seven questions to help find your values (@hpierrejacques 2021).

YOUR SWOT

The SWOT (strengths, weaknesses, opportunities, threats) model derived in the 1960s and early '70s by Albert Humphry at Stanford Research Institute (SRI). It is a tool developed to impact business strategy, but it can also apply to individuals pursuing goals and objectives (British Library, n.d.).

You can break up the SWOT model into two major subcomponents.

Internal factors

- Strengths

- Weaknesses

External factors

- Opportunities

- Threats

INTERNAL FACTORS

Strengths and weaknesses: There are things at which we are good and bad. These could be subject matter, athletic ability, talents, or personal attributes. Determining your strengths and weaknesses can come from internal introspection or simply asking people who know you well.

Strengths: Your Value Toolkit

What value do you bring to the table for any relationship?

As we look to build relationships, we need a deep understanding of the assets and value we can bring. These are the value tools within your *value toolkit.*

Below are some example areas of value or value tools you can bring to an individual or group as part of enhancing a relationship:

- Money
- Resources
- Information and insights
- Relationships
- Digital followers
- Experience
- Organizational power
- Your time to help them and volunteer

If you have minimal value tools within your toolkit you can bring to a relationship, that will limit you in growing and strengthening your network. If this is the case, the last bullet point, your time to help them, can be something of immense value, as people with goals appreciate people who are willing to help them.

STRENGTHS FINDER

There are lots of tools to discover your strengths. These include the Myers-Briggs Personality Test, free VIA Assessments, Leadership Circle Profile, Emergenetics, NeuroColor, and many more (Forbes Coaches Council 2018).

One of the more popular tools is Gallup's CliftonStrengths Assessment, where you answer 177 questions, and it produces a report listing your strengths across thirty-four dimensions, highlighting the top five strengths to focus on. You can find the website here:
https://www.gallup.com/cliftonstrengths/en/252137/home.aspx

EXTERNAL FACTORS

Opportunities and threats: These are areas considering your environment that you have minimal to zero control over but impact you. Opportunities are areas where you are not in now but can give you another way to accomplish your goals. Threats are things that can deter you from your mission and goals.

Some examples of opportunity and threat areas include:

- Macro-economy
- External event funding (coming in or going out)

- Culture
- New coworkers, competitors, and bosses
- Laws and regulations
- Pandemics
- Other

Once you have developed your SWOT you can leverage these analysis strategies:

- **Strength-opportunity strategies**—Leverage your strengths to maximize opportunities.
- **Strength-threats strategies**—Leverage your strengths to minimize threats.
- **Weakness-opportunity strategies**—Minimize your weaknesses to maximize opportunities.
- **Weakness-threats strategies**—Minimize your weaknesses to minimize threats.

Below are some questions to further help you develop your SWOT

- What am I good at?
- What do other people tell me I am good at?

- What am I not good at?
- What do people tell me I am not good at?
- Where am I strong and weak on my CliftonStrengths assessment?
- What are external factors I can leverage as opportunities?
- What are external factors that could be threats?

YOUR HAPPINESS

What makes you happy? It is a deep question and, for me, not an easy one to answer. This is another dimension to look at to understand yourself deeply.

And as it relates to networking, who wants to associate with or network with miserable, low-energy people? Happy people attract people, and as the center of their networks, they make their networks stronger and happier.

Being happy is also likely to increase your lifespan. Laura Carstensen, a lifespan developmental psychologist at Stanford University in Palo Alto, California, published research in the journal *Psychology and Aging* around a study of older people in the San Francisco Bay Area.

The study recorded their emotions five times a day for a week, then followed them for many years. For 111 people, she found that happier people lived longer than people who experienced more negative emotions (Fields 2011).

Happy people create and exude a force of power and attraction in their network.

Your Happiness: Tony Robbins on Happiness

Tony Robbins is an American author, coach, speaker, and philanthropist. Around the world, people know him for his seminars and self-help books. In an interview with Tony Robbins on the *We Study Billionaires* podcast, episode 505, Tony mentions the person who changed his life was his original mentor, Jim Rohn. "And he really taught me something interesting. You just got to put happiness first," Tony said.

So how do you ensure you are happy?

It's not money or fame. Tony said, "How many people have you seen who are incredibly wealthy who've taken their life just in the last few years alone?" He went on to discuss how you can think of fashion designers, hosts from CNN, and great comedians who have been taken away. Tony said, "You don't need a lot of homework to see that money doesn't make you happy."

Tony has interviewed more than fifty of the most successful billionaire titans of finance and said there were only a handful who appeared truly and consistently happy. Tony clarified, "I don't mean fake happy. I mean living in a state of gratitude, appreciation, and being able to find meaning."

In Tony's interviews and research, he found that having a meaningful life makes people happy. Tony said, "A meaningful life doesn't mean you're happy every moment. It means you have a sense that you're growing and you're giving.

"There are only two rules in the universe that seem immutable to me. They're not my rules. I just look around. Everything in the universe grows or dies. And everything in the universe contributes toward, or evolution eventually eliminates," Tony said (Green, n.d.).

When I reflect on my life, the moments where I am most happy is when I give money to charities, time to organizations, projects at work, or parenting kids. I also look back at all the milestones of knowledge and growth and how that also has made me happy.

Your Happiness: Arthur C. Brooks

Another way to look at happiness is from Arthur C. Brooks. Arthur teaches about happiness at Harvard and writes a regular column in the *Atlantic* magazine. In an article in the *Atlantic*, Arthur discusses his story about making a bucket list of things he hoped to achieve and that he thought would make him happy and satisfied. He found that nine years after making this list, he accomplished the items, but he stated: "But none of that had brought me the lasting joy I'd envisioned." He went on to describe neuroscience behind this constant desire for us to want more.

He also describes his research into Buddhism and Buddha's first noble truth: life is suffering—*duhkha* in Sanskrit, also translated as dissatisfaction—and that the cause of this suffering is craving, desire, and attachment to worldly things. Based on this research, he then discussed his own transformation to commit to stop trying to add more and more but instead start taking things away.

He then summarizes the whole article in one simple equation:

Satisfaction = What you have / What you want

There is a lot of focus on the top (what you have) and gathering more and more. His big takeaway was to focus on the "what you want" portion. "The big lever is our wants." He said, "By managing what we want instead of what we have, we give ourselves a chance to lead more satisfying lives" (Brooks 2022).

EXAMPLE OF A LEADER WHO PULLS IT ALL TOGETHER

Guillermo Diaz, former chief information officer at Cisco Systems and CEO of Conectado, is a very solid and focused leader who spends a lot of time on self-reflection. In my interview with him, he discussed that he created his own personal compass based on several of these self-assessment components. This compass helps guide his life and gives him direction. It is a simple graphical model that one can use to visualize the relevant self-assessment areas.

His purpose:
Accelerating access to opportunities that improve the lives of the underrepresented.

His passion:
Always remember where we came from: imagine the future.

His platform:
The digital community *metaverse* for opportunities: digital and cultural knowledge to visualize safer, simpler, and sustainable connections.

His perspective:
You can be what you can see: knowledge, experiences, and grit.

Additionally, one thing he does that I admire is at the end of each year, he looks at the next year and comes up with a word to describe what that year is going to mean for him and lives it. It is a word he focuses on every day.

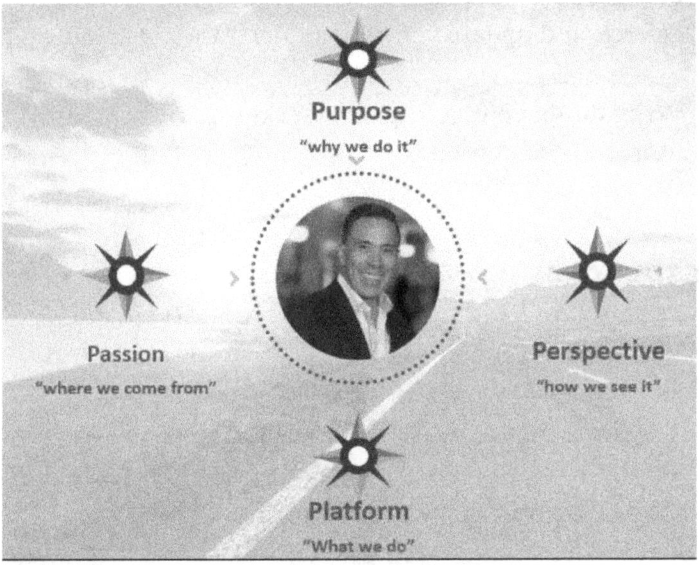

SUMMARY

These areas of self-understanding are interrelated and change over time. I highly recommend setting aside some daily or weekly time to evaluate all of these and update them as life occurs and each area evolves. People who are achieving networking excellence deeply understand themselves to provide strength and focus to their relationships.

EXERCISE:

- Write down your vision, mission, purpose, ikigai, goals, SWOT, value, and what makes you happy.
- Conduct a CliftonStrengths Assessment.
- Perform a Myers-Briggs Test.
- Schedule periodic time in your calendar to review, reflect, and update your self-understanding areas.
- Write down your strengths, weaknesses, opportunities, and threats.

RESOURCES:

- *Vernon Can Read* by Annette Gordon-Reed and Vernon Jordan
- *A Message from Garcia* by Charles P. Garcia
- *Purpose Driven Life* by Rick Warren
- *The 7 Habits of Highly Effective People* by Steven Covey
- *48 Days to the Work You Love* by Dan Miller
- *The Blue Zones* by Dan Buettner
- *Emotional Intelligence 3.0: How to Stop Playing Small in a Really Big Universe* by Dr. Tomi Bryan

- *Ikigai: The Japanese Secret to a Long and Happy Life* by Hector Garcia

- *Find Your Why* by Simon Sinek

- *From Strength to Strength* by Arthur C. Brooks

Myers-Briggs (Source: https://www.myersbriggs.org/my-mbti-personality-type/mbti-basics/)

CliftonStrengths Gallup—The assessment takes about one hour to complete, and you will see 177 paired statements. From each of these statements, you can choose which ones best describe you. Once you complete the assessment, you will get a report that identifies and ranks all your strengths. Here is a sample of the output: https://www.gallup.com/file/cliftonstrengths/en/260807/CliftonStrengths_34_Report.pdf (CliftonStrengths, n.d.).

STEP 2

HAVE SMART GOALS

It always seems impossible until it's done.

—NELSON MANDELA

"If I don't know where you want to go, how can I help you get there?"

This is typically my response to the many people I mentor after hearing their typical answer to my common question, "What are your goals?" The answers I get back are very telling in their depth and precision. But once the answers come in, my mind goes to work on how my network, experience, value toolkit, resources, and strategies can help them. A disciplined approach to goals is the main ingredient for not only successful people but for people who achieve networking excellence.

Throughout my life, I have heard about the importance of goal setting. However, in all that discussion of how important it was, no one discussed how to follow through on those goals effectively. I could accomplish many goals but had no discipline about setting or focusing on them. As I looked at how I allocated my time across many years, I don't regret anything, but I could have been more deliberate on how I spent my time focused on tasks and the discipline of goal setting. That additional and deeper focus on goal setting could have put me on a different trajectory and helped me accomplish more.

All these thoughts around goal setting came together for me in the early 2000s. I was obtaining my masters in business administration (MBA) degree at Notre Dame Mendoza School of Business and listening to Tom Mendoza, benefactor of Notre Dame's Mendoza School of Business and member of the board of directors Varonis and VAST Data, and other successful leaders like Charles P Garcia, Managing Partner at R360 and author of the book *A Message from Garcia*. I heard over and over how very successful people are very disciplined about goals and goal setting.

As I did more research on goals, I came across several books, *Think and Grow Rich* by Napolean Hill and *The Power of Positive Thinking* by Dr. Norman Vincent Peale, that reinforce and expand on these goal-setting principles.

With all these inputs, I then executed a disciplined plan and saw amazing results.

Create SMART Goals

The first model I focused on was setting SMART goals. The smart goal concept developed in 1981 via a paper titled "There's a SMART Way to Write Management's Goals and Objectives" by George T. Doran, a consultant and former director of corporate planning for Washington Water Power Company (Haughey 2014). I did not see an accelerated change in my goal accomplishment until I started using SMART goals, which is why I lead and love this model.

S—Specific: Include the details of what you want to accomplish.

M—Measurable: You should be able to measure your progress and accurately determine whether you've accomplished your goal.

A—Attainable: Your goal should be one that can be attained within a reasonable time. It should be within reach and not too difficult to obtain.

R—Realistic: A realistic goal is one you can reach given your current mindset, motivation level, timeframe, skills, and abilities. Realistic goals help you identify not only what you want but also what you can achieve (Indeed Editorial Team 2022).

T—Time bound: Your goals should have a date by which you wish to accomplish them with mini goals along the way measured in days or weeks (Haughey 2014).

Make Sure to Add Stretch to Your SMART Goals

We underestimate what we can accomplish and what we can do. For example, in the early 1990s, while in college, my goal was to make $40,000 a year and have a home and a car, and I would be happy for life. Forty-thousand dollars was more than my mother and father made combined. Forty-thousand dollars is what the above-average engineer made at the time. I have been fortunate to have earned well over that annual amount.

I also ran the Chicago Marathon in 1998. When I first thought about running eight miles, let alone twenty-six miles, it was daunting, and I thought there was no way I could do this. Little by little, with training and mini goals along the way, it amazed me what I accomplished. In addition to the three to six-mile runs several days a week, long runs occurred on Sundays as part of the training that progressed weekly from six to eight to twelve to fourteen to sixteen to twenty miles each week. After each long run, I reached a new distance milestone, providing me with a strong feeling of accomplishment. I finished the marathon in October of 1998, and the milestones and accomplishments along the way made it more rewarding.

To compensate for this limitation we put on ourselves, we should stretch ourselves, our thinking, and our goals. Stretch goals are ambitious, bold, and scary and cause our minds to think of new ways to obtain them.

Ted Turner, the successful American entrepreneur who founded TBS and the Cable News Network (CNN), the first twenty-four-hour global cable news channel, encouraged others to stretch themselves.

You should set goals beyond your reach so you always have something to live for.

—TED TURNER

Although your goal should be attainable, you should not be afraid to set a stretch goal. You will be amazed at what you can accomplish when you stretch yourself.

STRETCH GOAL SETTING TONY ROBBINS:
Tony Robbins focuses on big stretch goals in terms of contribution to philanthropy.

- He has executed a goal to provide fresh water to a million people a day in India.
- He owns a plane and knows this has a carbon footprint of about 3,000 trees. He has committed to planting one hundred million trees and is at about seventy-one million (as of 2022).
- He sees hunger as one of the world's biggest challenges. He has given out around a billion meals. He has a one billion meal challenge for sustainability he is doing with the XPRIZE with a $20 million prize to figure out how to solve this on a world level.

He loves the challenge and loves making extraordinary things. As it relates to what he loves most, Tony says it is "seeing the impact on people's lives and then seeing that I can utilize those resources to do things that can shift the quality of life for people I don't even know" (Greene, n.d.).

Charlie Garcia on Stretch Goals

In his book *A Message from Garcia*, Charles P. Garcia has a specific message around goal setting and stretch goals that have positively impacted me and my career.

> It is important to set goals. Don't set goals that are so low that they are easy to reach. Set your goals high

enough so that they require you to work and to stretch yourself. This is how you improve and get better at doing certain things. Coasting down the hill is fun, but riding up along the ridge gives you the best view of all, and to reach it requires work. Regardless of your goals, the one ingredient that will give you the drive to achieve them is Ganas. Nothing is impossible if you're burning with Ganas. The fire in the belly, the passion you will need to remain steadfast in the pursuit of your dreams. Ganas will help you and will keep you focused when the going gets tough. This passion will help you attract the right people to achieve your dreams and will help you overcome the most challenging obstacles (Garcia 2003, 53).

Writing Down Your SMART Goals

SECRET SAUCE OF GOAL SETTING

According to Tech21Century.com, we receive the equivalent of thirty-four gigabytes of information daily (Andrea, n.d.). To filter this information and prevent us from becoming overloaded, we have the reticular activating system (RAS) in our brain, and this acts as the gatekeeper. The reticular activating system are the nerves in our brain that help us filter out unnecessary information and enables the necessary and important items to come through (Van Schneider 2017). The RAS is responsible for our wakefulness, our ability to focus, our fight-flight response, and how we perceive the world. It can control what we perceive in our consciousness and is essentially a gatekeeper of information.

Therefore, the RAS is important for goal setting, as you can train your brain to filter out things that are not relevant to your goals and increase your brain's focus.

Now, here is the secret sauce. Write, reflect, and strategize on these SMART goals daily! By focusing on daily reflection, you program your brain's RAS to help you filter out things that don't align with your goals and spot more opportunities that do align. The act of writing these goals down and reflecting on them sharpens the filter of your RAS.

While strategizing, it is important to visualize and see yourself accomplishing these goals. This strategizing should include leveraging all your senses on what it would look like when you accomplish this goal, like how the environment would smell, the touches of people shaking your hand, and so on (Thomas, n.d.).

Through mentoring relationships and interaction with many individuals throughout my career, I believe very few people have goals. Those few who have goals have them in their head and are not well thought out. The next level of people has their goals written down, but they likely sit on a desk gathering dust or are not looked at frequently enough to impact their RAS. The true goal warriors and those who achieve networking excellence have their goals written down and reflect and strategize upon them daily. They look at each day and figure out the best way they will use and optimize the hours to accomplish their objectives (or move them closer to their goals), see if there are any synergies or ways to accomplish their tasks more efficiently, and help others in their network accomplish their goals. They look at short-term tactical things and long-term strategic things they can do.

STEVE HARVEY ON WRITING DOWN GOALS

On TV host Steve Harvey's YouTube channel, Steve mentions a major reason people don't have what they want is they don't have it written down. Steve says, "This is a very, very important piece to success. It's a principle of success." Steve mentions he doesn't know anybody wealthy who does not have these items they want written on a piece of paper. Steve recommends creating a vision board with your ambitions written down (Harvey 2019).

To emphasize how important writing things down are, Steve even discussed a scripture verse from the Bible, Habakkuk 2:2. Steve paraphrases it and says, "Write the vision and make it plain so that he who reads it will run to it. And even though it terry (which means that it may take a long time), wait, for surely it will come at an appointed time" (Harvey 2019).

GOAL SETTING FROM TOM MENDOZA, FORMER PRESIDENT AND VICE CHAIR OF NETAPP AND BENEFACTOR OF NOTRE DAME'S MENDOZA SCHOOL OF BUSINESS

(Summarized from article: https://www.forbes.com/sites/netapp/2015/02/11/90-day-goals/?sh=33fde8e66260)

Tom Mendoza, former vice chair and president of NetApp and benefactor of the Mendoza School of Business of Notre Dame, shared his thoughts on goal setting around 2004, having a profound impact on me and others. It can work for you. He wrote a blog post for *Forbes* online in 2015 that details his approach to goal setting entitled "90-Day Goals Changed My Life: Here's My System."

Although I believe you should have ninety-day goals and goals that should be one, three, five, and ten years out, Tom Mendoza's goal focus centers around ninety days because Tom believes anything longer than that will cause procrastination. "You have to set a goal with a time limit that causes you to take action *today*," Tom says.

Tom also focuses on how you define the goals. "The key to setting a goal for anything is to make them time bound, measurable, and written," he states.

In the *Forbes* article, it states that 90 percent of high-performing people:

- set *specific* goals—with outcomes,
- set a *deadline* for their goals, and
- *write them down.*

Tom Mendoza, through his life experience and results, believes goals should be set at the beginning of each quarter, and they should include three professional goals and three personal goals.

PERSONAL GOALS

Tom mentions his personal goals are truly *personal,* and you shouldn't share these with anyone.

As you set the goal, you should ask yourself: *What can I accomplish over the next ninety days that will make me feel good about myself?*

This is important because when you feel good about yourself, you carry yourself differently, creating a personal feedback loop that changes you.

PROFESSIONAL GOALS

Professional goals center around the question, "What I can achieve that impacts my business or profession?" You share these goals with the boss and the people you serve. These are time bound and measurable. For validation, Tom says, "I ask my boss and my team how they'd feel if I were to achieve the goals over the next ninety days. Most times, they feel good about my choices, but at times I get great feedback about the goals." The feedback is great because you can adjust *before* you begin working on them.

FINALIZE YOUR GOALS

Step 1—Set the goals aside for a day.

Step 2—Review your goals and ask yourself if you would be proud if you achieved these goals. After this reflection, you might tweak it a little higher to stretch yourself. Tom says, "You are not setting these goals to make others proud. You're doing this to make *yourself* proud. Once you realize this, it's like a breakthrough in your mind."

Step 3—You need to make these goals your highest priority and include the time in your schedule. It does not move off your agenda because it is the most important thing of the day.

END OF NINETY DAYS

At the end of ninety days, you can assess your progress and how you feel. It is not a failure if you don't meet all your goals. Tom said, "The first time I did this, I hit four of the six goals. But I was ecstatic: I'd aimed at something and made tremendous progress. Then came the realization that I could aim higher."

And you'll realize you can do more. You'll expect more of yourself, as will others, as you begin your next ninety days and repeat the process of shooting for higher goals. For example, I set relationship and financial goals I have been able to build on and grow. After accomplishing a specific milestone, I move on to the next one.

TOM MENDOZA GOAL SETTING SUMMARY

Tom executed this system around goals for more than twenty-five years. This system has worked for Tom, many others, and me, and it can work for you (Mendoza 2015).

As soon as I heard Tom mention this technique, I began to put his approach into action. The ninety-day check-in and deadline focus on goals impact me the most. These goals continue to build off each other to accomplish my longer-term goals.

Goal Importance to Networking Excellence

You can network with many people in this world, and there is no limit. However, you don't have unlimited time.

In fact, a LinkedIn survey discovered that about 49 percent of participants said they didn't have enough time to network (LinkedIn Corporate Communications 2017).

You want to network with people who align with your goals, purpose, mission, and ikigai.

The goals you set help focus your time and energy on networking so that you can maximize the use of your precious time.

NETWORKING AND GOALS

In my interview with Marcelo De Santis, the chief digital officer at ThoughtWorks, he mentioned an old proverb: If you want to go fast, go alone. If you want to go farther, go with others. Marcelo said, "I like the quote because the quote implies you have a destination. Goals help anchor you to this destination with others or your network to help you get there."

Persevere through Adversity to Achieve Your Goals

Life has many ups and downs. As you set your goals, there will likely be obstacles, roadblocks, and reroutes you will need to take to achieve your goals. Steve Harvey has a story that helps highlight this point.

When Steve Harvey was ten years old, being on TV was his goal. He had a stuttering problem as a youth and an unsupportive teacher. One day his teacher asked the class what profession they wanted when they grew up. Steve said his goal was to be on TV. The teacher asked him, "Why did you write this on your paper?" Steve listened but couldn't say anything due to his stuttering. The teacher said, "Who in the school has ever been on TV?" Steve tries to get a word out but stutters. The teacher then said, "Who in your family has ever been on TV?" The teacher finally mentioned to

Steve, "With your stuttering, how are they ever going to put somebody like you on TV?"

As Steve got older, adversity continued. He flunked out of school. He got divorced multiple times and was homeless for three years. But since he was ten years old, he had a laser-like goal to appear on TV.

As his life story continues, it was a Thursday night in 1991, and he lived out of his car in Pensacola, Florida, with $35 to his name. Steve then said a prayer asking God to make his goal and dream come true of being on TV.

He was going to call his dad but first decided to punch in a code and call his answering machine to get his messages. The recording said, "Hey Steve, this is Chuck Sutton with *Showtime at the Apollo.* We saw a tape of you. You're very funny. If you could get here Sunday night, we'd love to put you on television. Call me back. Let me know if you can make it."

He had no money for a flight to New York, making him sad and depressed. He wanted to give up, as being on TV was his goal. As he checked the message to confirm the Apollo Sunday date, a voicemail came in, and he got a call from Comedy Caravan comedy club in Jacksonville asking if he could perform and make $150 for Friday night. He drove three hours from Pensacola, Florida, and had a great performance. Then they asked him to perform a second night and ended up finding a $99 flight to New York from Jacksonville so that he could be on *Showtime at the Apollo.*

He arrives in New York on Sunday, and that evening while waiting to come on the show, some major stars begin to enter the Apollo. D.L. Hughley entered first. The second person to come in was a comedian named Dwayne "The Rock" Johnson. Then comes Jamie Foxx. They did not know each other. It was 1991, and none of them were famous at that time. As they handed out the lineup, Steve saw he was last. They were all very nervous, as the Apollo was a tough audience. The audience booed all three acts before Steve, making him even more nervous.

So, Steve walks out on stage and tells this joke about boxing legend Mike Tyson and how he got in a fight in Harlem with this heavyweight boxer named Mitch Green. Steve wrote this joke such that Mitch's eye starts talking, and as the punch from Mike Tyson came, the eye started screaming. Steve said, "They went crazy. They lost it, and I got a standing ovation."

Steve's successful performance provided a key enabler for him to become the host of Apollo. He did it for eight years, making it the longest host in *Showtime at the Apollo* history. Steve persevered through adversity to achieve his goal.

He said he sends his grade school teacher a TV every year to make sure he can see him on TV (Harvey 2019).

USE SYMBOLS TO VISUALIZE YOUR GOAL(S)

Years ago, Jim Carrey set a goal to become a movie star and sign a deal worth $12 million. To keep himself focused on the goal, he wrote himself a check for $12 million and put it in his wallet as a symbol he could look at regularly. He gave up stand-up comedy and went on the show *In Living Color.* His career continued to progress in the movie industry with several successful films. Jim Carrey realized his goal when he starred as the Joker in *Batman Forever* and made $12 million (Garcia 2003, 146).

In 1970, actor Bruce Lee wrote himself a letter predicting he would be the best-known Asian movie star in the United States by 1980 and would have earned $10 million by that time. Although Lee's life ended tragically as a young man, he did reach his goal before he died (Garcia 2003, 146).

Both Jim Carrey's check and Bruce Lee's letters are examples of useful symbols to help you accomplish your goals.

HUSTLE FOR YOUR GOALS

American singer and songwriter Taylor Swift is a huge superstar today. When she started, she really wasn't someone you could have predicted would succeed in this way. She was fourteen years old and in country music. All those things did not make her destined to become a global superstar.

Rick Barker, who was Taylor's first manager, attributes her success to hustle. When Taylor was young, she came to him and said, "I want a gold record." This is an example of a pretty big stretch goal. Rick told her she would have to sell 500,000 albums to meet this goal. Rick mentioned to Taylor that for her to sell that many albums, she would have to meet, hug, and shake hands with 500,000 people. Taylor made this happen, and she would play anywhere. She would play at places like church picnics, county fairs, and malls. She would do all those things behind the scenes and hustle. She leveraged Myspace and social media and spent a lot of time getting to know her fans and connecting with them (Barker 2020; Wilson 2020).

In the early days, Taylor would do these after-show meet and greets to connect with fans, and these would be three and three-and-a-half-hour sessions. Richard says, "She had the choice, just like every artist, to stay back on the bus and hang out with everybody and talk about the show, but instead, she wanted to spend as much time with her fans."

One time on the bus after losing an award, Taylor asked, "Rick, what is the award based on sales?"

Rick said, "It is the Billboard Music Award."

She said, "Then I want to win a Billboard Music Award. I want to love on all these fans so much and outsell everyone." She went out that year, outsold everyone, and won the Billboard Music Award. Her focus has been more on her fans than on sales, and her hustle has enabled her to accomplish so many goals (Barker 2020).

STAY CURIOUS IN GOAL SETTING AND APPROACH

David Wieland is a very successful entrepreneur and investor. He has goals, but they are not as structured. His approach to personal goals is more about constantly staying curious and learning about new things. David said, "This aligns with my professional role, which is to take a lot of information from many different areas of life, synthesize those into some general themes and frameworks, and then apply those to decisions and investments."

You now have a deep understanding of yourself and where you are going. You have created the strength at the center of your network and have a list of SMART goals that stretch you. This part of the foundation is in place and provides input into another key component of the networking excellence foundation—your brand.

EXERCISE:

- Write down your SMART goals.
- Create a periodic time where you review these actions you will take to accomplish to move closer to the goal.
- Track the time you spend each day and the time you spend doing things that don't align with your goals.

RESOURCES:

Tom Mendoza, https://www.forbes.com/sites/netapp/2015/02/11/90-day-goals/?sh=9838fe162602

- *A Message from Garcia* by Charlie Garcia
- *Unshakeable* by Tony Robbins
- *Think and Grow Rich* by Napoleon Hill
- *Power of Positive Thinking* by Dr. Norman Vincent Peale
- *It Works* by R. H. J.
- *Wisdom of the Unconscious Mind* by John K Williams

STEP 3

DEFINE AND REFINE YOUR BRAND

Personal branding is about managing your name—even if you don't own a business—in a world of misinformation, disinformation, and semi-permanent Google records.

—TIM FERRISS

When Steve Jobs returned to Apple, rejoining as its CEO in 1997, he gave a passionate speech about branding and Apple's image.

Steve said, "This is a very complicated world. It's a very noisy world. And we're not gonna get a chance to get people to remember much about us."

Steve mentions the importance of being very clear on what we want people to know about us as it relates to branding. He said, "Apple, fortunately, is one of the half a dozen best brands in the whole world, right up there with Nike, Disney, Coke, and Sony."

He mentions that great brands need investment and care if they are going to retain relevance and vitality. Steve discussed how prior to launching the branding and marketing around the famous "Think Different" commercial that Apple had to do a bit of self-assessment.

Steve said, "Our customers want to know who Apple is and what we stand for. Where do we fit in this world?"

Steve continued, "Apple, at the core, its core value is that we believe that people with passion can change the world for the best. That's what we believe. Those people who are crazy enough to think they can change the world are the ones who actually do."

This self-assessment, focus on values, and focus on the goals Apple wanted to accomplish led to not only a successful branding and marketing campaign but also the start of a run that helped Apple become one of the best companies in human history (Jobs 1997).

As you deeply understand yourself, your values, and your goals, you can now ensure you are building a brand to help accelerate your dreams. Your brand will signal to the world and, more importantly, to your network what you stand for and what your values are.

A brand is an intangible marketing or business concept that helps people identify a company, product, or individual. People often confuse brands with things like logos, slogans, or other recognizable marks, which are marketing tools that help promote goods and services. The best way to think of a brand of an individual or leader is to think of statements useful to describe them (Kenton 2022). I view these words as the current brand of that person.

Hanna Larsson, director of sales EMEA at Remote, details five good reasons why brand is important in her LinkedIn feed.

1. A personal brand stays with you regardless of where you work.

2. A personal brand makes it easier to create and maintain a powerful business network that will open doors for you.

3. A personal brand grows stronger over time and will unlock opportunities.

4. A strong personal brand is your safety net and power.

5. A personal brand will help you stand out from the crowd when you look for a new job.

She summarizes and mentions that you own your brand and navigate it (Larsson 2022).

As you think about your brand today, you should look at your current brand. As you reflect on your goals and where you want to be, you should also consider your future brand. Below are a couple of dimensions around brand self-understanding to help you.

- **Your Current Brand**
  - How do people perceive you and your image?
  - When they think of you, what are the top five words that come to their mind?

- **Your Desired Brand**
  - What do you want your brand to be? This is a derivative of all the self-understanding areas described earlier in the book, with a big focus on your vision and goals.

PICK THREE TO FIVE UNIQUE WORDS TO DESCRIBE YOUR BRAND

I interviewed Juan Carlos "JC" Gutierrez, head of solutions architecture and customer success—Latin America and Caribbean for Amazon Web Services and a former Oracle and PWC executive.

On branding, he said, "When I think about brands, I think about a quote from Ralph Waldo Emerson that goes something like, 'Who you are speaks so loudly, I can't hear anything you are saying.'" Juan emphasized being authentic and real with your brand and that your actions should align with this.

I then asked Juan how he goes about building his brand, and he said, "I work to keep my brand simple and authentic. When one is building their brand, they should start with three to five words and then expand the explanation of each as it relates to their brand." For Juan, his three are technology, global, and servant.

Below expands on each of his brand areas.

Technology—For technology, he has worked for world technology leaders and serves on a technology leadership board.

Global—From a global perspective, he has traveled the world with close to ten million airline miles and has three nationalities from three different countries spanning the US, South America, and Europe. He has run divisions in Latin America and worked at global firms.

Servant—From a servant perspective, Juan serves his customers and his team, serves on boards, and serves his community. He is also working on a book about servant leadership.

When I asked Juan if he could give me an example of somebody who he has really seen transform their brand, he mentioned Marilyn Ehrhardt, who was a former technology senior executive at Oracle and is now an executive coach and author of the book *In the Valley of the Shadows of Success: From Leaning In to Kneeling Down Women Are More Precious than Rubies.* She was a mentor to Juan, and she has changed her brand over time.

Juan said, "She changed her brand from being a corporate executive focused on climbing the corporate ladder, winning at all costs, to now kneeling down, serving, having a spiritual change, and having God at the center."

Juan describes how that change in brand requires a lot of courage. Juan said, "You can imagine the change. Her *why* and her values changed, and the people she works with, her network, and her brand have changed and are not the same."

Marilyn's story illustrates how changes in the foundational areas of self-assessment values and purpose can manifest in changes to goals and brand when building a foundation for networking excellence.

FILLING THE GAP BETWEEN THE CURRENT AND DESIRED BRAND

There will likely be a gap between your current brand and your desired brand. You can take actions to fill that gap. Below is a list of some that can get you closer to your desired brand.

- Communicating
- Speaking
- Posting on social media
- Social media profiles
- Associating with people who share your desired brand
- Execution and action

Here are some additional tips to consider as you build your brand (Pope 2020).

- **Be authentic**—Twenty percent of consumers have unfollowed a brand on social media because they thought the content was too corporate or not authentic enough.
- **Leverage video**—Sixty-four percent of consumers make a purchase after viewing a branded social video.
- **Leverage online**—Thirty-three percent of millennials, compared to 20 percent of Gen X and 6 percent of boomers, say things they see online influence their purchasing decisions.

- **Leverage Instagram**—Forty-three percent of consumers feel the urge to make a purchase after viewing an advertisement on Instagram.

GALE WILKINSON ON HER BRAND AND LEVERAGING SOCIAL MEDIA

Gale Wilkinson, founding director of IrishAngels, has leveraged social media to amplify her brand. In my interview with her, she said, "I tell my friends, especially in venture, we all have to be building our brands in the physical and digital world. I firmly believe this. I wish I would have thought about it much sooner."

Gale's social media outreach has helped her with connections and amplifying her brand. She mentioned that people would come up to her at events, introduce themselves, and tell her they saw and liked what she put online.

As an example of how she has built her brand and social media following, Gale started in August 2020 when she decided she would do one post a day. And at that time, she had about 3,000 followers on Twitter, and it took her two to three months to get into a groove. She remembers the first time one tweet went viral, and she said, "Oh my gosh, this is crazy. Because I am only on it for ten to twenty minutes a day."

That was the inflection point for Gale, who got to about 10,000 Twitter followers on July 4, 2021. And there was another inflection point for that. By the end of 2021, she had 25,000 followers. She is currently at around 40,000 followers, and you can follow her at @GaleforceVC. Gale says, "The fact that I picked a fun/

unique handle @GaleforceVC has helped me to grow my brand versus just my name 'GaleWilkinson' or something similar."

Being authentic to her brand is vital for Gale. She said, "I'm a builder. So, I talk about early stage company formation issues, like what's going on in the macro environment like how to raise money." Gale also talks about the future of work and about DEI (diversity, equity, and inclusion) within early stage venture. Gale also has a rule that her posts always have to be positive and helpful.

Gale's other rule for her brand is that it has to be something that came up today. Gale said, "So, like today, where the market is tanking, I tweeted about the uncertainty in the market and layoffs and all the stuff that's happening, and that's because people have been talking to me about that."

She continues, "If I'm in a founder conversation, and I teach something based on a question they have about a financial model, I might tweet it. So, I'm not sitting here being like, *Oh, what should I tweet today?* That's the wrong way to do it. It's authentic to what I'm already doing. And I think that has created momentum for me personally."

Gale summarizes her brand as a successful, very helpful, approachable early stage investor with an expertise in the future of work. She emphasized how approachability is very key for her.

MY PERSONAL BRAND

My desired personal brand has changed over my life. Currently, my focus is on three legs of a stool:

1. Technology disruption enabler
2. Unicorn investor
3. Networking excellence

These three legs of the stool support each other. For example, networking excellence helps me see and support the best companies, and networking with other investors helps me be a better unicorn investor. Also, technology disruption is the enabler for unicorn investments. As I communicate on social media, public events, and traditional media, I am putting more focus on these areas.

Your brand will help be the magnet by which people in your network and desired network will gravitate to you. By executing the foundational components of self-assessment and SMART goals, you ensure your brand has the right focus, and you are doing this in an optimal way. Now, it is time to power your networking excellence foundation with rituals and routines!

EXERCISE:

- Ask those close to you to provide five unique words that describe you.
- Ask those close to you what they think your brand is.
- Ask those close to you what they think your desired brand is or what it should be.
- Detail the current and desired channels you are using to amplify your brand.

RESOURCES:

- *Start with Why* by Simon Sinek
- *Reinventing You: Define Your Brand, Imagine Your Future* by Dorie Clark
- *Think and Grow Rich* by Napoleon Hill
- *Wisdom of the Unconscious Mind* by John K. Williams

STEP 4

EXECUTE DISCIPLINED RITUALS AND ROUTINES

Excellence is never an accident. It is always the result of high intention, sincere effort, and intelligent execution; it represents the wise choice of many alternatives—choice, not chance, determines your destiny... Excellence is a habit.

—ARISTOTLE

We all have twenty-four hours in a day. How many of those hours are consumed by rituals, routines, and habits?

Habits power about 40 percent of our daily lives (Macka 2019). This is great if the 40 percent are good habits. The challenge is that most of us have habits that don't align with our goals.

Daily rituals are important because they can help put habits around self-awareness, spiritual health, physical health, mental health, and your focus on your goals. With your SMART goals in place and written down, you can now leverage rituals and habits to help accelerate the accomplishment of these goals and be the strong center of your network.

Tony Robbins states on his website, "Habits put our brains on autopilot, freeing up our concentration for bigger things. They are the rhythm of our daily lives, the backdrop to everything else we do. Going for a morning run is a routine. Watching three hours of Netflix before bed while eating popcorn is also a routine. The difference is that one of these daily routine examples helps us feel energetic and productive, and the other depletes our energy" (Team Tony, n.d.).

Tony goes on to mention on his website that creating habits that last can take up to eighteen weeks. When you do the math, eighteen weeks is only 0.5 percent of the average American lifespan. It is such a small percentage of time to make such a big impact on better health, achievement, and fulfillment (Team Tony, n.d.).

ON HIGH ACHIEVERS AND RITUALS

Tony said in *Business Insider Magazine,* "High achievers provide ideal daily routine examples. There's a reason successful people all seem to work out, eat healthily, and practice mindfulness: these routines work. And you can make them work for you."

Here are some tips:

- Make it a must—Put it in your calendar and visualize yourself doing this daily. Don't let other things cause you to move it.

- Start Small—Start small and increase over time.

- Stay consistent—Don't start and stop. Stay focused and be consistent.

- Get the right tools—Track these in spreadsheets and leverage tools like Tony Robbins's Rapid Planning Method to map out your day and focus on the most productive tasks (Robins Research International, n.d.).

- Fuel up—Make sure you are eating healthy and have proper hydration.

- Meditate—Spend time to clear your mind and also reflect on making the habit a permanent behavior.

You can find these tips here: https://www.tonyrobbins.com/productivity-performance/making-a-daily-routine/ (Team Tony, n.d.).

In my interview with JC Gutierrez, he mentions that when he thinks about consistency and tools, he highly recommends organizing your time and leveraging your calendar. JC says, "I schedule my daily, weekly, monthly, quarterly, and annual rituals and important dates into my calendar. This helps me be efficient and disciplined."

Daily Rituals from IT Works

I also came across a great book called *It Works* by Roy Herbert Jarrett. The book is only twenty-eight pages long but is full of great content. The key message in this book is that you don't get what you want. You get what you subconsciously think you deserve, so you have to condition your mind and your rituals if you want to meet your goals.

The book recommends that you write down a list of all your goals. The book is less focused on the *how* to achieve the goals with the idea that if you want something bad enough then you continuously reflect on it. The how will eventually come to you. Although the book states this approach, I like both approaches together. Have a plan to achieve the goal you are working toward and continuously reflect on it, so it comes to you.

One of the book's lessons is to be as specific as possible as you write these goals. Direct your conscious mind to that which you desire. For example, if you have a certain desired income in mind, identify the exact dollar amount. If you have a sales record, list the specific sales goal and the detailed prospects and how much you plan to sell to each prospect.

Another lesson is that you can program your subconscious mind by looking at your results and training yourself. The subconscious mind is powerful and can give you what you desire.

Now that you have a list of these goals, you must do three things:

- You must read these goals in the morning, noon, and night every day.

- Think of these goals as much as possible throughout the day. The more you think about these goals, the more likely you will achieve them.

- You must keep these goals to yourself. This will help avoid any negativity from others that may discourage you along the way (Jarrett 1992).

I don't look at my goals three times a day, but this approach does have merits and might work for you. The key is using this approach to train your subconscious mind to focus on what you want and filter out items that are irrelevant.

Tony Robbins Daily Ritual

Looking at rituals for successful people and those who coach successful people on rituals is also important. Tony Robbins is a successful author, coach, speaker, and philanthropist. He has a morning ritual that can help shape your rituals. You can find the details on this website: https://www.businessinsider.com/tony-robbins-morning-routine-meditation-and-workout-2017-10.

He Spends Ten Minutes Meditating.

Robbins created a ten-minute daily exercise called priming based on techniques found in yoga and Buddhist mindfulness (Feloni 2017).

1. Meditation (one minute)

He begins by sitting straight with his eyes closed. He inhales deeply through his nostrils while simultaneously lifting his arms in a shoulder press motion, and then exhales forcefully through his nostrils while bringing his arms back to his body, palms up. He performs the breaths in quick succession. Robbins does this shoulder press and breathing three sets of thirty, with a brief break in between each set.

2. Express gratitude (three minutes)

He spends one minute on three things for which he is grateful. There are many things that one can be grateful for. You can look over the last day to see if something stands out or over the last year. You can be grateful for your health, the things you have, your family, and countless other items. Being grateful and appreciative will keep you in a high-energy state throughout the day

3. Experience connection (three minutes)

He imagines a light flowing in through his head and to the rest of his body, feeling as if the light is energizing and healing him. In this visualization, the light flows back up to his head and then flows outward to the rest of the world, reaching his loved ones as well as strangers.

4. Visualize success (four minutes)

He then spends a minute each imagining what it would feel like to accomplish three of his goals. He focuses on how these accomplishments not only benefit him but allow him to help others.

DAILY RITUALS (TONY ROBBINS)

Daily rituals help drive your goals, purpose, and happiness. Your daily rituals should also focus on caring about people, which helps improve your quality of life and the quality of your relationships. Your daily ritual should also focus on serving. Tony states in *The Investor's Podcast: Richer, Wiser, Happier*, "Did you know hero comes from the Latin word servo?" When we think about heroes, we think of large muscular type superheroes. True heroes serve and care about people, so please include this as part of your daily ritual. The serving part is vital to your network because you are serving to help them accomplish their goals (Green, n.d.).

Include Hunger in Your Daily Ritual

Tony has studied hundreds of world-class leaders, and in his view, the one thing that sets them apart from others is *hunger.*

Tony mentions in *The Investor's Podcast: Richer, Wiser, Happier,* "It's hunger that separates people. The hunger to grow. The hunger to give. The hunger to master. The hunger to go to another level." Tony references leaders like Marc Benioff at Salesforce, Ray Dalio, and specifically calls out Sir Richard Branson, who is more driven today in his sixties than he was at sixteen starting Virgin. He has that hunger to be more, do more, give more, share more, and not settle. Hunger is the factor because it'll get you to maximize everything else (Green, n.d.).

DEEP THINKING INTO DAILY RITUALS

In my interview with Marcelo De Santis, he discussed that incorporating deep thinking into daily habits and rituals is very important. Marcelo said, "If you talk to a Buddhist monk, they will always get back to what you are thinking right now."

He said, "According to Buddha, our thoughts are very powerful. They determine our mental states (such as happiness or sadness). These mental states impact our lives and the people around us. It is important to realize these thoughts and incorporate these into our daily rituals."

Marcelo said, "That is why a Buddhist monk will ask you, 'What do you think?'" Thinking is vital because:

1. What you think drives your actions; and

2. Your actions drive your results or outcomes.

So, if you want extraordinary results, you need to go back to extraordinary actions that come from extraordinary thinking.

Marcelo said that to improve your thinking for extraordinary results, you should include in your habits and rituals different points of view. Incorporating this can be difficult. Marcelo said, "Sometimes you feel triggered by different points of view because you want to defend your point of view. In my experience, different points of view on whatever you are thinking sharpens your thinking and improves the outcomes you desire."

Marcelo said that in Buddhism, they connect with others and give a lot of value to human connection.

Marcelo said, "One of my favorite concepts in Buddhism is metta: this word translates as *loving-kindness*, but its root meaning is *the nature of a friend*." Marcelo continues, "Metta is a very nourishing quality, and when we show it to others, we're also nourishing ourselves. This is a classic case of treating others as you would like others to treat you. Modern life expects us to be so up-together all the time: one blessing of friendships is that you should feel safe to show your failings, admit them, and still feel valued." My interview with Marcelo helped reinforce the incorporation of thinking and acts of kindness into rituals.

MEDITATION AS PART OF YOUR RITUALS

As you create your habits and rituals, you should consider incorporating meditation, as it can improve your thinking. Meditation can thicken the prefrontal cortex. This brain center manages higher-order brain functions, like increased awareness, concentration, and decision-making. Changes in the brain show that with meditation, higher-order functions become stronger while lower-order brain activities decrease. You have the power to train your brain via a meditation routine (Ask the Scientists 2022).

In my interview with engagement manager strategist Carlos Coto, he said, "Just like you need to reboot your computer to clear up memory, quirky processes, and random issues, the same thing needs to happen to the brain with meditation. Meditation recharges and refreshes the brain to perform at a higher level."

HAVING DOWNTIME AS PART OF YOUR DAILY RITUAL

In my interview with David Wieland, he said how he puts downtime as part of his daily ritual. It could be time for daydreaming, deep thinking, or meditation. David likes to carve out thirty minutes to go for a walk or sit and do nothing. David said, "I think the reason it's called daydreaming is that in the evenings, when you fall asleep, your brain is sort of clearing out the RAM and clearing out your short-term memory and categorizing the things that happen during the day and placing that into your long-term memory and trying to make sense of the world."

David likes to do a similar activity during the day. Especially if he is working through a big problem he has spent a lot of time on and is feeling a little frustrated. David said, "I literally will just purposely stop thinking about it and try to think about nothing and kind of let my subconscious go to work."

TIP: CLOSE DOWN WHEN YOU DON'T HAVE THE TIME

There are periods for David when things get very busy. He said, "There are definitely periods like right now where I can't talk to anybody. I am not open to any new meetings." David gets daily requests asking him to tell his career trajectory to the venture capital industry or people looking for jobs. David will reluctantly say, "Listen, honestly, I just can't right now. Maybe let's connect in a couple of months," David said that he would not have anything meaningful to talk about if he is not able to focus on his own job in this moment.

MY DAILY RITUAL:

I have a daily ritual that I work to stick with. Like anybody, things like doctor's appointments, travel, vacations, and family events sometimes impact this routine. But I feel this routine gives me an optimal morning and has me charged up for the day.

My daily ritual includes the following:

- Shut down from work and or screens at 9:00 p.m. on average.
- Fall asleep around 10:00 p.m.
- Wake up around 5:00 a.m.

I then hit the day with the *G*s

- God: I thank God for another day of life—one minute.
- Good morning: Look outside at the beautiful world and mentally create optimism for the day—one minute.
- Gospel: I listen to the Gospel via the Hallow (Hallow.com) app on my iPhone—five minutes. I grab a coffee during this time.
- Gratitude: I identify ten things I am grateful for—one minute.
- Guide: I reflect on my personal mission and vision statement—one minute.
- Goals: I reflect on my goals and think about things I will do within the day to bring me closer to my goals—eight minutes.
- Gente (*people* in Spanish): Quick network review on who in my network I need to connect with today—three minutes.

- Guidance: I reflect on eight leaders I admire and want to model. Eight is the optimum number for me. These eight leaders have shifted over time, and I think about them and how I can spend the day modeling myself after them—three minutes.

- Gym: Exercise for thirty to forty-five minutes.

- Growth: Reading the news (macro to micro)—*Wall Street Journal*, *Chicago Tribune*, *Gary Post Tribune,* and social media review and comments—thirty minutes.

- Grub: Eat breakfast, which has transformed over the years to currently mostly a healthy shake—fifteen minutes.

- Get going: I feel charged up and ready to go. I begin my workday!

- Finish work around 5:30 p.m. on average.

- Family dinner around 6:00 p.m. when I'm not traveling.

- Close down screens at 9:00 p.m.

From a weekly ritual perspective, every Sunday I attend church, visit a family member, and I have one hour scheduled to review and update my network, including ways I can help them accomplish their goals. Every quarter I do the Tom Mendoza goal review. I also think about ways I can be most efficient. For example, if I do an action, how could it have a broader impact? Part of your daily ritual should be looking at your network and determining who you will be giving value to and helping today and what the most efficient way to add as much value to your network as possible is.

These are different approaches to rituals and routines you can use to create one that works best for you. As an example, I don't schedule downtime and usually have it when I am stuck in traffic or waiting for appointments.

Pablo Picasso said, "We can only reach our goals through a vehicle of a plan, in which we must fervently believe, and upon which we must vigorously act. There is no other route to success."

Habits and rituals help accelerate the path toward your goals and need to be a vital part of your plan and networking excellence foundation. With a self-assessment, SMART goals, your brand, and rituals in place, you have built a strong foundation to leverage and achieve networking excellence.

EXERCISE:

- Document your daily, weekly, monthly, quarterly, and annual rituals.
- If not already, try meditation.
- Is your daily ritual focused on service?
- Increase the times per day you reflect on your goals.

RESOURCES:

- *It Works* by R. H. J.
- *Think and Grow Rich* by Napoleon Hill
- *A Message from Garcia* by Charles P. Garcia

EXECUTION

STEP 5

IDENTIFY THE RIGHT PEOPLE

If you want to go somewhere, it is best to find someone who has already been there.

—ROBERT T. KIYOSAKI

Who are the one or two hundred or so people most important to you to help you accomplish your goals?

I ask this question to those I mentor. The answer, in the beginning, is a list of a handful of people but not very well thought out. Those practicing networking excellence are deliberate about this list and, more importantly, working on ways to help these people accomplish their goals.

With deep self-introspection, complete a list of your SMART goals, your brand, and rituals in place to solidify your foundation. It is now time to identify who the people in or not yet in your network who can help you achieve your goals are.

The book *Never Eat Alone* by Keith Ferrazzi is a top ten book for me and helped shape my networking philosophy and approach.

Keith has a deep focus and discipline around identifying the people to help you with your goals. He said on his YouTube channel that many people have to-do lists to help drive the productivity of tasks, but sadly most people don't have a people plan to build relationships to accomplish goals. Keith mentions that putting relationships into practice is critical to your success in business and in life. Great networkers are proactive and efficient and have a process in place to do this. Keith Ferrazzi calls this his relationship action plan (Ferrazzi 2020; Howes 2014).

The first thing to focus on is identifying the critical individuals to build relationships with to achieve your goals. Keith says if relationships are critical, they need planning, and we need to be proactive about them. "Planned and purposeful does not mean to be fake. There's nothing fake about the relationships that I purposely decided to build," Keith says (Howes 2014).

How to Identify People per Goal

In the spirit of being purposeful and not fake, it is important to look at your goals and the respective people who can help you per goal. Take your first goal and identify the three to five people who can best help you accomplish this goal and are critical to influencing the achievement of that goal. Repeat this process next to every goal. These can be people who can help drive the outcome or people who are very knowledgeable on the goal area and can teach you. These people are the key individuals to help you accomplish your goals in life.

As you look to identify these people, the first place to start is your current network. It is important to list the people within your current network who are in the best position to help you with your goals. You will find that some people within your current network are not in the best position to help you with your goals and priorities. You will have to prioritize your time with them accordingly.

I come across more people who don't align with my goals than those who do. These could be at the bar, fitness center, family events, or shopping. As I interact with them, I am very pleasant, kind (practicing that from the foundation section of the book to help me live longer), and helpful. I am also very conscious of the amount of time I am spending. It is highly unlikely I would be at a bar chatting with somebody for two to three hours who is not within my network or does not have the potential to be in my network.

As an example of how I prioritize my time around people, I enjoy Notre Dame football, but whether they win or lose has little material impact on my goals. I will attend tailgates for networking and catching up with people in my social circle. However, going into the stadium for the games, although beautiful, is a five- to six-hour event with limited time to connect with people. I will typically leave as the game starts, arrive back home via an eighty-minute drive, and multitask, working to help my network while watching the game on TV in the background. I would likely only attend a game if I was with a couple of people in my defined network sitting next to me at the game where we were able to have a meaningful conversation.

There are always exceptions to advice about keeping a tight alignment with people who help you with your goals. One of those exceptions is a statement by Marcelo De Santis, who said, "I always force myself to connect with people who have absolutely nothing to do with the things I do or outside my profession. Because that contrast sometimes moves you out from your mold."

Now look at your goals and list people outside of your current network who will be key to helping you accomplish your goals. Include them in your list per goal as well.

TYPES OF RELATIONSHIPS

There are four types of relationships you can categorize these people into.

- **Supporter**—People who open up opportunities and provide you support for your goal.
- **Educators**—People who give you knowledge and wisdom toward learning about your goal. These are teachers who educate you toward accomplishing your goal.
- **Lifelines**—These are people you totally trust who keep you accountable to your goals; people with whom you can share your weaknesses; people you can feel comfortable letting know when you are failing. They are kicking your butt and driving accountability.
- **Connectors**—Connectors are people who know multiple people who align with your goals.

I would personally recommend a total list of eighty to two hundred across all these relationship types.

You can find supporters, educators, and connectors by looking in your network, searching on LinkedIn, asking your close friends, and asking new connections, among others. For example, if my goal was to run a four-hour marathon and I got connected to

Don Johnson, who was the president of the County Running club, I would ask him who the people are I should meet with to help me successfully accomplish my goal. I also think about what I can do to help Don and the people he mentions.

Below is an example of a table you can customize to help you track.

Goal	People	Type	Action	Date
Run a Four-hour Marathon on 11/5/2022	Coach Dan Smith	Supporter, Educator	Weekly connections to discuss my progress. Buy Dan his favorite coffee.	Weekly
	Maria Lopez (running partner)	Supporter	Daily run. Help Maria's son get an internship.	Daily
	Sally Trotter (fifty time Marathon runner)	Supporter, Educator	Connect with her at the marathon and discuss additional ways I can support the charity for which she is running.	12/3/2022
	Sara Jackson (author: *How to Run a Marathon without Hurting Yourself*)	Educator	Book Signing event at a local bookstore. Discuss how I can help her sell more books.	11/1/2022
	Don Johnson (President of the County Running Club)	Connector, Supporter, Educator	Monthly club meeting. Discuss how I can help bring more members.	11/15/2022

TO FIND YOUR LIFELINE:

Lifelines are people within your network who you unconditionally trust. Keith Ferrazzi says there are four core characteristics of lifeline relationships, and the best ones have to have all four things.

1. Intimacy to the point of vulnerability—Can I tell you when I am weak, down, scared, or up against a wall? Can I do this to the point of vulnerability?

2. Generosity—Do I really want to help you, and do you really want to help me? Do we care enough to help?

3. Candor—Will you tell me the truth even if it is difficult?

4. Accountability—Accepting responsibility to make sure you meet your goals.

Keith said, "Fifty percent of Americans say no one has their back and they have zero lifelines. And of those who say that no one has their back, 60 percent of them are married" (Howes 2014).

To find your lifeline, you are going to need to take your armor off and say what you are afraid of. You will also need to discuss your plan. At this point, you ask the person what they think and see how the person responds. Keith said, "Do they respond with candor? Do they respond with intimacy? Do they let their guard down? Do they respond with accountability at the end of the dinner? Are they saying to you, let's talk next week because I think you should do these two or three things, and I'm going to hold you accountable for them, dammit" (Howes 2014).

If after the dinner they don't call you the following week, then maybe they're not the right person for your lifeline.

Keith says that vulnerability is fearful because people have all the characteristics. They think that people are going to use it against them. Keith said, "You feel like you're going to be weak. You'll face judgment. That's all the sort of the primal reptilian brain fears and concerns associated with this."

With regards to lifelines and being vulnerable, Keith says, "If you don't get willing to push the boundaries of your social discomfort, then you will be mediocre. You will be mediocre in your life. You will not achieve what you deserve to achieve" (Howes 2014). Don't be afraid to be vulnerable, as it accelerates the relationship.

Lifelines do not have to be mutual, but in the spirit of networking, you should feel compelled to help your lifeline with their goals in the same way.

LEVELS TO THE NETWORK

In addition of categorizing your network, there is prioritizing. You can use several levels to prioritize your network.

- Lifeline three to five
- Top twenty-five
- Key 120 to 220
- Rest of world/social outreach

LIFELINE THREE TO FIVE

Identify the three to five people in your network who are your lifelines.

TOP TWENTY-FIVE

Identify the twenty-five most important people to your goals and success. You will likely spend most of your time interacting with these people.

KEY 120 TO 220

Joe Girard, author of *How to Sell Anything to Anybody* and "World's greatest retail salesman" by the Guinness Book of World Records for twelve consecutive years (Automotive Hall of Fame n.d.), said, "Everyone knows 250 people in his or her life that they can influence with their opinions and experiences—250!" This came up with asking people who attended funerals to attendees at a wedding.

Although not scientific, using Joe Girard's general rule, the highest number of relationships one can manage at any time is 250 (Girard 2014).

Although 250 is the number for the most you are likely to manage, use a number you are comfortable with. Gale Wilkinson says the max capacity for her contacts is about 150. Her firm has way more contacts than that, and her focus is on how to identify and prioritize these contacts and efficiently stay in touch with them. Gale said, "These include founders we're watching, our investors, and corporate execs that we know. We stay focused and intentional about driving value back and forth to these people."

My number is about 160. This number has varied up and down over the years depending on how my goals have shifted and life has changed.

UP-LEVEL THE LIST

Once you have your initial list of people inside and outside your network who align with your goals, see if you can put the name of a person who is one level higher in the organization or two levels higher in their influence toward your goal. I call this technique up-level.

Look at your list of people identified, and if it is the CEO of a company, you can also put the chairman of the board. This stretches your thinking, which aligns with stretch goals from the earlier chapter. Often, we do not push ourselves either because we don't know this person or are afraid of rejection. You will be coming to this person with value and in the spirit of helping them, which should minimize this fear.

When the type of services I sell gear toward the chief information officer or the vice president of information technology, there have been several instances where I have connected with board members I know at these corporations or presidents of divisions to help make connections, build relationships, gather more knowledge on the value my services can provide, and navigate the sales cycle. My approach with all this is finding how my value toolkit can be helpful to make them successful.

DON'T BE INTIMIDATED

As it relates to up-leveling, David Wieland says sometimes there will be somebody you are interested in meeting who is of a higher social status or level. You might think that person would never be interested in meeting with you. David said, "Ninety-nine percent of the time, that's false. They might be busy. But many times, they are actually quite interested in doing the same thing, which is just meeting interesting people and having a conversation. Maybe it goes somewhere. Maybe it does not."

David has never been hesitant to reach out to somebody out of his league. David believes we should balance this and also have meetings with people early on in their careers or folks who are also just sort of curious about what you're doing. David said, "I also try to meet with younger people or those starting out in their career as well and be helpful to them. These meetings have worked out quite well, been very helpful to me, and opened up doors. But the key is prioritizing."

DIVERSIFY YOUR LIST

Now, look at your list with a diverse lens. Does your network have a variety of perspectives to prevent your network from being too insular or becoming an echo chamber? Ensure it includes people from different gender, races, ethnicities, geographies, and ages. Push yourself to find these.

In my interview with Gale Wilkinson, she said, "I found that diversity is important. This includes people from different companies, different functional areas, different parts of the world, different age groups, and all sorts of types of backgrounds will make a richer experience and network." Diversity brings more innovation, different points of view, and experiences to solve problems.

Gale also highlighted networking across generations. She said, "There are differences as one builds relationships across generations. I found that in leading the IrishAngels angel investment group that building relationships does vary based on generation. It is important you can bridge the gaps."

As it relates to diversifying your network, in my interview with Dr. Robert Rodriguez, author of *Enterprise Resource Group Excellence*, he educated me on a tool from Harvard Business called the Harvard Developmental Network questionnaire. You can find the questionnaire here: https://store.hbr.org/product/developmental-network-questionnaire/404105

The tool is about $10 to purchase, and Robert takes the survey within the tool about every five years. The tool helps you see a schematic and almost a visual representation of your network. It also helps you identify some gaps.

"It helped me. It told me my academic network was lagging. That insight gave me the push to prop that up again, leading to some of the teachings I'm doing now," said Robert.

The tool helps you look at your network and measure it from different aspects. It ensures you look at various dimensions of diversity and where your network originates. It helps you measure how much value each member of your network provides for you and if they lean more toward a friend, ally, sponsor, or mentor. Value areas include opening opportunities, opening doors, sponsoring, and friendships. It then provides developmental networking maps from a past, current, and future perspective to help you map and optimize your network. I found the tool extremely valuable. I could see I had a very male network and was not getting enough sponsorship. It also was a useful tool with frameworks to help me map my network five years into the future.

MAP YOUR NETWORK INTO CITIES

Geography is a key component of your network. As you identify people, it is important to log what city or metro area they are from. You can then separate your network into locations to optimize when you travel to a city. For example, when I travel to a city, I will often look into my network and invite people I know in that city to a meal or a coffee. It helps you be efficient as you travel and creates connections among the people you invite.

LEVERAGE REFERRALS

As you identify people for inclusion in your network, there will be some people you do not know. Getting connections to people whom you don't know and want to know is difficult. Referrals are a key vehicle to meet these people and are even more important for people added via an up-level.

Adela Cepeda said, "Those aren't cold calls. You have to know someone, and someone has to refer you."

It is important to look at connectors within your network or use tools like LinkedIn and others to find people who know people within your desired network and ask for the referral.

DON'T BE OVERLY INTENTIONAL

As you identify the right people, more will be left off your list than on your list. You have to leave a little bit of room and can't be super rigid walking through life, ignoring people with blinders because they do not align with what you want to do and are not on your list. It's a little bit of a balancing act, and you should realize you can meet somebody new unplanned and that it is a game changer for your goals.

ROBERT J. RODRIGUEZ SECRETARY OF STATE OF NEW YORK NETWORKING STORY

Regarding identifying the right people in your network, Robert J. Rodriguez early on identified Adela Cepeda as a person in his network to help him get a job and support him in his political career. Through his hard work, care for his constituents, networking, Adela's help, and the help of many others, he is now Secretary of State of New York.

Adela Cepeda's firm won a contract with the city of New York. As part of the contract, the city wanted a firm that had a local office. As part of obtaining an office and staffing the New York team, Adela needed to hire New York based employees. This is when Adela hired Robert. He had a good job at Bloomberg and called on broker dealers, including those in Mexico. Educated at Yale, Robert has an MBA from Stern Business School at NYU. He felt excited about starting a new office, working with Adela, and the NYC contract. He was a hard worker and very reliable.

Adela Cepeda said, "Robert is a great networker, and I didn't realize he came from a family where the dad had been the first Puerto Rican elected to the city council from the Bronx." Robert ran Adela's New York office.

Robert mentioned to Adela he wanted to run for the assemblymen office representing Harlem, which is where he lived. Adela said, "I felt it's great to have political representation. So even though he was not going to be full time in the business, I thought that was important." The job of assemblyman was part time, so he could continue working for Adela's firm, and Adela allowed him to continue to work and fit his campaigning after work hours.

Adela states, "I strongly believe you have to let people grow even if it may not be the best thing for your business. You have to let the individual grow, and I will never regret that." Robert eventually won assemblyman and advanced in his political career. New York Governor Kathy Hochul nominated him as Secretary of State of New York in 2021.

EXERCISE

- List the three to five people who can help you (education, enable, lifeline, connectors) accomplish your goals.
- Review your network to ensure it is diverse.
- Purchase and execute the Harvard Developmental Network questionnaire.

RESOURCES:

- *How to Sell Anything to Anybody* by Joe Girard
- *Never Eat Alone* by Keith Ferrazzi
- *Who's Got Your Back* by Keith Ferrazzi

STEP 6

TARGET THE RIGHT NETWORKS

Find a group of people who challenge and inspire you, spend a lot of time with them, and it will change your life.

—AMY POEHLER

Last chapter we discussed identifying the right people to help you accomplish your goals and build relationships with. There is another key area to target to help you accomplish your goals, build relationships, and achieve networking excellence. They are networks—groups, organizations, clubs, and so on. Networks and groups are efficient ways to accomplish your goals more rapidly. These networks facilitate bringing like-minded people together versus you having to individually spend the time reaching out one by one.

There are many networks and groups to participate in and join. Your foundation and goals are important to help you prioritize which ones you should focus on. Below are different areas of networks that you can identify, prioritize based on your goals, and join. As you study these networks, in the spirit of networking, you should also consider the value you can provide to the network. If you are not a member already, then determine a way to join, and be a contributing and value-adding member of these networks. By building relationships, you may also identify individuals to add to your identified network.

The Networks That People within Your Network Belong To

When targeting the right networks to join and contribute to, the first place you should look and study are the networks that people within your network belong to. As you study each person to determine how to help them, you will find the networks they have been a part of and are currently in. Research the mission, vision, past events, upcoming events, members, leadership, and board of these networks to prioritize. Then take action and join!

Networks That Have Been Helpful for Me

I have been a part of many networks throughout my life. Some of these networks are looser, and some are stronger. A few networks have endured for a long time, and some have lasted only months. Networks have provided scale, diversity of ideas, and a network of support for me in good times and bad. They have helped me when I needed career advise, perspectives on issues facing me, and questions I had on different personal matters. My network has also helped me accelerate the growth of nonprofits, helped me grow start-up companies I have invested in, and opened doors for sales opportunities, among others.

Just as your goals and what you like will shift over your life, your networks will also shift.

To identify networks you are currently a part of, look at where you spend time and groups you are a part of and have been a part of. When you stop and reflect, you will be surprised by how many groups and networks you have been a part of over your life. You will find that you have many current networks you are a part of. You will also identify new networks that you should join.

TYPES OF NETWORKS TO JOIN

Here are several areas of networks you can join:

- Social networks
- Education/alumni networks
- Award networks
- Employers/employee resource groups
- Religious
- Culture/ethnicity/race
- Your kid's school
- Professional groups
- Nonprofits
- Political/government/community

SOCIAL NETWORKS

Did you know that 4.70 billion people, which is more than half of the people around the world, now use social media (Chaffey 2022)?

Social networks provide digital groups and ways to connect, learn, and interact online. There are many platforms and many groups within each of these platforms. Below are several to build your network and interact with those in your network. We will go into detail later in chapter 9.

- YouTube
- Facebook
- Twitter
- Instagram
- Discord
- Substack

I am on most of these but am more active on LinkedIn, Twitter, and Facebook than others. I am active by reviewing content, commenting, and sharing. You should seek subgroups within these social platforms that align with your goals. You can also prioritize which platform to utilize based on your goals and who is on the platform. Additionally, look at the platforms where the majority of the people within your network are and start on those platforms first.

EDUCATION/ALUMNI NETWORKS

Your alumni groups are an easy network to belong to because they share common values, educational experiences, and educational roots. This can be your grade school, high school, college, or graduate school, and also places where you took summer classes, certifications, and seminars.

I personally have served on the foundation board of my high school. I am a member of my college Rose-Hulman Sawmill Angels and Notre Dame affiliated IrishAngels. For Notre Dame, I served on the advisory board of the business school and the board of the Notre Dame Alumni Club of Detroit.

Some of my education and alumni networks include:

- St. John the Baptist
- Bishop Noll
- Rose-Hulman
- Notre Dame
- Purdue Northwest
- Bentley
- AWS Cloud Certification
- Harvard HACR Board Certification
- Alumni Society

Fun fact: Did you know Pennsylvania State is the college with the largest alumni network? Penn State has 616,000 alumni with over 172,000 dues-paying members worldwide (Penn State Alumni Association 2022).

From a university perspective, many families spend hundreds of thousands of dollars on university education for their children. In many cases, I see that once people graduate, they lose their connection to the university. I believe an easy way to get a return on your investment is to stay engaged and connected with your university. There are many people within my network from my universities, and these networks have been very helpful to me.

I interviewed Jorge Cabrera, president of the Rutgers Business School Alumni Association. Jorge said, "Rutgers has an alumni community of over 600,000 living graduates, most of them living in the New Jersey, New York City, and Philadelphia area. There is no reason for a Rutgers graduate living in New Jersey to struggle when looking for a new job, clients for their business, or capital for a business venture." Jorge says that tapping into your alumni circles is a very easy and extremely efficient way to expand your network. Since you already share a common experience, these new connections are *warm connections*, and the time it takes for both individuals to become comfortable and trusting of each other reduces significantly.

From an alumni network perspective, I also interviewed David Segura, CEO of VisionIT, a global IT service provider. David exemplifies building reciprocal relationships, finding commonality, and cultivating connection points. David and I have known each other for almost two decades. I have learned many networking skills from David and consider him a master networker. He recently became chairman of the University of Michigan Alumni Association.

David believes you can find common ground with members of your alumni network through your ethnicity, culture, sports preferences, skills, and educational background. Your alumni network connection makes for immediate familiarity and relatability. David says, "I view a key piece as you make connections is to be open to learning from an individual, find ways you can help them, and share things you are working on that might be valuable to them or guidance they can give through their network."

A great example has been David's ability to build a very diverse network through his alumni association. It started many years ago when the CEO of the Alumni Association of the University of Michigan had reached out to David and was impressed by the business he was building and invited him to lunch. They talked and got to know one another, and years later, they asked him to serve on the alumni board, which now reaches over 650,000 members and growing.

David said, "I felt not only would it be great to help the alumni association, but I knew it would provide me an opportunity to meet so many people who I probably would not meet in other settings where I was putting in an effort, like tech conferences, supplier diversity events, chambers of commerce as examples." In joining the board, David became much more active in the alumni network attending events, visiting local chapters around the country, attending major donor events at the university, and finding ways of being valuable to the university.

Along the way, David made new connections across many industries that helped him build his network. David said, "The members of the University of Michigan Alumni Association have a common love for our school. We have shared experiences from our education to attending football or basketball games and an immediate bond when we say 'Go Blue!'" David's many activities with the alumni society and dedication of his time led to the alumni association board appointing him chairman. David said, "I am thankful I added value and can further open more doors for others who want to connect more effectively into this powerful alumni network."

EMPLOYERS/EMPLOYEE RESOURCE GROUPS

Many of us will work for multiple employers in our careers. Each of these employers has a network of relationships you develop and are a part of. These can be relationships you keep directly with the people you work with or some organizations like P&G, Accenture, and others for formal alumni groups. Additionally, within these employers, there are specific employee resource groups. Some of these employee resource groups include military, female, African American, and LGBTQ+, among others. You do not have to be an identified member of a group to be an ally and join.

Some of my past employers include:

- Accenture
- Empower Solutions/Intelligroup/NTT Data
- Ford Motor Company

- Oracle
- Verizon
- Softtek

Employee resource groups I have been a part of:

- Hispanic Employee Resource Group
- Military Resource Group

The P&G Alumni Network group, whose website is www.PGAlums.com, is probably one of the strongest corporate alumni networks around the globe. They have local chapters, a foundation, a women's forum, a board of directors, annual reports, and formal events, among other value-added capabilities for their alumni. I interviewed Felipe Flores-Arango, executive vice president and CFO of Zug, Switzerland-based Pharmanovia. Felipe served on the board of directors of the P&G Alumni Network for ten years and has very good insights on how to build and value these employer networks.

Felipe and I first discussed the structure of the board. P&G's Alumni board met monthly via calls, and the board has various committees. These committees included mentoring, membership, and chapters. Felipe said, "The focus of all these committees was on executing the vision and strategic plan of the P&G Alumni Association." The P&G Alumni Association would get investment from P&G and do things like conducting market research, recruiting assistance, setting up events, and researching disruptive technologies. In major cities with P&G alumni, they would have formal chapters. Felipe said, "Chapters are the engine, but it comes down to people who plan the events in each chapter and pull it all together." Chapters are for local interaction, but every two years, all P&G alumni receive invitations to come together, and the location alternates between the US and Europe. Felipe said, "We get about 500 people from around the planet to come to this event every two years."

Felipe also leveraged the chapter structure while living in Europe and has attended events in London. He said, "I knew very few people in the first London event I attended. A lot of people were new, but that was nice because then you meet new people. You have this common P&G thing, and people don't care that you don't work in the UK because you have ultimately the common umbrella of we are all P&G alums."

We talked about networks and how to best leverage them. Felipe said, "You have your university, corporate, and platforms for networking, but ultimately it is up to you to use these and leverage these."

When I asked Felipe what other corporate alumni networks they admired and modeled were, he said, "As a board, we did analysis and benchmarking on which were some of the top-performing corporate alumni networks, and we also leveraged market research. We found that the best alumni network was McKinsey. They have a connection, and they really go out of their way to help each other."

OUTSIDE YOUR EMPLOYER

Many people have 90 percent of their network within their company. They are in the company running club, company mentoring circles, company ERGs, and more. They have dinners with their team and spend evenings and weekends hanging out with the same people from their work. It is important you look outside your company and measure your network outside your employer.

In my interview with Dr. Robert Rodriguez, he said, "Sometimes people focus so much on their job that they don't take a step back and focus on the network outside of their company." You should do a periodic scan outside your work network. This could be within your industry or similar industries.

RELIGIOUS

Many find a bond with their church as they share the same religious beliefs. Also, within the church, there are subgroups and committees you can join.

Some of my church groups over the years include:

- St. John the Baptist
- St. Thomas Moore
- Hallow
- Notre Dame
- Catholic Youth Organization

CULTURE/ETHNICITY/RACE/ TOWN OF ORIGINATION

Within this world, we have beautiful people, cultures, languages, places of origin, and ethnicities. No matter where you are in the world, these groups can bring together some familiarity. For example, my wife is originally from Colombia. When we moved to Michigan, she did not know anybody and barely spoke English. We found the Association of Colombianos de Michigan (ACM) and joined the network, and it helped her acclimate rapidly. Most of us within the United States can trace our family originations to other countries. There are many organizations and networks to help people from different origins. Below are a couple I have been a part of:

- Hispanic Chamber of Commerce
- Puerto Rican Arts Alliance
- Congressional Hispanic Leadership Institute
- Association of Colombianos de Michigan
- National Museum of Mexican Art
- Association of Latino Professionals for America (ALPFA)

One of the largest professional networks within the United States Latino Community is ALPFA. It has over 95,000 members and is a strong network for professional relationships. They have 157 students and forty-four professional chapters, as well as an annual conference that brings these members together with some of the largest corporations in America looking for talent. The current CEO, Damian Rivera, is a friend and a member with me in several mutual networks.

YOUR KIDS' SCHOOL

Your kids' school also provides a network of parents, teachers, and alumni who you can potentially include within your network.

Below are a few schools my kids have attended:

- St. Thomas More
- Shrine Catholic
- Marian Catholic
- Munster High School
- Purdue University
- Montessori

As an example, I am working with the Purdue Foundry to help identify start-ups that might be right for investment. They have offered me working space at their facilities any time I am visiting my son, and I am sharing with them my experience from investing in angel groups and technology disruption.

PROFESSIONAL MEMBERSHIP GROUPS

There are hundreds of professional organizations out there, some that align with your industry, your career level, and your functional area of expertise.

Some of the professional groups I affiliate and have affiliated with include:

- National Association of Corporate Directors
- Sawmill Angels
- Angeles Investors
- Latino Corporate Directors Association
- Indiana Venture Capital
- Detroit Economic Club
- Union League Club
- Chicago Club
- Chicago Blend
- IrishAngels

NONPROFITS

Many nonprofits have causes you might believe in that have associated networks and groups of people with similar values.

Some nonprofits I associate with:

- National Association of Corporate Directors
- WTTW—Windows to the World Communications
- Notre Dame Club of Detroit Alumni Board
- Node Chicago
- NSHMBA National Society of Hispanic MBAs
- HITEC—Hispanic IT Executive Council
- Angeles Investors
- NMMA—National Museum of Mexican Art

OTHER CLUBS AND SOCIAL GROUPS

You can join other types of networking groups based on your interests. Below are a few examples:

- Runners group
- Bike riding club

- Wine club
- Book club

AWARD NETWORKS

As you progress through your career, there is a high likelihood you will get awards. As we receive these awards, we become part of these networks where we have common goals, synergies, and life experiences.

Some of these award networks for me include:

- Crain's Tech Chicago Top 50
- HITEC (Hispanic It Executive Council) Hall of Fame
- Chicago United Business Leaders of Color
- Crain's Detroit 40 under 40
- Rose-Hulman Alumni Career Achievement Award
- Notre Dame Business School Distinguished Alumni Award

As it relates to awards, there is one piece of advise that has always stuck with me from Tom Mendoza, former vice chair of NetApp and Benefactor of the Notre Dame Mendoza School of Business. Tom mentions in a tweet to me:

> The question I ask people who think they want to go into leadership is, "Would you rather give a plaque

> or get a plaque?" Every great leader I have met that people want to follow gets more enjoyment out of the former (@TomMendozaTalks 2022).

I focus on giving awards versus trying to receive them.

POLITICAL/GOVERNMENT/COMMUNITY

I have supported many candidates, both Democrat and Republican, throughout my life and have friends and family in different political parties. It is what makes America the best country in the world. I have been involved with the Republican Party and various subgroups within the Republican Party since the early 2000s, which have enabled a broad national network. I have friends who have done the same on the Democratic Party side and have built a strong national network of business leaders, activists, and media. You can work to build these networks at the local, regional, and national levels.

Some of these networks for me throughout my career include:

- Commissioner, State of Indiana Minority and Women Business Enterprises Division
- Commissioner, White House Hispanic Prosperity Initiative
- Indiana GOP Leadership Diversity Advisory Committee
- Congressional Hispanic Leadership Institute
- Hispanic Coalition Leader for Michigan gubernatorial candidate Dick DeVos

CREATE YOUR OWN NETWORK

If a network does not exist that aligns to your goals, create one. I did this with HITEC and Angeles Investors. There are many examples of people who have created groups or networks to fit a need. Here are a couple of examples:

- Pablo Schneider created the Renaissance Dinners series to celebrate diversity and elevate diverse leaders.

- Paula Meinzer created LEEN (Latina Executive and Entrepreneur Network) and LEEN Golf Society. LEEN brings together a diverse group of high-growth Latina businesswomen from multiple organizations and backgrounds who are committed to a discussion of topics relevant to today's issues to educate and encourage women to reflect on their own goals.

- Greg Hedges, Managing Director at Protiviti, with win-win-win intentions, created the Notre Dame Executive Business Council of Chicago. This network connects Notre Dame alumni in Chicago, opens up business opportunities for the network, and strengthens the Notre Dame alumni network.

- Raymond Arroyo created PRIMER to help connect and elevate Latinos into positions of power.

- Chris Salvi, cofounder of Salvi Media, created the Chicago CEO Series. This is a video series that highlights leading CEOs within the Chicagoland area. Chris states, "Everyone's a winner. CEOs and the marketing team get a positive piece on leadership style, their business, industry, and the local community. Our business builds connections with the CEOs and marketing teams. A number of the subjects have become mentors, clients, or both."

These are just a few examples of leaders who put in the work, took the initiative, and created their own networks around their goals. They have had fun doing this, helped others accomplish their goals, and created a platform to help them accomplish their goals as well.

INVEST IN NETWORKS

There are times when you will look at your network and see four to eight people on your list, and in your research you see they belong to a networking group. As you consider joining the group, you might notice a price tag to join. This investment and price tag might cause you to pause or make your stomach drop. A simple way to look at the investment is to look at your time and effort to individually meet with these folks, the time to coordinate, the value of the relationship to your goals, and what an hour of your time is worth.

Be smart and wise with your money and resources but don't be afraid to invest in joining these networks. I have also volunteered to get into networks, which is another avenue for you if your resources are low. You can do this by understanding what the pressing needs of the organization are and where your skills can really help. You can also accomplish this by looking at committees and seeing where you can best volunteer your skills.

ADELA CEPEDA'S NETWORKS AND INVESTMENT

Adela joined the Chicago Network around 2005 and didn't realize how much value there was. This is a network of women who succeeded and are at the top of their firms. Adela said, "I've got to know a few women within the Chicago Network that I could actually go to for advice about my firm. Advise like whether I should sell my firm or whether I shouldn't. This came from network members who have gone through similar experiences. They provided a lot of business knowledge and could help me think about it."

Adela and I met through a mutual connection in the Chicago Network, Sheila Talton, CEO of Gray Matter Analytics and a member of the board of directors at John Deere, Sysco, OGE Energy Corp. Sheila was a cofounder of the Information Technology Senior Management Forum, and I was a cofounder of the Hispanic IT Executive Council, and our organizations have had a partnership. It was through this partnership I met Sheila, and she graciously connected me to Adela.

As an example, Adela is part of the following networks, among others:

- Harvard Club Alumni Group
- Chicago Network
- ADL—Anti-Defamation League
- Union League
- Soho House

- LCDA—Latino Corporate Directors Association
- The Alumni Society
- Angeles Investors
- Leadership Greater Chicago

When I asked her how many of these networks are paying memberships, Adela said, "Six to ten of these networks have paid memberships. You have to invest, as it is the cost of doing business." Adela feels the best thing about these networks is that she is a more senior member and can help younger people get in. Adela said, "I get the gratification of helping other people advance and having them become part of my network." Adela always has four to six younger women she is mentoring and giving some sort of direction. As it relates to family, Adela said, "I started by focusing on my daughters. I've been mentoring them for twenty-six years, as they haven't had a father mentor them." Adela's husband passed away shortly after their third child was born, and he was an iconic figure and networking leader.

TAKE AN ACTIVE ROLE AND ADD VALUE—OR LEAVE

Don't join these networks to take selfishly. Find ways to contribute and add value. This will help improve your leadership. Your passion, efforts, and results from these endeavors for these networks you join will give you the visibility to help you grow your network.

There are many networks to help you build relationships. These networks and perspectives are a starting point that you can use to strengthen your execution engine. The strong foundation you build can help you prioritize which networks to target as you achieve networking excellence.

EXERCISE

- List out the communities and networks you are a part of.
- Identify organizations with a membership fee that you should invest in and join to accelerate your goals.
- Have lunch with the head of one of the groups you plan to join.
- Research people in your network and determine what groups and networks they belong to.

RESOURCES

- *Never Eat Alone* by Keith Ferrazzi
- *Joining a Nonprofit Board* by Marc J. Epstein
- *Employee Resource Group Excellence* by Dr. Robert Rodriguez

STEP 7

BUILD RELATIONSHIPS WITH AND ADD VALUE TO YOUR NETWORK

It is literally true that you can succeed best and quickest by helping others to succeed.

—NAPOLEON HILL

With the right people and networks identified to accomplish your goals, it is now time to put together a people and relationship plan to help these people and groups accomplish their goals. This plan and the respective ways you can help your circle are with the intention of helping your network. Your intentions should focus on your success. This is not doing good expecting things in return, or manipulating the people in your network. Marcelo De Santis said, "It is important to note that this is not manipulation. It is about your intention, and you will not only help this person but also learn from this person."

STUDY AND RESEARCH YOUR NETWORK

Most, if not all, of the identified people within your network have goals they want to accomplish. This step is about deeply understanding your network to determine the best way you can leverage you, your value toolkit, and all your strengths to help them be successful. This includes understanding their histories, places they have lived, and their network of relationships. It is kind of like being a detective. Here are a couple of questions that can help you research your desired network:

- What groups or boards are they a part of?
- What is their role at their company?
- Are they on any videos on YouTube?
- Who do you know connected to them?
- Has anyone written about them or quoted them in any articles?
- What have they posted on social media?
- What political candidates have they donated to?

Here are some places and tools you can leverage to research:

- **LittleSis** (https://LittleSis.org)—Use to research who and what organizations the people in your network are connected to and how they are connected.

- **Google** (www.Google.com)—Use to find out what is publicly available on the person in your network.

- **Open Secrets (**www.OpenSecrets.org)—Use to find out political donations the person in your network has made.

- **LinkedIn** (www.LinkedIn.com)—Use to understand their career history, education, groups, boards, interests, connections, and posts of interest.

- **Facebook** (www.Facebook.com)—Use to understand interests and groups they are a part of, among others.

- **Blog posts** (www.Blogger.com, among others**)—**You can use them to determine their interests.

FORMULATE AND VALIDATE A HYPOTHESIS ON THEIR GOALS AND THE VALUE YOU CAN ADD

With all this background research, you can formulate a hypothesis or an educated guess on what you think are their three to five top goals. Additionally, you can find synergies around people you know, organizations you affiliate with, or common causes of interest. These synergies can be useful to rapidly establish rapport when you meet and help you identify ways you can help them.

Once you identify this hypothesis, you can look into your value toolkit and see if there are any matches you have to help this person. For each person on your list, detail the tools within your value toolkit that would be of most help for this person to accomplish their goals.

Keith Ferrazzi, on "The Secret to Networking in 2020: Relationship Action Plan" YouTube video, says, "You're curious for what it is that you can do to make them successful before you start asking what you need from those relationships" (Ferrazzi 2020).

With this hypothesis, write down what you believe their top three to five goals are. These are a hypothesis until you validate these goals with the individual in your network. You can validate this hypothesis with them in several ways. These include conversation, asking mutual acquaintances, meeting over a meal, and via email, among others.

An example below shows a way to connect with value via email and validate your hypothesis.

You can use this after meeting somebody at an event and after you have done research on their goals. This can be via email or adapted via a verbal conversation.

* * *

Person A,

Trust all is well. I understand you are looking to do (goal one) and (goal two).

FYI, I plan to be at (network A, or city B) on Y date. I plan to speak with person A about your goal there. I have done XYZ, which can help with goal one, and Jane Smith is a dear friend of ten years who has driven goal two very successfully. I am open to connecting you to Jane if you are open. Let me know if you are attending, and we can also synergize other ways I can help you with goal one and goal two.

Thanks.

* * *

To validate his hypothesis Keith Ferrazzi uses an approach called the five pockets of generosity, which looks to provide value to the person based on the research he has done. Keith said, "I've researched this individual, and I've identified five things that I think I could do to be helpful, which through the dialogue, I will figure out whether those five ways I can be helpful." If, through the dialogue around their goals, seeing if these five areas will help them or brainstorming additional or other ways he can be helpful, Keith feels he has earned the right to build an ongoing relationship. Once you have the right to build the relationship, you know you have to follow up or fail. Keith says, "Get back to them. Continue to be generous, continue to stay on the radar screen" (Ferrazzi 2020).

MAKE EVERY INTERACTION COUNT

Rushdi Ariss, executive director of enterprise applications and data platforms at Disney, said, "Networking is a give-and-take relationship. Every network, every interaction in the networking sense, is around getting to know the other person and figuring out what you can do for them."

Rushdi mentions that if he knows of a person who is writing a book, he will say, "That's fascinating. Is there anything I could do to help you? Would you like me to proofread it? Would you like me to give you some examples that will connect to somebody I might know?" Rushdi mentions the formula is simple: "You build a relationship, you make an investment, and then over time, you'll get those dividends out."

In Rushdi's opinion, the most effective networkers are those that make deposits in other people, make a connection, find something in common, and then invest themselves into the other person.

DON'T BE AFRAID TO ASK

As you begin to reach out and connect, you might be afraid and intimidated. Don't be afraid. One of the quotes Steve Harvey gives when he gives motivational speeches on YouTube is the Bible verse, "You have not because you ask not." If you are spiritual you can ask God, but this also applies to asking others (Harvey 2019).

CREATE A RELATIONSHIP VALUE PLAN

For each of the individuals and networks assigned to each of your goals, create a relationship value plan. This would include the date of your next interaction (email, in person, social posts, or other) and the deposit of value you will deliver to help them toward their goal. The plan will likely go out for a year or two and should include how frequently you're going to interact with this person as well as the value you will provide. It should be organized by each goal and each person.

Items of a Relationship Value Plan

People have their own priorities and their own self-interests. It takes work to build up value and deposits into the value bank account. Keith Ferrazzi said, "I had to bust my butt to get people to want to have a relationship with me. I had to work on charisma. I had to work on volunteering my time. I had to work on authentic flattery, letting people know how I admired them, make them feel good about themselves with me around" (Ferrazzi 2020).

Keith emphasizes that intimacy, generosity, candor, and accountability are components of great relationships. Intimacy and generosity are the two accelerants of the relationship. You lead with generosity and follow with care (Ferrazzi 2020).

You will need to look at each relationship as a long-term five- to ten-year relationship where you will help them and will have multiple opportunities to interact with this person.

Keith Ferrazzi uses the example of building a relationship with your child's teacher. He spends time periodically inviting the teacher over for dinner. He spends time popping in and saying hi to the teacher in the classroom. He sends cookies with his sons, knowing this would be beneficial to the teacher (Ferrazzi 2020).

Other techniques to help the people in your network include:

- Inviting them for a meal to discuss ways you can help them with their goals.

- Going out of your way to say hello (in person).

- Sending an occasional email with something they will find valuable.
- Connecting them to somebody who can help them accelerate their goals.
- Volunteering for a cause that is important to them.
- Partaking in group dinners, lunches, or breakfasts of people with common goals to help facilitate the accomplishment of those goals.
- Keith Ferrazzi sends a Thanksgiving card versus a Christmas card as Christmas is so cluttered (Ferrazzi 2020).

DETERMINE THE NEXT INTERACTION OR TOUCHPOINT

Look at your schedule and their schedule and find an event or a point where you both can interact. If one does not exist, you can look for somebody in your network to connect you with this person so you can bring the tools in your value toolkit to help them. You can also reach out via email, work to connect with them on social media, or think strategically about a point of value where you can both connect.

ADDING VALUE TO DIRECT INTERPERSONAL INTERACTIONS

As you build relationships with your network, there are various things you can do to build rapport more rapidly and accelerate the relationship. You can find many of these items in the classic book *How to Win Friends and Influence People.*

Here is a summary of tips from the book *How to Win Friends and Influence People* from a blog post of *Farnam Street* (Farnam Street, n.d.):

1. Give honest and sincere appreciation.

2. Become genuinely interested in other people.

3. Smile.

4. Remember that a person's name is to that person the sweetest and most important sound in any language.

5. Be a good listener. Encourage others to talk about themselves.

6. Talk in terms of the other person's interests.

7. Make the other person feel important—and do it sincerely.

8. Let the other person feel that the idea is his or hers.

9. Begin with praise and honest appreciation.

10. The only way on earth to influence other people is to talk about what they want and show them how to get it.

11. Get the other person's point of view and see things from that person's angle as well as from your own.

EXAMPLES OF EXECUTING A RELATIONSHIP DEVELOPMENT PLAN

ADD VALUE BY CONNECTING PEOPLE IN YOUR NETWORK

Around 2011, Luis Ubiñas was a person I put into my relationship action plan. Luis's background is extraordinary. He grew up in very humble beginnings. He attended Harvard Business School. He was a top student and a Baker Scholar. He was a divisional leader at the world-renowned management consulting firm McKinsey, and then he became the CEO of the Ford Foundation, which is one of the largest foundations in the world.

Luis was on the board of a company that was a client of mine. I researched his background and reached out to him via a cold email. The message was around mutual interests, which included our backgrounds, our passion for the US Hispanic community, and our passion for education with an invite for lunch. A month or so later, we had a great lunch discussing synergies, mutual friends, and shared values, and we kept in touch every six months or so.

As part of ways to bring more value to Luis, I introduced Luis to Adela Cepeda around 2016. They were both graduates of Harvard and had many synergies and common values. I was surprised they never met. It was very rewarding for me what happened over the next couple of years from this connection.

Adela mentioned, "Luis and I aligned on how we felt about Latino advancement and trying to do more for the community." Adela was serving as governance chair of Mercer mutual funds, and she had an opportunity to add a director to the Mercer mutual fund and asked Luis if he would be interested as he had deep expertise managing Ford Foundation investments and his learnings during the financial crisis.

In 2019, Luis joined the board of Mercer Funds, and I was glad to have made the networking connection between Luis and Adela to help facilitate that value.

EXECUTE AND ADD VALUE TO MEMBERS IN YOUR NETWORK

Here is a great story of pursuing goals, taking action, not being afraid to ask, adding value, and leveraging networking to accomplish your goal taken from *We study Billionaires Podcast* "503: The History of Bubbles, Mania, and Fraud with Jamie Catherwood," which you can find here: https://www.theinvestorspodcast.com/episodes/the-history-of-bubbles-mania-fraud-w-jamie-catherwood/

Jamie Catherwood is a client portfolio associate at O'Shaughnessy Asset Management. His road to this position is a classic story of executing a relationship plan. Jamie Catherwood was a history major but really wanted to break into a career in investing and finance (his goal). So, he reached out to a friend and asked for advice, and that friend recommended he listen to the podcasts *Invest Like the Best* by Patrick O'Shaughnessy and *Masters in Business* by Barry Ritholtz. Jamie took additional action of writing down every term he did not understand and looked it up later, building his financial knowledge over time. When he graduated from college, he ended up accomplishing his goal and getting a job in finance and investing, working for an institutional investment consultant in Washington, DC. To add further to the networking story and the power of thank you, Jamie had the courage to reach out to Patrick O'Shaughnessy of O'Shaughnessy Asset Management and thank him, leveraging a cold email. Jamie stated the email was something like, "You don't know me, but I kind of credit your podcast with helping me learn enough to get my first job in finance. And so, if you're up for it, I'd love to take you out to lunch or dinner to say thank you." The email also emphasized how much Patrick and his podcast gave to him and how he would just love to repay it. These are small deposits of value (Lockerbie 2022).

Patrick responded back pretty quickly, saying he would love to get lunch. Patrick didn't apparently realize that Jamie was in DC and O'Shaughnessy was in Stamford, Connecticut. Ironically, Jamie figured that since he already got one of the two podcast hosts that he listened to for a meeting, why not shoot the second one? So Jamie direct messaged Barry Ritholtz on Twitter with a similar thank you message and ended up getting breakfast meeting with him in New York that same day (Lockerbie 2022).

So, Jamie does the work, wakes up at 4:00 a.m., and drives up to NYC. He has breakfast with Barry and makes sure to figure out the Metro North train to get from his breakfast with Barry to Stanford to get lunch with Patrick. The worst thing for you to do when building first-time relationships is to arrive late to a meeting.

The breakfast and lunch meetings were a success, and Jamie stayed in touch with value-based interactions (Lockerbie 2022).

The story gets better. Eventually, through networking on social media and Twitter, Jamie got to know Jim O'Shaughnessy, principal, chairman, cochief investment officer, and portfolio manager of O'Shaughnessy Asset Management. Jim is a prolific and active user on Twitter, with close to 150 thousand followers (Lockerbie 2022).

Jamie gets to know Jim and stays connected with him with value-based interactions. Roughly two years into Jamie's first job, Jim gave Jamie a call and said, "Patrick and I decided that you need to come work for us."

Jamie then stated, "I then put in my two weeks the next morning." As of the publishing of this book, Jamie still works at O'Shaughnessy Asset Management (Lockerbie 2022).

As it relates to goal setting, Jamie's goal was to simply get a job in finance. He leveraged networking, social media, hard work, and his relationship plan to accomplish his goals and add value to his network. A couple of key lessons: Cold emails work, leverage the power of a thank you note, and don't be afraid to set goals higher.

BUILD RELATIONSHIPS BEFORE YOU NEED THEM, AND AVOID 911 NETWORKING

Dr. Robert Rodriguez also describes an anti-networking activity that he calls "911 networking."

In my interview with Robert, he told a story of a guy he put within his relationship action plan. Whenever Robert reached out to connect with him, he was always too busy.

Over the next eighteen months, Robert invited him to connect at various events multiple times: to meet for lunch, to come out golfing, to go to the Museum Galas, and many more. He never could attend and was always too busy. Right before COVID-19 hit, he reached out to Robert and said, "Hey Robert, old buddy, old pal, I'm in transition. Would you like to get together for lunch to discuss connections to your clients who can help me?" Robert thought to himself, *Now, all of a sudden, you got time for me?* Robert mentioned that when he tells other people the story, they ask him if he responded by saying he was too busy. Robert said, "No, I still met with him, but it came with a lecture and was a teachable moment." He said, "Hey, I get that you were busy. But guess what? I'm busy too." Robert told him, "I wasn't reaching out to you so you can help me. I wanted to get to know you and establish an ongoing connection. The only reason you were reaching out to me was so I could help you, not to establish a connection."

This is why Robert called this type of networking "911 networking." This is basically when you have built up no relationship capital and are asking for an emergency and immediate withdrawal.

As it relates to 911 networking and people reaching out to him for a favor after years of no interaction, in my interview with Felipe Flores-Arango, he said, "I'm very polite in scenarios like this, but I am also coaching. I tell people I will help you, but you cannot just show up after years of no interaction and just ask me for help because I know someone who you need to talk to or because you're looking for a job."

FINDING COMMONALITY AND CONTINUOUSLY KEEPING IN TOUCH

Rushdi Ariss was networking at a professional business association that he belongs to. He struck up a conversation with this one gentleman at dinner, and they had immediate chemistry. Rushdi said, "That initial meeting was about finding commonality. We spoke about the schools we attended, what we studied, our kids and their ages."

Rushdi identified commonalities and mentioned how he was intrigued to learn more about this gentleman. The conversation was captivating, and Rushdi didn't want it to end. Following the dinner, they had subsequent catch-up conversations, continuing to build the relationship.

Unbeknownst to Rushdi, this person had a broad set of C-level relationships, and some of his friends were looking for certain talent. This individual then ended up connecting Rushdi with two interviews for VP and above level positions with companies that Rushdi had no relationship with. He saw something in Rushdi that he thought these companies could leverage, putting his name and reputation on the line by connecting them to Rushdi. They had built a relationship based on trust, and the gentleman was willing to advocate for Rushdi in his absence.

Rushdi said, "You can't pay for that. You can't go looking for that. It's something that happens as a fruit born from building authentic relationships."

KEEPING THE RELATIONSHIP ALIVE AND GOING WITH VALUE

Marcelo De Santis, who, in addition to being the chief digital officer at ThoughtWorks, is an executive coach and Mount Everest climber, said, "Connecting the first time is not that easy, but you can do it. The harder thing is keeping the networking relationship alive and going." Marcelo mentions that networking is not a one-time event. He refers to it as a series of events that keep you growing like energy. Marcelo said, "I like to look at networking as putting energy into people. You have to continually put energy into the system. Once you pull the plug, maybe someone will ping you once, twice, but by the third time, they are gone." Marcelo believes if you put good energy into people, that energy will come back to you. Marcelo also says that the other person you are connecting with is also part of an ecosystem and spreading your energy around.

Marcelo said, "I made the connection to Joaquin to you and seven other people. Those connections were value-based connections that everybody learned from. One connection to seven people, and of those seven people, a few connected him to other folks. Your name and your energy floats around with that. With each connection you helped create, your name gets a little bigger and carries through those connections."

MOUNT EVEREST: BUILDING RELATIONSHIPS AND TRUST FOR SURVIVAL

Marcelo De Santis shares his story about climbing Mount Everest, building and leveraging relationships in the extreme environment of high-altitude mountaineering.

Marcelo said, "When you embark on an expedition to the Himalayas, you are up to two to three months of living in a remote, isolated place that is stripped of any of the pleasures of life, along with the fact that your body is dealing with oxygen deprivation."

Marcelo mentions during these long expeditions how most of the time, you will know half of the team since there are always new climbers who join. Expeditions to mountains like Everest, Ama Dablam, or Manaslu have a large degree of risk and a lot of responsibility on each climber to make sure personal actions do not endanger the lives of colleagues or impact other expeditions and teams around.

Marcelo shared that to build that common sense of responsibility and interdependence within the team, they conduct a very simple but powerful team-building ceremony which consists in each person sharing several things.

1. What are the climbing skills you're best at?

2. What are the climbing skills you need help with?

3. Why are you climbing this mountain?

The first two questions help to build awareness and understanding by knowing each other's strengths and learning opportunities. The third question—on *why*—builds an emotional connection across all climbers as they openly share the purpose behind the effort of climbing these difficult mountains. It is inspiring and humbling to listen to their personal reasons for climbing. Some do it because a family member passed due to an illness, others to break a personal record, or in the case of Marcelo, some do it to fundraise in support of UNICEF.

Marcelo said, "Building trust and interdependence in a climbing team is really important. It does not matter how strong and qualified you are individually as a climber in a place in which acting as a team is the only life insurance you have. Because at any point in time during the expedition, there could be avalanches, or someone might fall into a crevasse, and you want to know not only who has the skills to assist in the rescue but also be able to provide encouragement to the person being rescued who might be under a large amount of stress. That is when reminding that person of their 'why' might make a huge difference."

Marcelo shares, "In my second Everest attempt, I got a pulmonary edema at camp three, and my life was at risk. I was very close to death while climbing down the mountain, and I almost gave up halfway down. At that moment, my climbing partner showed me a picture of my wife that I used to carry with me in my backpack. He reminded me that she was one of the reasons I was climbing and that it was worth standing up on my feet and sort out the icefall, one of the most technical sections of climbing Everest."

He finalizes by adding, "Mountaineering teaches you how to be intentional in building trustworthy relationships in a very short time, since establishing those human bonds are priceless in a place in which everything is uncertain, and a large number of different risks are all around you, including the risk of losing your life and the lives of your climbing colleagues at any time."

IF YOU SHOW INTEREST IN PEOPLE, THEY WILL SHOW INTEREST IN YOU

Jason Calacanis is one of the world's top angel investors and the author of the book *Angel: How to Invest in Technology Start-ups—Timeless Advice from an Angel Investor Who Turned $100,000 into $100,000,000* which you can find at amazon.com/Angel-Invest-Technology-Start-ups-Timeless-Investor/dp/0062560700. He attributes a lot of his success to networking.

He attributes relationship building to finding great deals, getting his name on the capitalization tables for investments, networking to helping his portfolio companies, and finding other great networks as part of his investing syndicate. In his podcast episode 1409, he interviews JJ Foster, who added value to Jason by typing up the notes for ten of his podcast shows (power of accelerator series). This effort took JJ two hours per episode and about twenty hours total. This creation of value (the notes for Jason Calacanis) and knowledge helped him get a job at OnDeck, a nationwide technology accelerator.

To return the favor and in the spirit of smart networking, Jason allowed JJ on his podcast show and interviewed him. He has a couple of mentoring tips and networking techniques he shares with JJ. He used JJ as an example and said, "If you show interest in other people, they will show interest in you." JJ showed interest in Jason by writing up his notes. Jason also touched on the law of reciprocity. Jason felt compelled to give something in return (i.e., include him on the podcast).

Jason provides additional tips for networking with JJ. Although these tips are specific to the venture capital industry, the lessons can be useful across industries (Calacanis and Wood 2022).

1. Living in cities with networking density enables a ton of collisions with others

    a. Jason states, "If you want to do full court press in venture capital and investing, you should be in the top cities with lots of venture density. You just have to run to Austin, LA, Miami, and New York. Anywhere but a third- or fourth-tier city where there are no tech people."

    b. Jason says, "Get the smallest apartment you can in the lowest cost spaces and go to a town where there's gonna be a ton of collisions. For example, get a studio apartment in Redwood City or somewhere in Palo Alto and just go hang out in Palo Alto every day and have lunch there and just listen to conversations and meet people."

2. Always picking up the tab.

    a. Find a place where you can order a bunch of family style appetizers, and order drinks by the pitcher. This would be like sangria, beer, pizza, or Mexican food. You can raise the bar with sushi when you are making more money

    b. Invite two founders who you met and two other associates, and now you got five people at dinner. If it winds up being $40 versus $200, is it gonna kill you? Probably not. When you walk in the location, give your credit card to your host and pick up the tab for your networking guests.

c. You will be known for facilitating great dinner connections.

By studying the people in your network, determining the value you can add, and putting these into your relationship action plan, you are now in a great position to work and execute to add tremendous value to your network. The stories in this chapter reinforce how hard work and adding value to your network can create mutual success.

EXERCISE

- List out the various touch points of value you will have overtime with your network.

- Provide examples of connections you have made that have been able to help both parties.

RESOURCES:

- *How to Win Friends and Influence People* by Dale Carnegie

- *Never Eat Alone* Keith Ferrazzi

- *Who's Got Your Back* by Keith Ferrazzi

STEP 8

MEASURE AND INCREASE THE VALUE YOU PROVIDE

If you can't measure it, you can't improve it.

—PETER DRUCKER

MEASURE YOUR RELATIONSHIP VALUE VIA THE VALUE BANK ACCOUNT

You can measure relationships like a bank account. When we add value and do something positive for a person in our network, we add deposits into their respective value bank account. Whenever we make an ask of someone for something that does not align with their goals or do something that pulls our person in our network away from their goals or do something negative, it is a withdrawal or a debit. Over time you want to measure each interaction and measure if you are adding to or withdrawing from this value bank account for the people in your network. The larger the interaction that moves them closer to their goals, the larger the deposit. As you build more credits or deposits of value, you can ask for a withdrawal.

An example of a large deposit of value comes from my interview with Juan Carlos "JC" Gutierrez. JC was at a Hispanic IT Executive Council (HITEC), an organization I cofounded, event and was talking to Andre Arbelaez, who was president of HITEC at the time, when Andre got a call from a HITEC Board member and CEO of Next Generation Inc, Darrell Higueros, who was in distress. His mother had sadly passed away in the United States, and the family wanted to do the burial in Guatemala.

He was trying to send her body from the US to Guatemala, and they couldn't get an airplane or any support. Darrell called Andre for help, and JC, who is also a board member of HITEC, was next to Andre. Andre explained the situation to JC and asked if he knew anybody who could help. JC said, "Hey, I know the chief financial officer (CFO), Gerardo Grajales, of Avianca Airlines through my network and work in Latin America. Maybe he can help." JC had built a good relationship with him and thought he could help. JC reached out to the CFO, who was at the time traveling in Europe, and the CFO said he would check. JC said, "The CFO called me back, and it was late in Europe. That is a good thing." The CFO put JC in touch with one of his team members, and Avianca provided space on an airplane for the body. The body was able to arrive in Guatemala in time for the services. In summary, JC said, "We were able to help Darrell in this time of need, and this was all due to relationships, connections, and networking. Additionally, this aligns with our values of serving." This effort touched several people in their networks and deposited value to each other.

Steven Covey taught a similar concept in his book *The 7 Habits of Highly Effective People* around the emotional bank account. Every time we interact with someone, we tend to keep an accounting tabulation on the relationship of our emotions with them. If they do something we like, we give them a deposit, and for something we dislike, we give them a withdrawal. The receiver decides. Withdrawals and credits can be made without you being there by your reputation, both positive and negative (Viner 2013).

EXPECTATIONS AND PERFORMANCE ARE KEYS TO CREATING VALUE

Expectations are a vital part of determining whether something is valuable or not. We have expectations about a lot of things (the time it takes to get to work, how a person will treat us, a dentist visit, to name a few). When things don't meet our expectations, we tend to get upset, and when things exceed our expectations, we are pleasantly surprised and happy.

Expectations also play a role in adding to or subtracting from a value bank account. Every time your performance meets or exceeds an expectation from somebody in your network, you add a deposit to that value bank account. Every time your performance is lower than the expectation, you take a withdrawal and a debit from that value bank account. You can also view this by looking at the following two formulas:

$P \geq E = +$ (If your P [performance] is greater than or equal to $\geq$ the E [expectation] than it equals = a deposit +)

$P < E = -$ (If your P is less than $<$ the E than it equals = a withdrawal -)

Based on these equations, there are a couple of key value factors around expectations to increase deposits and minimize withdrawals.

- Understand expectations
- Lower expectations
- Increase performance
- Continually monitor and do the above three bullets

TAKING WITHDRAWALS WITHOUT DEPOSITS

Matt Wells is the associate vice chancellor for external engagement and development at Purdue University Northwest. In my interview with Matt, he shares his story on how not to approach networking and relationships via taking withdrawals without making deposits.

One of Matt's unique highlights of his professional career was where on multiple occasions when he was invited to the White House to meet with the president and senior staff to lobby for particular projects and legislation that were in his wheelhouse at the time. Matt states, "Those meetings, I can trace back to years of cultivating relationships that was almost like a trail of breadcrumbs."

There is a particular individual whom Matt got to know over the last few years. He is a very bright guy, probably in his late thirties, who has had some modest entrepreneurial success and talent to do bigger things. In his early thirties he had started a mildly successful local retail shop and built a pretty large network of influential public and private sector players. These relationships were both at the state level in Indiana and in DC before he worked for a very influential public figure.

In spite of his general charisma, Matt observed in a particular instance where he was looking to the campaign for a new position as the CEO of a prominent economic development organization, for which, at the time, Matt was helping run the search. To lobby for this role, this person attended every single board member over a span of probably two or three weeks and cold called these high-powered chief executives who sat on the board, articulating why he thought he'd be a great candidate and requesting a coffee meeting. He was displaying a level of familiarity with folks whom he didn't have any existing relationship with.

It was clear at the next board meeting that all seven or eight of the members had received basically the same message from this guy. The message was that he was trying to find some foothold with one person so that person could advocate for him to get an interview. Needless to say, he didn't get an interview. But ironically, Matt ended up meeting him in person after all this happened. He mentioned to Matt that he couldn't figure out why he hadn't gotten an interview. He said to Matt, "I went and tried to put myself out there and network, right? I can't understand why the networking did not work."

Matt suggested and said to him, "Perhaps, you know, you needed to be a little more intentional and strategic about how you made those approaches to people in positions of influence."

BUILD RELATIONSHIPS LONG BEFORE YOU WANT SOMETHING

Matt Wells mentions that really effective networking takes time to cultivate. Networking is not something transactional that you can do in a short time window. Matt said, "If your objective is to get an inside track (i.e., a career opportunity), your time to build a network for that is long before seeing the job advertised. It's a process that's continually ongoing. It stems more from what you have to offer others rather than what others can do for you."

WHAT COULD YOU DO DIFFERENTLY?

In terms of what could have been done differently to better position this candidate, Matt said, "If this is a position you are interested in, at some point, you needed to probably get involved with that organization over a period of a couple of years, show that you could offer some value to them, instead of just making a barrage of cold calls and harassing emails and phone calls to the board members saying how much you really want it." Matt continued saying, "Confidence is a great thing. But confidence that isn't backed up by real value, or intentionality, is a real liability."

NETWORKING AND ONGOING MEASUREMENT

There was someone who was an alumnus of the educational institution that Matt worked for who had grown up near the educational institution and had gone on to legendary success on Wall Street. One of the things Matt noticed is that most of the folks he worked with at the university saw dollar signs coming out of his eyes when they looked at him. They thought of him primarily as a donor prospect. Matt focused on developing a relationship to get to know him for who he was and to learn about his story. Matt states, "We discovered we had a lot of mutual interests and a lot of shared vision for where we saw the university and its surrounding region going in the future."

They struck up a real friendship, and in the following two or three years, that friendship opened more doors than I would have ever imagined. It connected Matt with another highly influential presidential adviser, who in turn connected me with a particular lobbyist whom I was able to retain to work on some of our high-priority projects, which in turn was mentoring one of the presidential senior staff members who were working on domestic policy. Matt states, "I can trace some of these really important meetings, these important transactions and, you know, opportunities. I can almost always draw a line. A relationship map back to where that originated."

Matt feels the most important thing in all of businesses is having broad and deep enough network of folks who genuinely know and trust you. He also feels you must have authentic quality relationships where you rely on each other for transactions from time to time, but it's because you have a mutual level of trust and respect. You know that person will be a good steward of a favor you ask, and vice versa. Matt's mentor, the Wall Street Titan, has impressed upon him over the years that the world runs on favors, and you do favors for people you care about and trust. Matt states, "Humans are social creatures, and it takes a level of time as well as a shared experience to build trust. It's just part of our DNA. It's how we're wired."

PATTI AND THE PITCH STORY

One of Matt's colleagues, who was a professor of management, wrote a case study called "Patty at the Pitch." It talked about two executives who know each other through the country club. One of them just got tapped for the CEO position of a fairly large corporation. And he is very welcomed by the board and the employees with much fanfare. He is a bright, young, dynamic talent who's got a bold and big vision for the future of the company. His first public appearance was the first shareholder meeting, and it was just dynamite. He gets up and delivers one of those presentations and speeches that gets the crowd totally fired up and inspires a lot of belief. The CEO mentioned to the group that he would be back in three months to unveil the new strategic plan and direction. The CEO let everybody know the best is yet to come. He goes to the club that night after the presentation and connects with his friend, Patti, for a drink. The club board recently elected Patti as chair of the board. The country club was losing members for several years, and their financial performance was weaker than expected.

Patti and he talk about what's next for them. Patti listens and hears this friend talk about this phenomenal presentation and all the support he's getting from folks inside his new company. The CEO dives into his work over the next couple of months with just ferocity and almost obsessiveness, spending time thinking through plans, brainstorming, refining ideas, and spending hours and hours every night at the office. The CEO was basically living at the office preparing for this big unveiling of where the company was going to go this upcoming quarter.

Every once in a while, he takes a break, goes to the club, and sees Patti just out there on the pitch hanging out with members and drinking in the bar. The CEO thinks to himself this guy is really going to need to turn it around or this club's in trouble. The CEO thinks to himself, *What the heck is he doing? He's wasting his time. I never see him at the desk. I never see him working. What the heck's going on?* The CEO, in his mind, says, "I'm glad I'm not making that mistake."

Fast forward a couple of months, and this keeps happening. The CEO is going at 1,000 miles an hour working on his stuff and seeing his buddy over there slacking off, chatting and laughing with the members on the pitch.

The next board meeting comes up for the CEO, and he feels fired up. He has rehearsed this presentation and has his lieutenants there to back him. He believes this presentation is just going to set the world on fire with this new strategic direction. He gets up there to present, and it's a total dud.

He can't figure out what the heck happened. He could not understand how they were on fire when he first came. He felt he gave them his absolute best stuff, and it just went flat, and nobody engaged with it. He goes to the club that night and runs into Patti. Patti has just come off the quarterly board meeting with the club directors, and Patti says, "We just had a total turnaround this quarter. Our membership numbers started trending upward, and we started to do better on collecting dues." The board of the club ended up extending Patti's term.

The CEO was a bit curious and surprised, and he said, "Patti, I don't get it. You didn't spend any time working these last several months and weren't doing anything. I never saw you working."

Patti said, "I was working the entire time. You just didn't know because that was my work. I was out there with my stakeholders listening to their input." Patti then mentions how he wove the conversations together into something that moved the club forward.

DR. ROBERT RODRIGUEZ'S FOUR LEVELS APPROACH TO CREATING AND MEASURING VALUE

In my interview with Dr. Robert Rodriguez, he says he likes to measure his relationships with people on four levels.

- First level—Knowledge. The person knows who you are.
- Second level—Preference. All things being equal. The person prefers to work and collaborate with you.
- Third level—Insistence. They get upset when somebody else gets a referral over you and want to partner with you on whatever they are working on.
- Fourth level—Sponsorship. They are there for you and speak highly of you even when you are not in the room. They value you and your work and will introduce you to others. You have built up enough relationship capital and deposits that they are confident you will do the same with whomever you receive an introduction to. Additionally, they know you'll sponsor them the same way.

BUILD ENOUGH VALUE SO PEOPLE ARE WEARING YOUR T-SHIRT

As it relates to measuring value and Dr. Robert Rodriguez's fourth level of relationship (sponsorship), Dr. Robert Rodriguez said, "Your presence is your leadership. But being present in a place and being present doesn't mean being physically present."

Dr. Rodriguez mentions that you want to build relationships and add enough value among people in the room that they say your name or reference you in their conversations without you being in the room. It is like a halo that follows you. The value you give to others is like compounding interest as they share that with others in their network and beyond.

Dr. Rodriguez refers to author Keith Wyche, who wrote the book *Good Is Not Enough.* He uses the term "wearing your T-shirt," which is where you inspire and empower others to speak for you and wear your T-shirt advocating and sponsoring you when you are not in the room. Robert said, "At the end of the day, it's about the relationships we can nurture and build. And, of course, you have to deliver results." It is important you are a good person and a hard worker, but sometimes people advocating for you is the differentiator.

Robert mentioned that he talks with many professionals, and they say to him, "Robert, I'm doing the work. I went back and got the MBA. I'm getting good ratings, but I'm just not moving ahead or receiving promotions."

The reason is that there are not enough people sponsoring or advocating for you or "wearing your T-shirt." You want to build value and relationship capital with key people such that they are always saying great things about you when you are not in the room. This creation of value and the networking associated with it will be a key differentiator in your career as you progress upward within your organization. Measure and increase the number of people who are wearing your T-shirt!

As I build relationships with people, I have a mental model of my relationships bank account with them, which is pretty much a gauge that spans from one hundred to zero to negative one hundred. I ask myself the following questions to adjust where that gauge is at for each person.

- Have I been asking for too many withdrawals without adding deposits of value?
- Do I understand their expectations, and should I lower their expectations?
- What would be a big easy way to help this person accomplish their goals?
- Are they wearing my T-shirt when I am not around?

Be laser focused on the value bank account with each member of your network and ways you can add value, increase it, and help them become more successful over time.

EXERCISE

- What is the relationship bank account with each of the people in your network?
- Who is wearing your T-shirt?
- Do you understand the expectations that each member in your network has of you?
- Are there examples in your life where you are working hard on tasks and not spending the time on the right relationships?

RESOURCES:

- *Good Is Not Enough* by Keith Wyche
- *The 7 Habits of Highly Effective People* by Steven Covey

OPTIMIZATION

STEP 9

MASTER NETWORKING EVENTS

You can have everything in life you want if you will just help enough other people get what they want.

—ZIG ZIGLAR

There I was, getting out of my car, ready to walk into my first Tercer Jueves (Third Thursday) monthly networking meeting for the Michigan Hispanic Chamber of Commerce. It was one of the top chambers in the country. I was nervous. I would be walking into a room of CEOs, business leaders, and corporate sponsors and not knowing many of them. They ran companies in the tens and hundreds of millions of dollars in revenue, and many were major suppliers to the big three auto companies. The CEO at the time was Armando Ojeda, and he welcomed everyone and welcomed me as a new member. He then asked everybody in the room to:

- Do a brief introduction;
- List three things they are looking for to help their business grow; and

- List three things that you could provide to help businesses grow.

This put me at ease because it helped facilitate meeting other people and letting people know what I could offer. It also helped set the stage. I attended these sessions regularly. I got to listen over time how these business leaders sharpened their pitch on the three things of need and value and how they thanked people in the room who helped their business. I also learned how these business leaders networked and how they mastered networking events. This was just one example that added to my building blocks of how to master networking events.

Networking events are a great vehicle to help add value to your network, meet new people, accomplish your goals, and have fun. With the map of your goals and your network, you can look at your calendar for the year and target the events that best align to help you connect and add value to your relationships and accomplish your goals. This takes time and planning, so focus on this well in advance and review it as part of your rituals. Additionally, there are things you can do during and after networking events to ensure you most optimally help your network, accomplish your goals, and build stronger relationships.

PREP BEFORE THE EVENT

IDENTIFY THE RIGHT EVENT

There are hundreds of networking events to attend. With your foundation in place, you can look at your calendar and identify the right ones to attend.

ATTENDING THE RIGHT NETWORKING EVENTS

In my interview with Gale Wilkinson, she said she has tried to be more intentional about the networking events she goes to. She attended every event when she started in the Chicago technology venture scene around 2011. She didn't know what was going to happen, but she felt she needed to go and learn about the ecosystem and start to create relationships. After a while, she was more focused and could be deliberate about meeting a specific founder or specific investor because she knew the lay of the land. Gale said, "I think many people want to skip that step or they stay in that step for too long."

Gale is also in a position where she is speaking at more events than she attends. Gale said, "So it's a strategy around attending quality of events that are in your strike zone that provides the opportunity to meet good connections and reinforce ones you already have. That's very important."

Be Selective on Attending Events That Don't Align with Your Goals

In some cases, you will receive invitations to networking events that do not align with your goals or will have people attending who are not part of your defined network. You can ask yourself the following questions:

- Is my time best spent here?
- Does this align with my goals?

I am not saying you shouldn't attend these events. But I am saying to be intentional with your time.

If you do attend these events:

- Be cordial.
- Be optimistic.
- Learn something.
- Take inputs from the event and become more selective about networking events you join in the future. Inputs can include the people you met and were able to help. Additionally, tracking what you learned and determining whether it helps you with any of your goals. Also, determine what was the opportunity cost of your time (would your time have been spent better doing something else).

It is okay to attend events that don't align with your goals. Remember that life is not always about you and your goals, and you might connect with somebody new at one of these events, which would be a great addition to your network.

DON'T GO TO AN EVENT IF YOU CAN'T FOLLOW UP

Realize that for every event you attend, you will need to schedule about fifteen to thirty minutes of follow-up for every hour at each event. My experience is the basis for this ratio. This could be a call, social media connection, or email to people you met or did not meet but want to follow up with. If you don't have the bandwidth and time to follow up after an event, I strongly consider you do not attend.

Gale Wilkinson said, "I just canceled a conference because I can't process all of the new people I am meeting." Gale strongly believes that every time she goes and meets with people, whether it's at events, conferences, or one on one, all that activity creates follow-up work, and that follow-up needs to happen.

RESEARCH WHO WILL BE AT THE EVENT

Once you decide which events to attend, it is important you do as much research as possible on who will be present and then study their backgrounds and find ways your value toolkit can be useful to them (Execution section). It may not be possible to get this data and might require you to formulate a hypothesis. You can consider board members, sponsors, and people who have attended the event in the past as examples of likely attendees.

In my interview with Salina Rivera, CEO of the Digital You powered by Miyan Media, she said, "The difference between people who do networking really well from others is that they go in with a plan. One should go with a goal in mind and think about whom they want to meet in the room." Salina said the goal could be as simple as saying hello to a person and sending a follow-up note delivering value and mentioning you both attended this specific event as a point of commonality.

REACH OUT PRIOR TO THE EVENT

Reach out to those you want to connect with prior to the event and touch on the value you would like to discuss at the event.

This will help facilitate and help you use your networking time more efficiently.

Salina says in advance of the event, you could say or write something like, "I look forward to speaking to you at the conference or hearing you speak at the conference on XYZ topic. I've been following your posts and sharing them with my network. Please let me know if there is anything I can do to help you reach more people who would benefit from your expertise." Salina continued, "You've made it all about the other person, and in the event you cannot connect at the conference, you can still follow up off the thread."

DURING THE EVENT

By ensuring you are at the right event, and with the preparation and research completed, you are now ready to enter the networking event. This could be a couple of people or a networking event with hundreds of people. Either way, the stories and tips below should help you leverage these events for mutual success.

HAVE AN OPEN MINDSET TO LEARN

In my interview with Adela Cepeda, she mentioned when she enters a business networking event, she hopes to make two or three connections that are business related. She also works to have time to listen to what other people are saying and doing, as those outputs can be very revealing. Adela said, "You can learn so much from people. It could be a vacation they took in a new location that would be of interest to you. It could be something about raising their kids that's relevant to you. It could be anything, but there is so much to learn from other people."

NETWORKING EVENT TIPS

TIP: HAVE AN APPROACHABLE POSTURE

The words you say are just 7 percent of what others perceive! In fact, 55 percent of communication depends on your facial expressions and posture, and the other 38 percent is from the way you speak (Georgiev 2022). Therefore, your physical body should indicate you are approachable. Looking at your phone or standing with your arms crossed does not give other people the appearance they should speak with you. Having a smile with positive energy attracts people. Also, have an open posture and make sure to dress to impress but dress appropriately for the venue.

TIP: MAKE EYE CONTACT WHEN YOU FIRST CONNECT

As you connect, you should have a firm handshake, a clear voice, and keep eye contact. Statistics show that to create an emotional connection and guarantee effective networking, you need to make eye contact at least 60 percent of the time (Georgiev 2022).

TIP: BE YOUR AUTHENTIC SELF

People want to get to know you personally, and vice versa. Be yourself! Chris Salvi, cofounder of Salvi Media, networks with some of the top CEOs. In my interview, he said, "You should be your authentic self when you are networking. Otherwise, it's exhausting. Networking is supposed to be fun. It is a lesson my parents taught me early on that I use to this day. This lesson has been very helpful as I have built my network with CEOs. As the individuals I truly connect with are willing to continue to get to know me, the others will avoid me. That's okay, though. Better not to waste time."

TIP: BE ENGAGED WITH THE PERSON WHEN SPEAKING

When you are speaking with a person or group, it is important you engage with that group and your eyes are not looking at the next person you want to speak with.

In my interview with Frank Carbajal, best-selling author of *Latinx Business Success*, he said, "I always advise people interested in networking to not look around the room when they're speaking with someone. Because what then happens is they're going to look like they're not very interested in building that relationship. This is a key part of being authentic."

TIP: ASK QUESTIONS TO FIND COMMONALITY

As you begin to connect, it is important to find areas of commonality. This could be current events, where you live, or family, among other areas. In my interview with Rushdi Ariss, he said, "When initially connecting, I'm trying to be intentional in trying to find something in common. Because if you're intentional about that, then you can build rapport much sooner."

Rushdi does this by finding out what the person finds exciting, is attracted to, or is looking to get out of the event. Once Rushdi has found that commonality, he might say, "Oh, hey, have you checked out XYZ? I saw them on the showroom floor. It might be something that aligns with what you are looking for." Rushdi is intentional about adding value to the relationship by investing and not seeking anything in return. "You are looking for ways to make a deposit of value. True dividends come over time."

TIP: MASTER SMALL TALK

When you are speaking one-on-one or with a group, there is an art of small talk. In addition to commonality, there are other techniques that can be useful. These include jokes, compliments, asking about family, and reinforcing their comments you believe are true.

Examples of questions that help facilitate small talk include:

- Hello, my name is X. What is your name?
- How are you doing?
- How is your family?
- Where is home for you?
- What are you looking to get out of this event?
- I like the agenda for this session. What are you most looking forward to?

- Do you know anybody else here? How did you first connect with that person?

- Thanks for pulling this event together. Do you need help with anything?

In my interview with Adela Cepeda, she said, "You need to join, and you need to develop these small talk skills for engaging in a conversation with people at networking events. Believe it or not, many people are uncomfortable doing that."

TIP: LISTEN MORE THAN SPEAK

Additionally, don't speak more than 50 percent of the time. We have two ears, two eyes, and one mouth for a reason. When you speak, ensure they are short and meaningful comments and conversations about how you can help them succeed and add value to their goals.

TIP: TELL YOUR STORY

Humans love to hear stories. The joy of listening to stories has been hard-wired into our DNA over thousands of years (Carson 2016). It would help if you had your personal story ready to use during these networking events. You should have a five-minute story, a fifty-second story, and a five-second story or headline. In my interview with Chris Salvi, he mentioned this is something he continues to work on and sharpen as it strengthens his personal brand and has a strong impact on his relationships and business.

When asked about her story, Adela Cepeda said, "I had a great story to tell at networking events. I had a women-owned firm that was going to change the complexion of money managers. It was very entrepreneurial, with great growth, and we had successful investors backing us. It was a fun and easy story to tell at networking events."

As it relates to storytelling, in my interview with Frank Carbajal, he said, "Storytelling is the most powerful ingredient of leadership. You need to have a good story about what you do. But the key is how you keep it as a succinct story that they can expand on when asked."

TIP: MOVE ON IF NOT ENGAGING

Frank Carbajal believes that when you speak to someone, and they kind of push you away a couple of times, then it's time to move on. This could be ignoring you, their eyes wandering at other people, very short answers, and no questions to get to know you. Frank said, "You have to move to folks who really want to commit to building that relationship. Because it is a commitment."

TIP: DON'T OVERCOMMIT

As you find synergies and ways your value toolkit can help a person, be careful not to overcommit. To follow through effectively 100 percent of the time, you must manage your commitments carefully. David Wieland said, "If I commit to helping them or doing something specific, I will do it 100 percent of the time, which means I have to be very careful about what I commit to."

TIP: FIND THE PERSON'S PASSION, AND DON'T MAKE IT ALL ABOUT BUSINESS

When networking, it is important to discover or lead with the person's passion and not make the conversation all about business. Chris Salvi said, "When I'm networking with people, 80 percent of it is about understanding their passion, and the rest of time is talking about my family, maybe interesting trials, tribulations, and triumphs in my life that somehow connect to their passion areas." Chris then touches on what he does professionally. Chris leads with his personal story and feels it's just a much better way of going about networking. Chris said, "Businesses do business with people. It comes down to two people trusting one another. And so that's why I like to lead with my personal self first."

TIP: GIVE CONFIDENCE TO OTHERS

As a facilitator of value and helping people, you might notice introverts, people who are shy, or those who are lacking confidence. Please go out of your way to connect with these folks, understand their goals, and determine any ways to help them.

Frank Carbajal was a recipient of this confidence, and it was very impactful for him. He was asked to be a keynote speaker, where Linda Ronstadt was an award winner. Frank was very nervous going into this speech because Linda is a famous singer who has earned eleven Grammy Awards, among other music awards.

Frank walked up to her, and he told her he was nervous. He mentioned that Linda said to him, "What are you talking about? You just published a book." Linda told him not to focus on her but focus on delivering the message of what you know and how you created a future leadership framework. She mentioned to Frank how important it is to share these stories from folks who started with humble beginnings and have achieved greatness. She reiterated to stick with this message.

Frank accepted the keynote, and it was the first time in his professional career he keynoted at that magnitude. Frank stated, "When I was up on that stage in front of Linda Ronstadt, I was so nervous."

During the speech, Frank looked over at Aida Álvarez, who is a friend and ran the SBA (Small Business Association). Frank said, "She looked over at me, gave me a wink, and gave me a thumbs up." This helped Frank feel a confidence from within. Frank said, "I delivered the keynote and crushed it. I had people in the room, cheerleaders believing in my message, and I think when that happens, you build the confidence to network with others."

You should do your part to make sure everyone in the room is comfortable and feels they belong. Frank Carbajal said, "Great leaders lift people up."

TIP: BRING YOUNGER, LESS EXPERIENCED PEOPLE IN

You should also look at networking venues and opportunities as ways to connect younger, less experienced people into the art of networking. Frank Carbajal said, "Bringing younger, less experienced people in is a form of giving back, which is in the spirit of networking." This is also helpful for those who may not be as confident.

TIP: DON'T BRING ANY NEGATIVITY, AND BE OPTIMISTIC

Negativity can bring down the happiness of other people and makes people less likely to want to interact with you and help you. I believe people who are happy and optimistic breathe life into a room and make the event a much more pleasant occasion.

TIP: DIPLOMATICALLY ENTER INTO A GROUP THAT IS ALREADY SPEAKING

In the event, if you are not able to connect in advance, and there are two or more desired people in a conversation, wait for a break in the conversation and ask their permission to join.

This entry point could be something like, "Excuse me, you are all leaders I admire and look forward to helping. Is it okay if I join this conversation?"

Ninety-nine percent of the time, they will say yes. Once they do, the key is to focus extra hard on listening and understanding how you can help any of the people who are speaking. You can make this easier by emailing and connecting before the event, letting them know you would like to discuss helping them with goal X at the event.

TIP: CONNECT PEOPLE

When you are at networking events, look for an opportunity to connect people who have similar goals or synergies to help each other easily and mutually. I will be at networking events and know, on average, 30 to 40 percent of the room. When I meet somebody new and understand their goals, I run through the people in my mind who could be helpful to them in the room and make the intro, or vice versa. It is a muscle you can work on building. When you make the perfect match, it is a double deposit of value for the same effort.

TIP: MANAGE YOUR TIME

You will often see people at a networking event who spend 90 to 100 percent of the time talking to the same people the whole event. Leaders who are excellent at networking can cover the room in a respectful way. Be respectful, be engaged, and determine ways to help but also be conscious of time.

TIP: THE POLITE MOVE ON

In the event you have been speaking with somebody longer than you would like, or the person is speaking more than listening, you could use a technique I call the polite move on.

> Thank you. It was great catching up and connecting with you. I look forward to finding out more about X and helping you with Y (always bring value). I have been planning to connect with another leader at this event whom I want to help. Let's stay connected to help you with Y.

TIP: PULL ON THREADS

Many people you speak with at networking events will have their story and elevator pitch, but when somebody mentions something interesting, it is important to "pull on that thread" and understand the comment a bit more.

David Wieland said, "I remember this guy, and during our conversation, he said he went over to Africa for six months to help develop a fintech super application, and I was like, whoa, you can't just go on talking without explaining that a bit more. And so, we just talked about that for, like, an hour on that thread." David has stayed close with this person, and they regularly interact on business matters, including a handful of coinvestments.

TIP: ASK QUESTIONS AND BE VULNERABLE

Don't be afraid to ask questions, ask advice, and be vulnerable. Frank Carbajal said, "Some folks want to wait before they ask questions. But there never is the right time. The right time happens when you push yourself." Frank shares that networking is not an easy process. It takes courage to walk up, ask questions, and be vulnerable.

TIP: DON'T RUSH A RELATIONSHIP

Frank Carbajal mentioned he had a conversation with his mentor, Robert Medrano, CEO of Beach View Capital, about how to network with top-level folks. Robert told him, "You can't be desperate. You can't speed up getting to know these folks. It takes time." Frank reinforces not to act desperate and focus on the value you bring.

TIP: BUSINESS CARD OR LINKEDIN CONNECTION

After connecting with somebody new at an event and you feel there is enough rapport, you can either provide your business card or use a LinkedIn feature where you can share your contact information via a QR code. If you are in a group of people, share this with all.

I remember when I was at a networking event in a group conversation, and at the end of the conversation, the one person speaking with the other person for the majority of the time gave her his business card and did not offer me one. I was like, wow, this person couldn't care less about building a relationship with me. Make sure you include those around you when you follow up with a business card or a social media connection.

Click on the QR code symbol in the search:

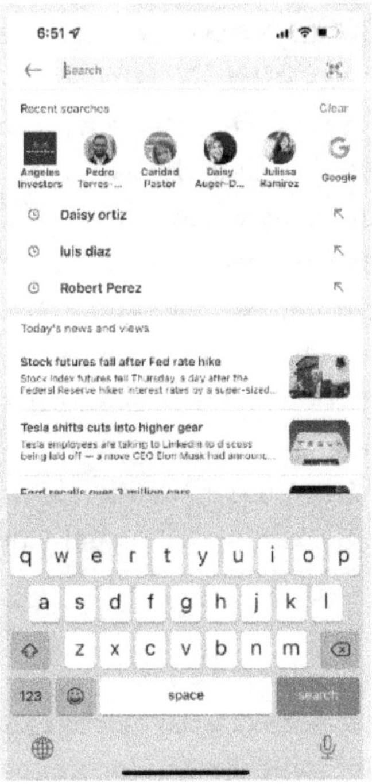

Then share your QR code to connect.

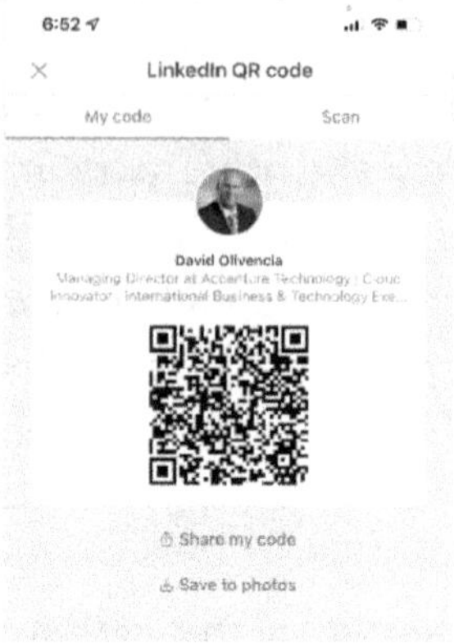

TIP: COMMUNICATE YOUR FULL NAME AND COMPANY WHEN CONNECTING VIA LINKEDIN

If the person doesn't have their phone with them, mention your intention to connect on LinkedIn. Salina Rivera gives an example of what she might say when she asks. She tells the person, "Hi, [Name]. It was nice meeting you. Are you on LinkedIn?" If they say yes, Salina will let them know to keep an eye out for a LinkedIn connection request from her. You can also repeat your full name and company here as another brand impression to reinforce who it will be coming from. Salina said, "If they have not been on LinkedIn for a while, this approach of letting them know it will be coming will usually draw them back."

TIP: STEP BACK AND ENJOY

As you attend the event, let it be natural and have fun. There are so many things to be thankful for. Be open to meeting new people and connecting with value. You never know who you may meet and how you can help each other obtain mutual success.

David Wieland believes it is enjoyable to meet like-minded people and have genuine conversations with them. David said, "I try not to put any pressure on myself or the situation to achieve anything at all." David believes it is important to go in, shake some hands, listen to people's stories, and try to absorb as much as possible and be helpful. This approach has worked well for David.

FOLLOW UP AFTER THE EVENT

After the event, it is important you follow up with those you connected with. It is very important you connect with value and tangible ways you can help them.

Salina Rivera said, "Follow-up is where most people fall through, even if they have some success in the room. For some reason, the follow-up seems to be one of the toughest parts I see for people." Digital and social media tools make it easier, but still, many people don't do the follow-up, and it leaves a lot of value on the table.

DEBRIEF

The first step of the follow-up is to debrief with lifelines, your coach, or internally with yourself. Some questions to ask yourself as part of the debrief include:

- Did you use these tips?
- Did you meet those you would like to?

- Did you connect with new people to add to your network?
- Were you able to help somebody?
- What and who are all the follow-ups you have?
- Did this network and event meet your expectations?
- How likely are you to attend this event again or recommend the event to a friend or colleague?

These answers should provide inputs for continuous improvement as you attend the next set of networking events.

FOLLOW-UP ACTIONS

After the debrief, it is time for action. Below are a couple of general suggestions you can do after the networking event and the debrief.

- Thank the host for a great event and a couple of ways you can accelerate the mission and vision of the organization.
- With those whom you connected with, reconnect with them via phone call, email, message, or a handwritten note. Connect with them with value and a tangible next step that not only helps them with their goals but is a win-win.
- Send handwritten notes, which are a nice touch.
- Here is a script that you can customize to follow up with somebody directly.

Person A,

It was great connecting at networking event B. I enjoyed our conversation about your goal A and goal B. Per our conversation, I thought the below points would be helpful:

- Attached is some research I saw on goal A.

- I will be following up with a connection to person C, who leads a center that focuses on goal B.

- I will connect you to a dear friend of mine who lives near you and has published a book around goal A and goal B.

I have an event coming up around (my goal C) on (date). Here is a link to the invite if you can attend.

Thanks,
Name
Title
(Links to social media)

LEVERAGE EMAIL AND THE CALENDAR TO FOLLOW UP

After each event, David Wieland connects with people he meets on LinkedIn and sends them an email. David said, "I try to recall some details for my own benefit and put that in an email." David's emails are typically, "Hey, I enjoyed talking about XYZ. I'm happy to do ABC." David then throws thirty minutes on his calendar sometime in the future to do the thing he committed to. David said, "I'll kick the can if I don't block out the actual time to do it." David leverages the calendar function to make sure it is on the schedule and gets done. I do the same.

The foundation and execution skills built along with these networking event tips can be useful to help you connect with value, master networking events, and achieve networking excellence.

EXERCISE

- What are the networking events you plan to attend over the next year?
- What networking events are you going to say no to attending?
- What tips will you focus on the most?
- How much time are you going to allocate to following up after each event?

RESOURCES

- *The 7 Habits of Highly Effective People* by Steve Covey
- *Never Eat Alone* by Keith Ferrazzi
- *A Message from Garcia* by Charles P. Garcia

STEP 10

SCALE THE VALUE TO YOUR NETWORK WITH DIGITAL AND SOCIAL MEDIA

"Build it, and they will come" only works in the movies. Social media is a "build it, nurture it, engage them, and they may come and stay."

—SETH GODIN

We live in an amazing time enabled by digital technologies and social media. At no other time in human history have you reached hundreds of millions of people instantly. Some of the great things about digital and social media are how they can amplify you and your brand, help you stay more connected to your network, and help you more rapidly accomplish your goals. Some of the bad things about social media and digital communications are that they can amplify bad messaging and brand if you are not prepared and do not have a strong foundation.

This is not an in-depth social media chapter. This topic is far too broad to cover here fully, and there are whole books written on this. Please go to Amazon.com and Google "social media and digital" or google the topic. This chapter will focus on a few ways to leverage digital and social for building relationships and networking.

As it relates to using social media and digital technologies, a study by *Forbes* asked 750 business executives about the top benefits of using technology for networking (Forbes Insights 2009). The top benefits of online networking were:

- Saves time (92 percent)
- Saves money (88 percent)
- More flexibility in location and timing (76 percent)
- Allows the participant to multitask (64 percent)
- Increases productivity (55 percent)
- Ability to archive sessions (49 percent)
- Less peer pressure (16 percent)

KEITH FERRAZZI ON DIGITAL AND SOCIAL MEDIA

Keith Ferrazzi believes we can now accelerate our relationships through online relationship building. He asks us to think of our relationships like a bullseye with your lifelines at the center. The next rung out is your A-level priorities, those most critical individuals to your goals and dreams in the next year. All the way out to your periphery is your online and digital network.

Keith said, "They are loose connections, and there is nothing wrong with that. You might follow them because you want to learn from them to accomplish a goal and are curious to hear what they have to say." When Keith has a question or wants to get feedback on a topic, he leverages this online network. Keith said, "I shoot it out to the world. And what I get back is a set of responses from individuals, and then I bring them one step closer." Keith might call them or do a webinar and bring them closer in. Keith said, "It's an immensely rich opportunity to nurture a field of relationships you can then draw in and out."

When you think about digital and social, you should regularly give to your community, share valuable content with those whom you follow, and send recommendations. It is about generosity and giving, just on a larger scale (Howes 2014).

AVOID SELF-INTEREST ON SOCIAL MEDIA

In our interview, Raymond Arroyo said, "Social media can also be very harmful. I find, for the most part, social networks, including LinkedIn, it's really not about your network." Raymond believes many on social who do it with self-interest and in a very self-serving manner are not looking to help others. Raymond also believes a network is real human-to-human connections that you have interacted with, not virtual connections. Raymond believes that social media is great but works hard for real face-to-face connections. This includes going out of your way to meet the people within your network in person with the intention of helping them.

OUTBOUND VERSUS INBOUND

There are two sides to social media called outbound and inbound. Outbound is what you actively put out to the world and is all the social media posting and engagement you do to add value to your network and beyond.

Inbound is what other people see and the perspective you give off when they search for you and your content. For example, when people search for your name on Google, likely the first thing that comes up is a link to your LinkedIn profile. LinkedIn has done a great job with theSEO (search engine optimization) algorithm such that your LinkedIn profile is usually one of the top two or three search results that come up.

From an inbound perspective, you can define yourself by a lot of things which include your personal life, your work, those around you, and more. Just like you can google this to research for others on what would create value for somebody, people can google you, and they will find your Facebook profile, your Twitter, your LinkedIn, and other items.

SOCIAL MEDIA PLATFORMS FOR NETWORKING

There are hundreds of social media platforms to help you connect with and add value to your network. This chapter is only going to focus on some of the top platforms that are currently out there and will only touch on the surface of how they can help with networking.

Some of the more popular social media channels for networking include:

- Twitter—Twitter.com
- YouTube—YouTube.com
- Facebook—Facebook.com
- LinkedIn—LinkedIn.com
- TikTok—TikTok.com
- Slack—Slack.com
- Discord—Discord.com
- Reddit—Reddit.com

LINKEDIN

As I view LinkedIn as a top tool for social media and business networking, I wanted to go into some of the details of its capabilities and how you can use it.

LinkedIn is a business and employment social media platform owned by Microsoft. It has about seventy million users and is the de facto platform for business and professional users (Dixon 2022).

YOUR PROFILE

Your profile on LinkedIn is your brand to the world. It is important it is current and has all the components you want to communicate. It also should portray the elements of your foundation and leverage brand enhancement.

It is important to make sure you use professional pictures to have the highest quality brand for your profile.

SEARCHING CONNECTIONS BY CITY

A lesson I learned from the book *Never Eat Alone* and watching leaders like Pablo Schneider and Jason Calacanis was that when you travel to a city, you look at your network in that city and invite them to a meal. In some cases, it is a "going Dutch" meal where everyone pays their way, or as Jason Calacanis in his Apple podcast says, you pick up the tab and buy pitchers of beer, pizza, and salad, which is something very simple (Calacanis and Wood 2022). LinkedIn has tools in the search that can help you filter your network by city. Once you have your network by city you can reach out and invite them to a meal.

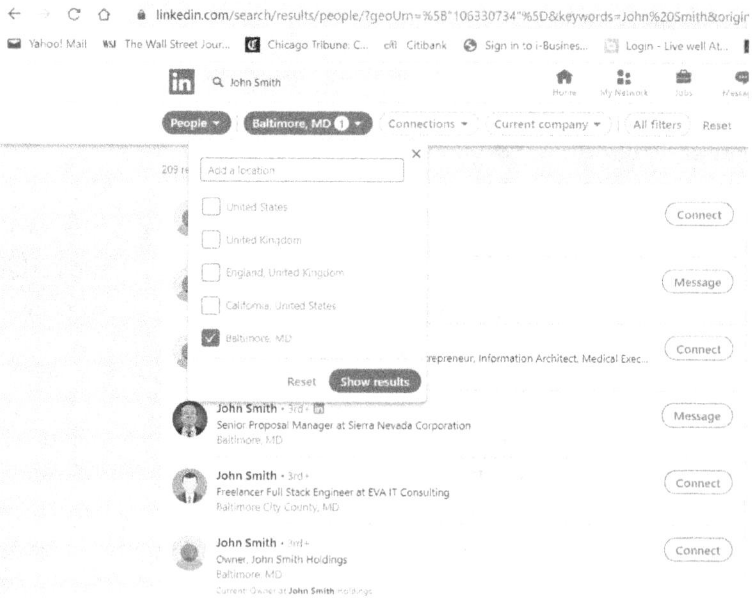

CONNECTING/CONNECTING WITH VALUE

When you want to connect with somebody on LinkedIn, please connect with value on why you are reaching out and how you can help them accomplish their goals. Also, try to connect with commonality.

Here is an example of some connection requests I get weekly that could be improved upon:

- Hi David, you have an interesting network, and I would love to connect.
- We have a B2B product that would be great for your customers. Let's connect.
- I saw we have many people in common. Let's connect.
- Hi David, I'm looking forward to connecting with you.

Connecting is great, but please work to reach out with context and value you can bring to the person you are connecting with!

ANALYTICS

LinkedIn has several layers of analytics that can be useful to you. This includes reviewing those who have looked at your profile and shares as well as likes and interactions with your posts. You can also boost and promote posts and check out the performance of those campaigns.

DIGITAL NETWORKING SKILL/TIP ENDORSE

A sincere digital endorsement of skills is a great way to give a deposit of value to somebody in your network. I say sincerely because it is also a reflection of you when you endorse someone, as your name and profile photo are added to each skill endorsed. Within LinkedIn, you can scroll down to the skills section at the bottom of the person's profile and click on the endorse button. As an example, below is the skills section for Salina Rivera, CEO of Miyan Media:

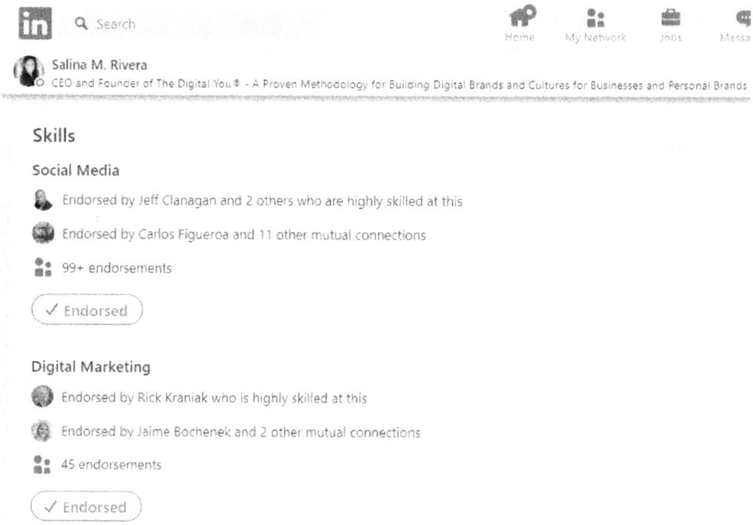

In my interview with Salina Rivera, she mentions as part of the relationship plan, you might add a calendar invite a month or two out as a reminder to endorse a respective person in your network. This will allow you to create additional digital touchpoints with a connection as notifications are sent to LinkedIn account holders each time they receive an endorsement.

From an inbound perspective, Salina mentions the skills section in your LinkedIn profile is important for you to fill out because you want to have people endorse you as well. At a minimum, Salina recommends being intentional about the top three skills you select, as they are always visible on your profile. The benefits include reinforcing your areas of expertise in a viewer's mind, introducing your top skills to someone who newly discovers your profile via a search, and helping with your SEO, or search engine optimization, on LinkedIn. But you also want to be able to endorse other people. You can review people in your network and find skills you believe they deserve endorsement for.

As one looks online and sees your endorsement for a skill, they are more likely to reach out and connect with you. Salina said, "I can't tell you how many times that has happened over a simple comment you make on someone's post or an endorsement."

Salina then told me about her social media and networking interaction with Jeff Clanagan, who is the CEO of Kevin Hart's Hartbeat, a global, multi-platform media company creating entertainment at the intersection of comedy and culture with a mission to keep the world laughing together. Jeff does his own social media, and Salina was surprised by that. He does digital touchpoints very well, and he keeps up with people on LinkedIn, but he does it very subtly. He gets great engagement on his posts. He endorsed Salina right away in the skill of social media, as they did a Harvard class togethe and that's where Salina first met him. If you go to Salina's profile, you'll see that he's one of the first endorsements she got for digital marketing.

LEVERAGE SOCIAL MEDIA TO INCREASE TOUCH POINTS WITH YOUR NETWORK

Salina focuses on teaching people how to develop in established touch points they would normally do in-person networking via digital. She says for those in your network or desired network that you want to be intentional about building a relationship with, research back and go about six months before, and look through their posts on LinkedIn. You can comment in a sincere way with value on their posts. Again, be sincere, and don't do these all at once and rush it.

Additionally, LinkedIn has this little bell in the right corner right below the pictures of your connection. Salina said, "To turn those bells on, you just click on that bell, and it will notify you when that person posts something on LinkedIn." See the bell in the upper right-hand side of the picture below.

Salina said, "You can be one of the first people to go and respond to a post. Your name will come up on their view that you commented on your post. People are always curious about seeing what someone has said or commented on. So, they'll go and see that."

Salina believes you need seven to twelve touch points to establish a brand in the mind of a potential consumer or whether you're meeting someone and trying to establish rapport. Those seven to twelve touch points in digital can happen. You just have to put on the right tools to make them happen. That notification and follow-up is one of them.

COMMENT ON POSTS WITH VALUE AND SINCERITY

There was a person who worked at a large Fortune 500 company, and this person was in charge of pulling together a large annual event. Salina knew the person was in charge of the budget for these events, and the person was on Salina's relationship value plan. This person wrote something about their family taking a break and going on vacation, and Salina made a comment on the post. This person wrote Salina back almost within a minute and said, "Salina, how are you? You know, thank you so much. And I wanted to reach out to you, and then I saw your name on LinkedIn. And it signaled me to connect. I wanted to talk to you about the Digital You program you have. We want you to bring that to our company." Salina ended up delivering this digital content to this Fortune 500 as a paid event. This happened because of a relationship value plan and commenting on social media.

Social media is a less intrusive way to establish touch points. Directly calling or texting someone may seem a little too personal for some folks. LinkedIn is one of the best places to continue those digital touchpoints of networking without being too intrusive with people, and there are things you can do on your own timing as part of your plan and time it with when you will next connect with them.

LEVERAGE YOUR PERSONAL BRAND AND PICK ONE SOCIAL CHANNEL TO START

Gale Wilkinson recommends picking one channel that makes the most sense for you. It could be a video. It could be podcasts, blogs, LinkedIn, Twitter, or TikTok. "For me, it's Twitter," she said. She tries to remember to also cross post to LinkedIn but mentions Twitter is definitely the best channel for her personally.

CREATING POSTS

LEVERAGE 3 X 3 MODEL TO PLAN POSTS

Here is a framework to utilize to help determine what to post. It is a 3 x 3 model Ethan Turer, author of *The Next Gold Rush*, taught me in a social media session for New Degree Press.

The first step is to identify the main three brand identities or roles you play. In my case, they are currently: unicorn investor, technology disruption enabler, and networking excellence.

For each of these roles, you want to create a post that teaches, celebrates you or somebody in that space (preferably not you), and surprises.

Here is an example of my framework.

		Teach	Celebrate	Surprise
	Technology Disruption Enabler			
	Networking Excellence			
	Unicorn Investor			

LEVERAGE A STRUCTURE FOR POSTS

Ethan Turer also recommends a structure for posts that I like. Your posts should have a hook, tag an entity or person, a body of text, hashtags, and a call to action with a media attachment. Instagram is more about the graphics and posts with lots of hashtags.

LEVERAGE HASHTAGS

A hashtag, or # symbol, is a way to categorize posts. It helps index how you can search content on social media. Anything after the hashtag is a topic you could use if you a posting about travel. Therefore, people looking for posts can help easily find content related to the topic after your hashtag. You should use hashtags to help people find your posts, content, or information.

Instagram lets you use up to thirty hashtags. LinkedIn has a smaller amount of around five. Twitter is about two to three, but you can add more in a reply. A great hashtag generator tool for Instagram is inflact.com/tools/instagram-hashtag-generator/#/search.

LinkedIn also has its own hashtag generator. You can visit the site: https://www.all-hashtag.com/hashtag-generator.php to identify all the main hashtags for what you are looking to amplify.

SOCIAL MEDIA STRATEGY FOR DAVID WIELAND

In my interview with David Wieland, he mentioned how he has focused on understanding his audiences and sharing things that are relevant to them but also meaningful to him. If you review his LinkedIn feed, the posts fall into three categories. The first is sharing updates and start-up venture capital news. The second is promoting Motivate Venture Capital portfolio companies. The third are things that are personally interesting to David that usually fall under the personal growth or self-improvement category. David's goal here is to help people share things he thinks are helpful, meaningful, and insightful to them and also help David gain some credibility.

David has seen results. He said, "I get a ton of deal flow and investor inquiries purely from LinkedIn. The sweater deal we did was a cold email from the founder. I probably have three investors in our fund who say, 'Hey, I have been watching your LinkedIn profile for, like, three years, and when you guys are raising capital, please let us know.'"

On timing, David doesn't set aside a specific time every day to post. He uses Google Chrome, and it's one of his persistent tabs. When he gets three or four minutes between calls, he will open the tab and see what's going on in the world. Sometimes he will go down a rabbit hole if there's something he needs to share with one of his portfolio companies or reviewing notifications. David doesn't spend dedicated time on it.

CREATING DIGITAL CONTENT

Chris Salvi, cofounder of Salvi Media, believes content creation can be a great lead into networking with others. He has used content creation via his CEO Series on YouTube to help build a network of CEOs. In my interview with Chris, he said, "It's crucial to always start with their best interest in mind." Chris asks the following questions when he considers creating content.

- Does it add value to others?
- Does it enhance our brand?
- How can it be used by our networks?
- Is anyone else making this content?
- Can we monetize the content?

POSTING ON SOCIAL MEDIA

DIGITAL AND SOCIAL MEDIA TIPS

Below are some general tips you can apply across most platforms. You can apply this as you reach out and share information with your network and use social media.

TIP: ENGAGE WITH YOUR OWN POSTS

As you post on social media and people like and comment, please take the time to engage, thank, and like others' comments. Salina said, "All people want acknowledgment. When it comes to acknowledgment through social media, it does not have to be complicated or time-consuming. A simple like or a quick reply of 'thank you' can lead to ongoing, engaging discussions both online and offline."

TIP: CONSIDER COMMENTING ON OLD POSTS

Don't be afraid to comment on old posts of people in your network. You're actually going to revive that post. Salina said, "You're gonna give that post a blood infusion because once you comment on it again, even if it was two months ago, that person is gonna be like, Oh, I wonder whom this person is that commented on a post." The person won't care it was two months ago. Salina continues and says, "They are generally curious about themselves and what people are writing about them and will review."

That's a great way to do it because not only are they notified that someone commented on their post, but everyone else who commented on it and liked it are also notified that someone else liked this post. So, it's great to go back and look at old posts that you can still comment on to keep connections going.

While you can utilize this tip on LinkedIn, it may not be the proper etiquette across other social media platforms.

TIP: KEEP THOSE TOUCH POINTS ACTIVE

Look at your network, and over time continue to connect with them, engage with value in their posts, and help them be successful. Use the touch points of value to increase your bank account with them. You should be thinking about the next seven to twelve touchpoints and interactions you will have with your desired network.

TIP: BOOLEAN SEARCH FOR EXPERTS ON YOUR GOALS

You can use Boolean searches on LinkedIn to connect with people or find people who are experts in your goal areas. You can run a Boolean search on LinkedIn by combining keywords with operators like *and*, *not*, and *or* during your search. Here is a link with more LinkedIn search tips: https://www.linkedin.com/help/linkedin/answer/a524335/using-boolean-search-on-linkedin?lang=en

TIP: GIVE

The rule of reciprocity works very strongly in social media, so give something. This giving can be knowledge, tips, insights, assistance, connections, and more. Salina said, "Repeatedly give, and then when you need it, your network will help you. It's just natural that human beings want to pay something back, right? If somebody does something nice for you, you want to do it for them. It works so awesomely in the digital space." Salina said, "You have to work in the digital space of finding those meaningful touchpoints and connections, but you'd be surprised at how many people you can turn into what you call fans."

TIP: HAVE YOUR OWN PERSONAL RITUAL

Marcelo De Santis has developed a strong social media presence with quality connections, but surprisingly, that was never his goal. Marcelo has approached social media driven by his desire to learn from others. He said, "I never designed an actual plan to 'grow my social media followers.' However, I do have a social media learning ritual. Every quarter I set a list of themes that I want to learn about, topics that are important for my career or topics I am simply curious about. I set my Google alerts to capture articles and news on those topics, and I read the results daily with my morning coffee. This ritual allows me to keep the focus on the themes aligned with my learning priorities. It also indirectly contributes to building my personal brand in social media given I often share those articles after adding my reflections, which often triggers interesting conversations, reactions, and more learning."

TIP: BUILD A SPACE FOR OTHERS TO SHINE

Marcelo De Santis was doing some research on Web3 and the Metaverse. He read a report from a principal at Razorfish. Marcelo searched her profile on LinkedIn and sent a connection request complementing her research and asking a few clarifying questions since he found her insights and conclusions about these technologies very thought provoking. As they began to discuss and share content on these topics, they built a good working relationship, and Marcelo's company—ThoughtWorks—invited her to present on Web3 and Metaverse during one of their global internal events.

Marcelo said, "I think she was responsive to my connection request because I was not trying to sell her anything. I also did my homework and showed her I had studied her research and even compared it with other similar reports. I truly made an effort to prove I was genuinely interested to better understand her thoughts on Web3, which were really unique and insightful."

Marcelo believes if we can respectfully and openly ask for help and create a safe space for others to shine with their superpowers, most people will engage because the motivation to have a positive impact in the lives of others is rooted deeply into our human DNA.

TIP: GET STARTED AND BUILD A PROCESS THAT WORKS FOR YOU

Ethan Turer has done a lot of innovative things in digital and social media. Ethan didn't come from this place of having this big online network but was systematic about building it. He is a regular feature on podcasts and has become a thought leader around all things digital. Ethan said, "So I hit the ground running, testing things. And along the way, I produced processes that worked for me."

Ethan believes understanding your audience, your brand, and what kind of social media content you like is important as you decide what you want to put out into the world on social media.

TIP: UPDATE YOUR BIOS

Your profile needs to resonate with your brand and goals. As you build your network, the outer rung of people in your bullseye network are going to want to find you and connect with you. It is important your profile resonates with them to leverage the magic of the crowds to solve any goals you might have. LinkedIn is usually the first thing that shows up when someone searches. So, it is important you have an updated bio. Wikipedia is another location people can find information about you. However, you need to have a high level of visibility and followers for Wikipedia to feature you.

TIP: BE AUTHENTIC

Be yourself when you are posting and interacting with posts.

TIP: LEVERAGE GRAPHICS DESIGN TOOLS LIKE CANVA

Most people prefer looking at graphics versus text. You can leverage free tools like Canva (www.Canva.com) that allow you to work with photo editing, design layout, and more, all within an easy-to-use platform to create graphics for your posts.

TIP: DO TRIAL AND ERROR

Post consistently, measure how well your posts and graphics are doing, take that input, and use that for your next set of posts in the spirit of continuous improvement.

TIP: LEVERAGE GRAPHICS FOR YOUR WEBINAR BACKGROUND FOR BRANDING

We spend much more time on webinar platforms like Zoom, Microsoft Teams, Google Hangouts, and others. While you are on these platforms, please ensure your background has key components of your brand.

TIP: BLOCK OUT TIME AS PART OF YOUR SOCIAL ROUTINE

Eric Koester, founder and CEO of Manuscripts and adjunct professor at Georgetown, has a tip for social media. He timeboxes. He doesn't scroll through social media all the time. In fact, he very rarely scrolls. He uses about thirty minutes every morning and spends time updating things and putting stuff together. Eric spends time on it every single day because it's important, but he doesn't spend all his time because it's distracting that way.

TIP: CONSIDER PAYING FOR UPGRADE FEATURES

Some social media platforms provide a higher level of service and reporting for a fee. LinkedIn has additional capabilities and features that one can purchase.

Here are examples of some additional features you get when you pay for premium:

1. With the free version you get one hundred profile searches, while the first level of paid gives you three hundred profile searches.

2. Ability to see who's viewed your profile across the last ninety days, as compared to the free version that shows only five days.

3. More saved searches, which is beneficial to a sales pipeline.

4. Better advanced searches into things like company size and seniority level. There are up to eight filters you can apply for targeted search.

5. LinkedIn Premium also offers four features only available on this level, multi-featured InMail, keyword suggestions, applicant insights, and open profile.

TIP: GIVE CREDIT AND DEPOSIT VALUE WHEN SHARING

If you share content from another source, please highlight where you got content. This can also help you make connections or add value to current connections. For example, sharing a link to an article on Twitter and then tagging the author of the article in your discussion of why you found the article useful could be a great way to add value to those in your network. Additionally, from an image perspective, make sure you give and not use images without proper permission

TIP: LEVERAGE SOCIAL EVENTS TO SCALE YOUR VALUE AND IMPACT

Across social media platforms, there are various live event streaming features. Twitter Spaces, LinkedIn Events, Facebook Live, and YouTube Live are all examples. These digital platforms allow you to scale your message. The scale occurs by leveraging the platform to build momentum and reach hundreds to thousands of people who can learn and further share your content. As an example, you can give a webinar on a title you are knowledgeable about, or you can feature somebody in your network and have them share their expertise.

TIP: SCHEDULE YOUR POSTS

If you don't have the time every day to post and it is easier to do posting in one setting, you can use tools like Buffer (Buffer.com) and Hootsuite (Hootsuite.com) to schedule posts. These tools can take a single post, schedule it, and post it out to platforms such as LinkedIn, Twitter, Facebook, and YouTube. The more you post, the better the search engine algorithms will be and help you show up in more searches

TIP: JOIN NETWORKS WITHIN SOCIAL MEDIA PLATFORMS THAT ALIGN WITH YOUR GOALS

Go to your preferred social platform(s) and see which groups you subscribe to. Look at the various networks you belong to that align with your goals and ensure you are following them online. Search for other groups that you should be a part of. Meetup.com is a place where you can go to find similar networks aligned with your goals and interests. When you join these networks, it is important you add value and contribute.

TIP: LEVERAGING SURVEYS AND POLLS

Surveys and polls are great tools to gather insights and engage your audience.

TIP: USE SOCIAL MEDIA ANALYTICS TO MEASURE PROGRESS

Several social media platforms have great analytics tools to help you measure your reach, engagement, and other key social indicators. LinkedIn and Twitter have great tools. You can use these to iterate and improve your content and posts.

BLOGS, EMAIL, AND EMAIL NEWSLETTERS

Email and newsletters are great ways to connect and stay connected to your network. Email follow-ups with value should be an integral part of your relationship value plan.

Xinjin Zhao was managing one of ExxonMobil's global businesses. He traveled around the world and built up a strong network of hundreds of customers and partners. About five years ago, he went to China for this assignment. He was thinking about how to maintain that network being so far away. He thought, *I have a network of hundreds of people working around the world, and I need to think hard about the best way to stay visible and stay connected with everyone from China.* Xinjin said, "That's when I decided to start a LinkedIn weekly blog, and it has turned out to be a wonderful way to keep the connections. It keeps the conversation going, and I have been doing it for the last four years."

Social media and digital tools are great vehicles to help you optimize your network and make your network more successful. Technology keeps rapidly changing, which will enable new tools in this space. You should keep an eye on these tools to help most efficiently optimize your networking excellence.

EXERCISE

- Create three times the number of posts for the month.
- Determine the times per week you will do social media and schedule it in your calendar.
- Review your social analytics and determine two to three areas you will improve on to meet your goals.
- Google yourself.

RESOURCES:

- *Get to Reach the Right People with LinkedIn* by David Martinez Calduch
- *How to Harness the Power of LinkedIn on Building Business Relationships* by Nick Bardales
- *Build Your Influence On LinkedIn* by Berta Kaneko

CONCLUSION

As I finish this book and reflect back on moments in my life, relationships built, goals accomplished, and career achievements enabled by networking, I am thankful to the mentors, coaches, employers, and teachers from whom I learned many of these skills. I am thankful to the authors of the many books I read about networking, relationships, creating value, and leadership. I'm also thankful to those who took the time for me to interview and share their perspectives in this book.

As networking is so important for career and life success, I am continually surprised why more schools and universities do not teach this. I am hopeful this book is an education platform for you to use, and the tips, framework, and stories can help you accelerate learning networking principles and also help you rapidly accomplish your goals in life and help others.

Prior to this book, I had no framework or mental model about how I holistically did networking. The writing of this book helped me think of the vital areas of networking and pull together a framework around foundation, execution, and optimization, which you can use to approach networking more easily. They are vital components to be excellent at networking that have not only helped me but have also helped others who I have highlighted in this book.

Writing this book also made me improve my networking skills, especially my foundation, and gave me a great reason to reach out and connect with many in my network who have been very helpful to me. This book also helped me grow closer to the people I interviewed as well.

As you become excellent at networking, I look forward to seeing you leverage these key three sections of the book:

Foundation—The foundation gives you the focus and strength to ensure you are networking in the right areas, ensuring you deeply understand yourself and leverage that understanding to define SMART goals and a brand you can build habits and rituals around to help you have a very strong foundation.

Execution—The execution is the work you will have to put in to build off that strong foundation to achieve networking excellence. As you execute, you will identify the right people and networks to not only help you with your goals but also, more importantly, you help them via your value toolkit to achieve their goals. You should always execute networking with the right intentions to help them first but also think win-win and measure the value you are giving them on an ongoing basis.

Optimization—With your foundation in place and executing through delivering tons of value to the people and networks within your network, you can focus on optimizing. This includes being efficient before, during, and after networking events. Optimization is also about leveraging tools like social media and digital to add more value to your network and also reach and help more people. Optimization is also about continuing to ensure your foundation is up to date with where you are at in life and that you are updating your network and relationship value plans over time.

I wrote this book with the intention of leaving the reader with tools, techniques, and a framework to be excellent at networking. My intention is that this leaves you with some new pieces of information and reinforces others you already know. If these nuggets of value around networking have been helpful to you, I ask that you share them with your network to help them.

Finally, being excellent at networking requires work and is not easy.

- Professionals who allotted 6.3 hours per week to networking activities said it played a crucial role in their success (Chang 2022).

So please remember to put in the "work" in networking. It will pay off!

To continue the learning around *NetWORKing Excellence*, please feel free to follow me on social media, and don't hesitate to tag me or send me a message on any tip that was helpful. I regularly travel around the United States and to Latin America, speaking on networking and other topics. Let's stay connected, and keep me posted on other ways I can help you be successful!

APPENDIX

INTRODUCTION

Apollo Technical. 2022. "Important Networking Statistics Everyone Should Know (2022)." Accessed September 22, 2022. https://www.apollotechnical.com/networking-statistics/#.

Fisher, Julia Freeland. 2020. "How to Get a Job Often Comes Down to One Elite Personal Asset, and Many People Still Don't Realize It." Accessed September 22, 2022. https://www.cnbc.com/2019/12/27/how-to-get-a-job-often-comes-down-to-one-elite-personal-asset.html.

LinkedIn Corporate Communications. 2017. "Eighty-Percent of Professionals Consider Networking Important to Career Success." LinkedIn Pressroom. Accessed September 22, 2022. https://news.linkedin.com/2017/6/eighty-percent-of-professionals-consider-networking-important-to-career-success.

WHAT IS NETWORKING AND WHY IS IT IMPORTANT?

Bloom, Linda, and Charlie Bloom. 2015. "Honoring the Rule of Reciprocation." Stronger at the Broken Places. *Psychology Today*, October 2015. https://www.psychologytoday.com/us/blog/stronger-the-broken-places/201510/honoring-the-rule-reciprocation.

EToro. n.d. "The Definition of Leverage and Margin." Accessed September 22, 2022. https://www.etoro.com/trading/leverage-margin/.

Ferrazzi, Keith. 2007. "Keith Ferrazzi: What is Networking?" BetterLifeCoaches. June 6, 2007. 1:23. https://www.youtube.com/watch?v=cTU2FkVyoUw.

Ferrazzi, Keith. 2011. "Keith Ferrazzi: Networking Guru, CEO, Author of Never Eat Alone." EaglesTalent. July 27, 2011. 5:59.
https://www.youtube.com/watch?v=8MsdKzS-8b8.

Garcia, Charles P. 2003. *A Message from Garcia*. New Jersey: Wiley.

Harding, Kelli. n.d. "The Rabbit Effect." Accessed September 22, 2022.
https://www.kellihardingmd.com/the-rabbit-effect.

LinkedIn Corporate Communications. 2017. "Eighty-Percent of Professionals Consider Networking Important to Career Success." LinkedIn Pressroom. September 22, 2022.
https://news.linkedin.com/2017/6/eighty-percent-of-professionals-consider-networking-important-to-career-success.

Sinek, Simon (@simonsinek). 2022. "The True Value of Networking Doesn't Come from How Many People We Can Meet, but Rather How Many People We Can Introduce to Others." Twitter, February 18, 2022, 8:45 a.m.

Ted Ideas Worth Spreading. 2017. "Susan Pinker, the Secret to Living Longer May Be Your Social Life." Accessed September 22, 2022.
https://www.ted.com/talks/susan_pinker_the_secret_to_living_longer_may_be_your_social_life?language=en.

Wilkinson, Gale (@galeforceVC). 2021. "One of My Favorite Professors @ Chicagobooth Was Ron Burt. His Research Showed That 50%+ of the Value an Individual Created at Work Was Due to Their Network of External Connections." Twitter, September 11, 2021, 4:03 p.m.

STEP 1: DEEPLY UNDERSTAND YOURSELF

Alaili, Abdallah. 2022. "Imagination Is Everything. It Is the Preview of Life's Coming Attractions." "Entrepreneur Post" (blog). November 18, 2020.
https://www.entrepreneurpost.com/2020/11/18/imagination-is-everything-it-is-the-preview-of-lifes-coming-attractions-albert-einstein/.

Barker, Rick. 2020. "The Truth about Taylor Swift." Rick Barker. February 19, 2020. 11:04
https://rickbarker.com/the-truth-about-taylor-swift/.

Biography.com. 2017. "Mother Teresa." Biography.com. Accessed September 22, 2022.
https://www.biography.com/religious-figure/mother-teresa.

Blakemore, William B. 2022. "St. John Paul II." *Encyclopedia Britannica*. Chicago, IL: Encyclopedia Britannica.
https://www.britannica.com/biography/Saint-John-Paul-II.

British Library. n.d. "What Is SWOT Analysis?" British Library. Accessed September 22, 2022.
https://www.bl.uk/business-and-ip-centre/articles/what-is-swot-analysis#:~:text=The%20SWOT%20framework%20is%20credit,the%201960s%20and%20early%201970s.

Brooks, Arthur. 2022. "How to Want Less." *The Atlantic*, March 2022. https://www.theatlantic.com/magazine/archive/2022/03/why-we-are-never-satisfied-happiness/621304/.

CliftonStrengths. n.d. "Live Your Best Life Using Your Strengths." Gallup. Accessed September 22, 2022. https://www.gallup.com/cliftonstrengths/en/252137/home.aspx.

Dalai Lama. 2007. *How to See Yourself as You Truly Are.* New York: Simon and Schuster

Fields, Helen. 2011. "Happiness Associated with Longer Life." Science.org. Accessed September 22, 2022. https://www.science.org/content/article/happiness-associated-longer-life.

Forbes Coaches Council. 2018. "Best Tests to Help You Understand Your Strengths and Weaknesses." *Forbes*, January 2018. https://www.forbes.com/sites/forbescoachescouncil/2018/01/22/best-tests-to-help-you-understand-your-strengths-and-weaknesses/?sh=5431ca72495a.

Garcia, Charles P. 2003. *A Message from Garcia.* New Jersey: Wiley.

Green, William. 2022. "RWH001: The Life Force Revolution with Tony Robbins." Recorded March 1, 2022. Podcast, 57 min. https://podcasts.apple.com/za/podcast/rwh001-the-life-force-revolution-w-tony-robbins/id928933489?i=1000553250714.

Hicks, Carl. n.d. "How to Create a Personal Purpose Statement." Accessed September 22, 2022. https://www.thehicksfix.com/_files/ugd/444e00_739bd9c524d145058ba45a3688e9ab19.pdf.

Kenny, Stuart. 2019. "Ikigai: The Secret Towards a Life of Fulfillment." *Travel* (blog), RedBull. February 3, 2019. https://www.redbull.com/au-en/ikigai-japanese-concept-secrets.

Lewis, David L. 2022. "Martin Luther King, Jr." *Encyclopedia Britannica.* Chicago, IL: Encyclopedia Britannica. https://www.britannica.com/biography/Martin-Luther-King-Jr.

Mitsuhashi, Yukari. 2017. "Ikigai: A Japanese Concept to Improve Work and Life." BBC. Accessed October 9, 2022. https://www.bbc.com/worklife/article/20170807-ikigai-a-japanese-concept-to-improve-work-and-life.

Nanda, B.R. 2022. "Mahatma Gandhi." *Encyclopedia Britannica.* Chicago, IL: Encyclopedia Britannica. https://www.britannica.com/biography/Mahatma-Gandhi.

Nobel Lecture. 2022. "The 14th Dalai Lama." Lecture for the Nobel Prize by the Nobel Foundation, December 11, 1989. https://www.nobelprize.org/prizes/peace/1989/lama/lecture/.

Pierre-Jacques, Henri. @hpierrejacques. 2022. "7 rules for self-discovery." Twitter, April 24, 2022, 7:40 p.m.

Pratap, Anita. 1997. "Calcutta Slum Dwellers Grieve for Mother Teresa." *World News Story Page* (blog), *CNN*. Accessed September 22, 2022. http://www.cnn.com/WORLD/9709/10/teresa.first.slum/index.html?eref=sitesearch.

Ramsey Solutions. 2021. "How to Write a Personal Mission Statement." *Personal Growth* (blog), Ramsey. September 23, 2021. https://www.ramseysolutions.com/personal-growth/mission-statement-101.

Ravindra, Kumar. 2008. "Mahatma Gandhi and His Quest for Self-Realization." *Opinion* (blog), Worldpress.org. January 30, 2008. https://www.worldpress.org/asia/3057.cfm.

Sinek, Simon. 2021. "Find Your Why | Simon Sinek." Simon Sinek. Oct 6, 2021. 4:53. https://www.youtube.com/watch?v=tF7YLGpOoz8.

Tomi Llama. n.d. "Personal Core Values: The Definitive Guide." Tomi Llama. Accessed September 22, 2022. https://www.tomillama.com/personal-core-values#pcv3.

STEP 2: HAVE SMART GOALS

Andrea, Harris. n.d. "The Human Brain is Loaded Daily with 34 GB of Information." *Tech 21 Century* (blog). Accessed September 22, 2022. https://www.tech21century.com/the-human-brain-is-loaded-daily-with-34-gb-of-information/.

Durando, Jessica. 2013. "15 of Nelson Mandela's Best Quotes." *USA Today*, December 2013. https://www.usatoday.com/story/news/nation-now/2013/12/05/nelson-mandela-quotes/3775255/

Green, William. 2022. "RWH001: The Life Force Revolution with Tony Robbins." Recorded March 1, 2022. Podcast, 57 min. https://podcasts.apple.com/za/podcast/rwh001-the-life-force-revolution-w-tony-robbins/id928933489?i=1000553250714.

Harvey, Steve. 2019. "Imagination Is Everything | Motivated + | Steve Harvey." The Official Steve Harvey. September 15, 2019. 8:14. https://www.youtube.com/watch?v=TbEMIw3ecGI.

Harvey, Steve. 2019. "The Apollo Story | Motivated +." The Official Steve Harvey. December 16, 2019. 10:25. https://www.youtube.com/watch?v=9igSh9IwMAc.

Harvey, Steve. 2019. "Write Your Vision | Motivated +." The Official Steve Harvey. September 15, 2019. 8:44. https://www.youtube.com/watch?v=DlMAIYd7-J4.

Haughey, Duncan. 2014. "A Brief History of Smart Goals." Accessed September 22, 2022.
https://www.projectsmart.co.uk/smart-goals/brief-history-of-smart-goals.php.

Indeed Editorial Team. 2022. "How To Set Realistic Goals." Indeed. Accessed September 22, 2022.
https://www.indeed.com/career-advice/career-development/how-to-set-realistic-goals.

LinkedIn Corporate Communications. 2017. "Eighty-Percent of Professionals Consider Networking Important to Career Success." Accessed September 22, 2022.
https://news.linkedin.com/2017/6/eighty-percent-of-professionals-consider-networking-important-to-career-success.

Mendoza, Tom. 2015. "90-Day Goals Changed My Life: Here's My System." *Forbes*, February 2015.
https://www.forbes.com/sites/netapp/2015/02/11/90-day-goals/?sh=33fde8e66260.

Thomas, Paul. n.d. "Reticular Activating System and Goals | How to Use Your Unconscious Mind to Achieve your Goals." Self Help For Life. Accessed September 22, 2022.
https://selfhelpforlife.com/reticular-activating-system-and-goals/.

Turner, Ted. n.d., "You Should Set Goals Beyond Your Reach So You Always Have Something to Live For." Safetynet. Accessed October 22, 2022.
https://www.safetynet-inc.com/bio/jeffrey-fulton/.

Van Schneider, Tobias. 2017. "If You Want It, You Might Get It. The Reticular Activating System Explained." *The Desk Magazine* (blog), *Medium*. June 22, 2017.
https://medium.com/desk-of-van-schneider/if-you-want-it-you-might-get-it-the-reticular-activating-system-explained-761b6ac14e53.

Wilson, Lana, director. 2020. "Miss Americana." Tremolo Productions. 1 hr., 25 min.
https://www.netflix.com/title/81028336?source=35.

STEP 3: DEFINE AND REFINE YOUR BRAND

Jobs, Steve. 1997, "Steve Jobs Talks About Brand Apple."

bestofstevejobs. June 23, 2012.
https://www.youtube.com/watch?v=TNYbcqyyj68&t=30s.

Kenton, Will. 2022. "Brand: Types of Brands and How to Create a Successful Brand Identity." *Marketing Essentials* (blog), *Investopedia*. March 24, 2022.
https://www.investopedia.com/terms/b/brand.asp.

Larrson, Hanna. 2022. "Why is Personal Branding So Important." LinkedIn. Accessed September 22, 2022.
https://www.linkedin.com/feed/update/urn:li:activity:6928248108405428224/?updateEntityUrn=urn%3Ali%3Afs_feedUpdate%3A%28V2%2Curn%3Ali%3Aactivity%3A6928248108405428224%29.

Pope, Lauren. 2020. "90 Branding Statistics to Help You Make a Good Impression." Learn Hub. Accessed September 22, 2022. https://learn.g2.com/branding-statistics.

STEP 4: DAILY RITUALS AND ROUTINES

Ask the Scientists. 2022. "Change Your Mind: Meditation Benefits for the Brain." *Ask The Scientists* (blog). Accessed September 30, 2022. https://askthescientists.com/brain-meditation/.

Feloni, Richard. 2017. "Tony Robbins Starts Every Morning with an 'Adrenal Support Cocktail,' a 'Priming' Meditation Exercise, and a Workout Involving a 'Torture Machine.'" *Business Insider*, October 2017. https://www.businessinsider.com/tony-robbins-morning-routine-meditation-and-workout-2017-10.

Green, William. 2022. "RWH001: The Life Force Revolution with Tony Robbins." Recorded March 1, 2022. Podcast, 57 min. https://podcasts.apple.com/za/podcast/rwh001-the-life-force-revolution-w-tony-robbins/id928933489?i=1000553250714.

Jarrett, R. H. 1992. *It Works: The Famous Little Red Book That Makes Your Dreams Come True!* Camarillo, CA: DeVorss & Company.

Macka, Jory. 2019. "You Can't Be Productive without Routines and Rituals. Here's Why." FastCompany. Accessed September 26, 2022. https://www.fastcompany.com/90293936/benefits-of-daily-routines-and-rituals.

Robins Research International. n.d. "RPM™ System Box Set." Tony Robbins Store. Accessed September 27, 2022. https://store.tonyrobbins.com/products/rpm-3-pack.

Team Tony. n.d. "Making a Daily Routine." Tony Robbins. Accessed September 26, 2022. https://www.tonyrobbins.com/productivity-performance/making-a-daily-routine/.

STEP 5: IDENTIFY THE RIGHT PEOPLE

Automotive Hall of Fame. n.d. "Joe Girard: Inducted 2001." Automotive Hall of Fame. Accessed September 30, 2022. https://www.automotivehalloffame.org/honoree/joe-girard/

Ferrazzi, Keith. 2020. "The Secret to Networking in 2020: Relationship Action Plan." Keith Ferrazzi. July 8, 2020. 6:53. https://www.youtube.com/watch?v=Yyxsk-AnMhc.

Girard, Joe. 2014. "Girard's Law of 250." *Joe Girard* (blog). March 1, 2014. https://www.joegirard.com/posts/girards-law-250/.

Howes, Lewis. 2014. "Keith Ferrazzi with Lewis Howes—How to Build a Powerful Network—School of Greatness." Lewis Howes. December 24, 2014. 39:26. https://www.youtube.com/watch?v=wCe3myrWNbI&t=863s.

Kiyosaki, Robert. 2010. "If You Want to Go Somewhere, It Is Best to Find Someone Who Has Already Been There." Facebook, April 5, 2010, 10:45 a.m. https://www.facebook.com/RobertKiyosaki/posts/if-you-want-to-go-somewhere-it-is-best-to-find-someone-who-has-already-been-ther/111017142258990/.

STEP 6: TARGET THE RIGHT NETWORKS

Chaffey, Dave. 2022. *Global Social Media Statistics Research Summary 2022.* United Kingdom: Smart Insights. https://www.smartinsights.com/social-media-marketing/social-media-strategy/new-global-social-media-research/#:~:text=4.70%20billion%20people%20around%20the,social%20media%20is%202h%2029m.

Lifestyle Desk. 2021. "'Find a Group of People Who Challenge and Inspire You:' Amy Poehler." *Lifestyle* (blog) *The Indian Express*, August 12, 2021. https://indianexpress.com/article/lifestyle/life-positive/find-a-group-of-people-who-challenge-and-inspire-you-amy-poehler-7448882/.

Mendoza, Tom. (@TomMendozaTalks). 2022. "The Question I Ask People Who Think They Want to Go Into Leadership David Is 'Would You Rather Give a Plaque or Get a Plaque.' Every Great Leader That I Have Met That People Want to Follow Gets More Enjoyment Out of the Former. #Leadership." Twitter, February 15, 2022, 6:07 p.m.

Penn State Alumni Association. 2022. "Alumni Association Making It Easier to Interact Where and When Alumni Like." *Alumni Association* (blog), Penn State University. September 29, 2022. https://www.psu.edu/news/alumni-association/story/alumni-association-making-it-easier-interact-where-and-when-alumni/.

STEP 7: RELATIONSHIP BUILDING AND ADDING VALUE TO YOUR NETWORK

Calacanis, Jason, and Molly Wood. 2022. "Ex-FB Diem team builds Aptos blockchain, Metamask parent ConsenSys raises $450M, Mojo's athlete betting market, Zero Grocery shutdown | E1409." Recorded March 16, 2022. Podcast, 1 hr. 29 min. https://podcasts.apple.com/us/podcast/this-week-in-startups/id315114957?i=1000567136222.

Farnam Street. n.d. "The Best Summary of How to Win Friends and Influence People." *fs* (blog), Farnam Street. Accessed September 30, 2022. https://fs.blog/how-to-win-friends-and-influence-people/.

Ferrazzi, Keith. 2020. "The Secret to Networking in 2020: Relationship Action Plan." Keith Ferrazzi. July 8, 2020. 6:53. https://www.youtube.com/watch?v=Yyxsk-AnMhc.

Harvey, Steve. 2019. "Write Your Vision | Motivated +." The Official Steve Harvey. September 15, 2019. 8:44. https://www.youtube.com/watch?v=DlMAIYd7-J4.

Lockerbie, Trey. 2022. "TIP427: The History of Bubbles, Mania & Fraud W / Jamie Catherwood." Recorded March 3, 2022. Podcast, 1:13:05. https://www.theinvestorspodcast.com/episodes/the-history-of-bubbles-mania-fraud-w-jamie-catherwood/.

STEP 8: MEASURE AND INCREASE THE VALUE YOU PROVIDE

Lavinsky, Dave. n.d. "The Two Most Important Quotes in Business." *Growthink* (blog). Accessed October 4, 2022. https://www.growthink.com/content/two-most-important-quotes-business.

Viner, Greg. 2013. "ELDC Emotional Bank Account." Greg Viner. Apr 1. 2013. 4:59. https://www.youtube.com/watch?v=Y1ugYimvfhQ.

STEP 9: MASTER NETWORKING EVENTS

Carson, Emily. 2016. "Holy Everything: 'Storytelling Is Written into Our DNA.'" *Lifestyle* (blog), *Post Bulletin*. June 3, 2016. https://www.postbulletin.com/lifestyle/holy-everything-storytelling-is-written-into-our-dna.

Cordis. 2018. "Story Telling in Our Genes?" *Society* (blog), Cordis EU Research Results. January 22, 2018. https://cordis.europa.eu/article/id/122780-story-telling-in-our-genes.

Croxton, Sean. 2022. "Zig Ziglar: 'To Reach Your Goals You Must Have the Right Mental Attitude.'" Recorded on October 13, 2022. Podcast, 12 min. https://seancroxton.com/quote-of-the-day/015/.

Georgiev, Deyan. 2022. "73+ Surprising Networking Statistics to Boost Your Career." *Resources* (blog), *Review42*. October 11, 2022. https://review42.com/resources/networking-statistics/.

STEP 10: SCALE THE VALUE YOUR NETWORK WITH DIGITAL AND SOCIAL MEDIA

Calacanis, Jason, and Molly Wood. 2022. "Ex-FB Diem team builds Aptos blockchain, Metamask parent ConsenSys raises $450M, Mojo's athlete betting market, Zero Grocery shutdown | E1409." Recorded March 16, 2022. Podcast, 1 hr. 29 min. https://podcasts.apple.com/us/podcast/this-week-in-startups/id315114957?i=1000567136222.

Dixon, S. 2022. "Number of Users in the United States 2018-2022." Statista. Accessed October 7, 2022. https://www.statista.com/statistics/194471/number-of-linkedin-users-usa/#:~:text=In%202022%2C%20professional%20networking%20platform,strengthen%20their%20professional%20social%20network.

Forbes Insight. 2009. *Business Meetings: The Case for Face-to-Face.* Jersey City, NJ: *Forbes.*
https://images.forbes.com/forbesinsights/StudyPDFs/Business_Meetings_FaceToFace.pdf.

Godin, Seth. n.d. "Build It and They Will…" RelicsWorld. Accessed October 7, 2022. https://www.relicsworld.com/seth-godin/build-it-and-they-will-come-only-works-in-the-movies-social-author-seth-godin.

Howes, Lewis. 2014. "Keith Ferrazzi with Lewis Howes—How to Build a Powerful Network—School of Greatness." Lewis Howes. December 24, 2014. 39:26. https://www.youtube.com/watch?v=wCe3myrWNbI&t=863s.

CONCLUSION

Chang, Jenny. 2022. "45 Significant Business Networking Statistics: 2022 Conversion Rates & Challenges." *FinancesOnline* (blog). November 5, 2022. https://financesonline.com/business-networking-statistics/.

CPSIA information can be obtained
at www.ICGtesting.com
Printed in the USA
LVHW022330260523
748159LV00004B/1104

9 798889 264064